MW00780920

After Sound

After Sound

Toward a Critical Music

G Douglas Barrett

Bloomsbury Academic
An imprint of Bloomsbury Publishing Inc

B L O O M S B U R Y
NEW YORK · LONDON · OXFORD · NEW DELHI · SYDNEY

Bloomsbury Academic

An imprint of Bloomsbury Publishing Inc

1385 Broadway	50 Bedford Square
New York	London
NY 10018	WC1B 3DP
USA	UK

www.bloomsbury.com

BLOOMSBURY and the Diana logo are trademarks of Bloomsbury Publishing Inc

First published 2016

Library of Congress Cataloging-in-Publication Data
Names: Barrett, G. Douglas, author.
Title: After sound: toward a critical music / G Douglas Barrett.
Description: New York: Bloomsbury Academic, 2016. | Includes bibliographical
references and index.
Identifiers: LCCN 2016000521 (print) | LCCN 2016002614 (ebook) |
ISBN 9781501308116 (hardback) | ISBN 9781501308109 (ePUB) |
ISBN 9781501308093 (ePDF)
Subjects: LCSH: Sound in art. | Silence in art. | Art and music. |
Music–Social aspects. | BISAC: MUSIC / History & Criticism. |
MUSIC / General. | PHILOSOPHY / Aesthetics.
Classification: LCC NX650.S68 B37 2016 (print) | LCC NX650.S68 (ebook) | DDC
700.1/08–dc23
LC record available at http://lccn.loc.gov/2016000521

ISBN: HB: 978-1-5013-0811-6
PB: 978-1-5013-0812-3
ePDF: 978-1-5013-0809-3
ePub: 978-1-5013-0810-9

Cover design by clareturner.co.uk

Typeset by Deanta Global Publishing Services, Chennai, India
Printed and bound in the United States of America

Contents

Introduction

Music After Sound

This book seeks to reimagine music as a critically engaged art form in dialogue with contemporary art, continental philosophy, and global politics. Represented by a diverse set of artists and musicians working during the past ten years, the artworks and analyses herein interrogate religion, gender, sexuality, HIV/AIDS, education, debt, finance, speculation, and labor. The discussions that follow will question received ideas about music and rework some of its basic tenets. Before proceeding, then, we must suspend the notion of music as a series of discrete sounds identifiable as tones, or "notes" with determinate pitches, etc., and which, taken together, compose what is commonly referred to as a musical work. For not only is the "work-concept" exemplified by the late-eighteenth-century musical score put into question, but here musical tones also remain optional. In fact, sound does not form the primary focus of the artistic practices pursued in this book. The first two chapters, for example, are dedicated to silence, the very absence of sound—or, more precisely, the two rather different configurations of post-Cagean silence found in the experimental music collective Wandelweiser and contemporary art and AIDS activist group Ultra-red. But isn't music composed of sound?

One may object to the idea that silence can figure as a *music without sound* by arguing, for example, that John Cage's 1952 composition 4′33″ refers to sound through its absence: by presenting the concert hall, the audience, and a musician who remains silent, sound is alluded to precisely by its withholding. Sound, in this argument, functions as the irreducible condition of music: music is seen as the aesthetic form that gives sound its proper seating.[1] What happens, though, when sound is radically rescinded as the epistemological grounds upon which music is situated as an art form? What if music had never been a "sound art" in the first place?

It might come as a surprise, but the very notion of music *as* sound is a relatively recent invention. With its roots in the writings of a group of German thinkers in the early 1800s, the equating of music with instrumental sound severed from language and social meaning, which was later termed "absolute music," has remained with us to this day. Now solidified and expressed at the level of everyday language, the concept is tacitly accepted any time someone says, "I didn't care for the lyrics, but *the music* was great." For prior to the advent of absolute music, the concept of music *included* language ("lyrics," for example) within the premodern tripartite *harmonia, rhythmos,* and *logos*—or harmony, rhythm, and language, or rational thought. Note that "sound" does not make an appearance in that trio.[2]

Absolute music, further sedimented in the mid-nineteenth-century musical aesthetics of Eduard Hanslick—particularly his notion of the "specifically musical" (as opposed to the "extra-musical")—would undergo its most exhaustive sequence in the music of the nineteenth and twentieth centuries, expanding to include electronic sound and recording technologies among other formal and technological innovations. This music, which stretches from Beethoven to Boulez, but also includes Ruth Crawford Seeger, Pierre Schaeffer, and Karlheinz Stockhausen, worked through the same artistic modernism that brought us abstract expressionism and the subsequent debates around medium specificity in the visual arts. (It was "the same" artistic modernism because the birth of absolute music, as many would have it, was also the birth of artistic modernism.)[3] Beginning in the 1960s, conceptual art would initiate a dismantling of medium specificity that extends to recent debates around the "postmedium condition" and beyond.[4] Yet while postwar ("visual") art exceeded medium to incorporate conceptual and discursive strategies, the concept of music as a "medium" composed by sound would never quite receive such questioning.[5] Furthermore, language (including conceptuality, "*logos*," etc.) has remained categorically excluded from music, thereby precluding such discursive forms.

How, then, can music *become critical* (in and of its own form)?

Whither Criticality?

Critical music turns on the question of language because for critical engagement of any kind, *meaning* is necessary. Language is distinct from meaning, but the two nonetheless rely on one another since language forms the substance and expression of meaning. Ideas leave traces, carve impressions into the world. Constituting a specific kind of matter(ing), concepts impose a consequential materiality: ideas *matter*, to paraphrase philosopher Slavoj Žižek. It was, for example, by adopting conceptual art's self-reflexive incorporation of language, along with the strategies of critical negation inherited by the historical avant-garde, that contemporary art would—at best—become capable of intervening in a broader cultural, political, and artistic field. The framework through which we may conceive of this potential can be formulated as what I term (in Chapter 3) *materialist conceptualism*: the notion of a conceptual art that acknowledges the inherent discursivity of artistic practice while taking into account the material impact language and ideas have on the real. But does this mean that critical practice is possible today?

Considering the historical present, in which everything up to and including thought itself has proven commodifiable, is not the very notion of criticality a naive and outmoded concept? If critical art strives, in Chantal Mouffe's words, to "contribute to unsettling the dominant hegemony,"[6] is it possible to "unsettle" a system that so radically reincorporates the logic of its own unsettling? For the prospect of locating *any* form of contemporary critical (art) practice—not only music—seems, if not impossible, at least paradoxical. Perhaps critical art may take the form of what Boris Groys describes as "paradox-objects,"[7] works that appear simultaneously to contain thesis and antithesis. If the tension that arises through such a contradiction leads to a *crack* in the existing order, an opening onto a special kind of difference, then perhaps in such a case a critical practice might emerge.

As such, critical art is circumstantial, provisional, contextually dependent, and historically specific; it requires reflection and reflexivity, intention and enunciation. "Critical in its content," writes Guy Debord in 1963, "such art must also be critical of itself in its very form."[8] As a form of critical art, critical music is critical *in and of its own form*. Not limited to discourse and beyond unquestioned forms of representation—critical music requires more than simply music "about" various issues—such an art must question its forms and their respective histories. Critical music not only reinvents existing aesthetic forms, but also intervenes into the broader cultural, political, and social universe that surrounds them. Critical music takes risks; it is engaged. Yet this is not to restrict such a notion of engagement or commitment to the discursive, but rather to recognize, through the critical legacy of conceptual art, that art—especially contemporary art—is necessarily constituted by (and is an instantiation of) concepts and language.[9] And so to achieve this kind of engagement, music's concept as (nonlinguistic) sound requires revision. Or at least circumvention.

Sound Art?

Sound art, and its related discourses, represents one such attempt to circumvent the formal boundaries that have prevented this kind of a reorganization or transformation of music. As early as the 1960s, long after music had begun to conceive of itself as "organized sound,"[10] sound art sought to establish a novel category based on many of the formal and technological innovations that had already taken place in music.[11] Multimedia installations, tape work, spatialized audio, sculptural forms, intermedia, site-specific sound, and other forms were pioneered by composers such as Cage, Schaeffer, Alvin Lucier, and Maryanne Amacher—artists for whom music remained an acceptable category for contextualizing their work. Nonetheless, it was through the work of one or several of these composers that sound art theory defined itself by way of a distinct break with music, a tendency that musicologist and anthropologist Georgina Born has identified as a "year zero" phenomenon: for curators, artists, and theorists alike, sound art represented a "radical new paradigm" that simply awaited discovery.[12]

Following a recognition of this supposedly new paradigm, sound art faced a twofold legitimation crisis. First, sound art would need to provide a critique of music to legitimate its existence as a category. What could "sound art" offer that music, the existing "art of sounds," could not? Theorists could, for example, criticize music as an essentially "Greenbergian" art form incapable of situating itself within the kind of expanded field first proposed by visual art—for example, in sculpture in the 1960s.[13] However, such a notion of music would fail to account for music's status prior to artistic modernism and the advent of absolute music. And, if taken literally, this transhistorical concept of music would prevent its further transformation. Criticizing this straw man version of music, Brian Kane has referred to such an approach as "musicophobic."[14] Secondly, sound art would have to establish itself as a "medium" of contemporary art, a domain that, by many accounts, had already transcended autonomous and "specific" mediums. This issue continues to appear in sound art debates. Responding to MoMA's 2013 *Soundings* exhibition, for example, art historian Branden W. Joseph writes: "Today, one questions the benefits of shoring up the independence of a category like sound art."[15] Nearly a decade and a half after Rosalind Krauss's inauguration of the postmedium condition (and almost a half-century since conceptual art began its critical interrogation of medium), sound art appears regressive, if not anachronistic.

Even from the outset, sound art had been complicated by the basic categorical difficulty of construing sound—at once a phenomenon, material, and sense—as an artistic medium. Would such a medium be limited to sound recordings, installations, sculptures, or objects that make sounds? Would it include performance, poetry, film, video, or even dance? Would Fluxus and Happenings be considered sound art? Considering similar questions, Max Neuhaus criticized sound art's taxonomical short circuit between material and medium by suggesting that in any other form the determination would appear ridiculous:

> It's as if perfectly capable curators in the visual arts suddenly lose their equilibrium at the mention of the word sound. These same people who would all ridicule a new art form called, say, "Steel Art" which was composed of steel sculpture combined with steel guitar music along with anything else with steel in it, somehow have no trouble at all swallowing "Sound Art."[16]

Neuhaus's critique of sound art appeared as a short text in the sound art exhibition *Volume: Bed of Sound* held in 2000 at MoMA PS1. As an artist often included in these kinds of exhibitions, Neuhaus's site-specific installations and architectural interventions are cited by sound art theorists as forerunners of the genre. Yet despite his background as a musician and his variegated practice, Neuhaus's works continue to be grouped around what the artist calls an "unremarked commonality": sound.[17]

In form, sound art parallels absolute music. Although "sound art" appeared over a century and a half later and lacked the metaphysical pretensions of absolute music, both movements sought to posit an essentially "medium-specific" art form based on sound. Absolute music and sound art point from different perspectives to the same construction: sound as an autonomous medium. This is not to reduce the category to what Seth Kim-Cohen calls "sound art fundamentalism"[18]; but even in its most "expansive" forms, sound art proceeds, by definition, from sound as an artistic category—a distinction shared by both absolute music and "new music." It should come as no surprise, then, when Neuhaus maintains that what is typically called "sound art" is "essentially new music."[19] But more than an incidental categorical overlap, sound art and new music similarly reflect absolute music's primary determining feature: sound. Sound art *is*, essentially, absolute music.

Toward a Critical Music

So what, if not sound, is music, broadly conceived? This book will address that question by insisting that music is a historically mutable, contingent, and ultimately revisable art form that, when radically conceived, exceeds any strict adherence to specific mediums or material forms including sound itself. The artistic practices analyzed throughout this book share various references to music's formal structures—its historical modes of aesthetic organization and self-understanding. Pussy Riot, Ultra-red, Wandelweiser, Hong-Kai Wang, Peter Ablinger, Cassie Thornton, Pauline Boudry and Renate Lorenz: these artists are to be distinguished from existing "new music" because they privilege criticality and challenge the notion of music as autonomous sound. But they are not "sound art" because these artists are not limited to sound as a medium (or context). Many of these art practices are not typically classified as music, while other artists self-identify as musicians. In any case, they incorporate strategies that include conceptualism, social practice, performance, and activism, and engage a host of political, cultural, and aesthetic subjects.

What, then, do these artists have in common? Ultimately, through their practices of mobilizing bodies, staging participation, and organizing collectivity, these artists, I argue, deploy forms of *composition*: they recognize a broader need to put together and assemble, to construct and compose radical forms of commonality.[20] Importantly, this conception of composition departs from the term's meaning in "new music" institutions—and, moreover, requires a break with sound (art) and absolute music.

Such a break is conceivable only by acknowledging the historical finitude of absolute music. Indeed, despite its widespread acceptance, absolute music is to be understood as a historically specific concept: it has a determinate beginning, and, as German musicologist Carl Dahlhaus insisted, "What has come about historically can also be changed again."[21] Such a change could represent a radical shift in musical thinking and practice. Music could become untethered from sound as an autonomous medium, left, at an extreme, without sound. Self-reflexive conceptual and discursive strategies could take the place of a (premodern) musical *logos*. Sound could be deprioritized in favor of the wider methodological scope necessary to formulate music as a critical art practice. No longer adherent to the primacy of sound, this "music beyond sound" could finally become a music *after sound*.

Such a concept of music nevertheless finds itself at odds with the dominant contexts in which music is situated (or excluded) today, namely "sound art," "visual art," and "new music." We can summarize here three interrelated points of departure:

1. *The explosion of "sound art."* A proliferation of sound art theories, sound art exhibitions, sound art conferences, sound art awards, sound art MFA

programs, sound art residencies, and sound art galleries has peaked at what Jim Drobnick labeled in 2011 as the "sonic turn" in the arts and humanities.[22] Importantly, the artworks, performances, objects, installations, and practices that form sound art's objects of inquiry are considered *not* music. They are not music because, as implied by the subtitle of the 2012 ZKM exhibition *Sound Art: Sound as a Medium of Art*, these artworks represent a *medium* that belongs to contemporary ("visual") art.[23]

2. *The crisis of medium in contemporary ("visual") art.* Long before the announcement of the "sonic turn," contemporary "visual" art, it was proclaimed, was no longer visual. What began with Duchamp's famous "non-retinal" formulation found expression in the conceptual art of the 1960s and 1970s and continues in the discursive and postconceptual practices of today. But while conceptual art has radically transformed the status of art, medium remains for many "*the* problem" of contemporary art.[24] Craig Dworkin, for example, has gone so far as to abandon the notion of medium altogether, while David Joselit proposes an art beyond postmedium as a kind of "universal currency."[25] "Sound art" would figure unambiguously as a *regression* in these models, while music, I contend, remains *productively problematic.*

3. *The decline of Western art music* to the point of critical paralysis in the face of global crisis. Amid the twin threats of global economic and environmental collapse, a profound silence has befallen music and its institutions. Music has steadily devolved from its status as one of the most culturally relevant and aesthetically radical art forms—playing a decisive, if not foundational role in the development of movements such as conceptual art, Fluxus, performance, intermedia, site specificity, and social practice—to an unprecedented level of cultural conservatism, political impertinence, and artistic regress. With few exceptions, (new) music has become the last place to listen for new forms of engagement.[26]

Music is in need, then, of both a new concept and context. To answer this need and to address the three points listed above, I propose the category of critical music.

This book considers contemporary art practices that reconceive a music beyond the limitation of sound. It is titled *After Sound* because music and sound are, in my account, different entities. While musicology and sound art theory often limit music to pure instrumental sound, or absolute music, I posit a conception of music as an expanded field of artistic practice encompassing a range of different media and symbolic relationships.[27] The works discussed in *After Sound* use performance, text scores, musical automata, video, social practice, and conceptualist strategies, while they articulate a novel artistic space for a radically engaged musical practice. Coining the term *critical music,* this book examines a diverse collection of art projects that intervene into specific political and philosophical conflicts by exploiting music's unique historical forms. Through a series of intimate studies of artworks surveyed from the global visual and performing arts of the past ten years, *After Sound* offers a significant revision to the way we think about music. The book as a whole offers a way out of one of the most vexing deadlocks of contemporary cultural criticism: the choice between a sound art effectively divorced from the formal-historical coordinates of musical practice and the hermetic neo-absolute music that dominates new music circles today.

Critical music is not a fixed object of study, but rather a mutable site for resistance; it recomposes music's codes, materials, and forms and listens for strategic assemblages and formations in the making. Consider, for example, John Cage's silent composition, *4'33"*, performed alongside statements made on the AIDS crisis. Or witness a group of artists staging a punk prayer in central Moscow's Cathedral of Christ the Savior. Hear a concerted scream by a group of artists saddled with student debt, or see a video documenting listening and recording exercises conducted by retired sugar factory workers in present-day Taiwan. A common feature uniting these scenes exists not only in their individually expressed senses of political urgency, but also in the insistence upon a broadened musical field necessary for their adequate contextualization and analysis. Here this terrain covers the themes of collectivity, language, authority, and speculation, and is mapped through engagements with poststructuralism, queer theory, and new materialist philosophy. The artworks in *After Sound* interrogate music's historical modes of technological reproduction and elaborate new forms of instrumentality. They refigure music as a site for political agency by challenging and exfoliating its forms.

After Sound is concerned with rethinking music as a critically engaged art form in which sound appears as one resource among many. I am not interested, for example, in so-called "visual music" (even though I touch briefly upon synesthesia), since such a category largely proceeds by grafting onto visuality the same kind of medium-specific logic inherent to "sound art." It is important to note that this study is partial; it is not intended as a survey or history of "non-sonic" music, but rather pursues a heterogeneous model for critical music through a selection of artists working during the past ten years. There are other artists from the last century who could be cited as additional precedents for a "music without sound," including, for instance, Manford L. Eaton and his "biomusic."[28] I do not intend to trace a genealogy, yet I include a number of important historical touchstone artists such as Cage, Schaeffer, Julius Eastman, Christian Wolff, Pauline Oliveros, Yoko Ono, John Baldessari, and Arnold Schoenberg. Historical avant-garde movements such as the futurists, Situationists, Fluxus, and Vienna Actionist artist Otto Mühl's Aktionsanalytische Organisation also appear alongside activist groups like ACT UP, Gran Fury, and Strike Debt.

Overall, this project responds to a broader need to bridge the disciplines of musicology, art history, and sound studies, especially as they relate to the music and art of the past decade. Scholars like Born have recognized, along similar lines, a need to strengthen dialogue between the fields of musicology and sound studies. *After Sound* extends this call to include related work in art history and theory. Already in art historians such as Liz Kotz, Branden W. Joseph, and Diedrich Diederichsen, and musicologists such as Ben Piekut, Volker Straebel, and Holly Rogers, can we find scholarship that situates postwar music within a broader arts context without recourse to "sound art."[29] The Toronto-based Occulture group (Eldritch Priest, Marc Couroux, and David Cecchetto) similarly offer cross-disciplinary engagements with music, continental philosophy, and contemporary art. Concerning sound art theory, Kim-Cohen has provided an alternative definition as a kind of "passage between discourses."[30] If such a passage involves an integral reconsideration of the relationship between music and sound, then it too represents a dialogue in which this book engages.

Each of the following six chapters stages an encounter between the work of an artist or collective and a constellation of related political, philosophical, and artistic concerns. These chapters were developed over the course of more than six years and at times represent different approaches. A couple of the chapters feel like mini-books on their own, while others are somewhat more exploratory. Each chapter builds on the others but is intended to stand on its own; I will therefore reintroduce in different contexts ideas that were developed in previous chapters. Overall, the book is organized in three sections based on a series of thematic pairings that emerge through the subjects under consideration: silence and collectivity, language and authority, and speculation and sense.

What forms of social, political, and artistic organization can emerge when music is stripped of sound? The first two chapters explore relationships between silence and collectivity through the significantly divergent interpretations of Cage found in the Ultra-red and Wandelweiser collectives. Chapters 3 and 4

[handwritten notes:]
Sections:
① silence and collectivity ③ speculation and sense
② language and authority

provide contrasting responses to the problems of language and authority: Žižek's hailing of Russian art collective Pussy Riot as "conceptual artists," and Peter Ablinger's iconoclastic "talking" player piano featuring the voice of Schoenberg. Finally, we move to speculation and sense in the work of artists Cassie Thornton and Hong-Kai Wang. Thornton's social practice work around student debt invites a dual consideration of philosophical and economic speculation, while sense— conceived as a counterpart to speculation (and conceptualism)—is foregrounded in Wang's participatory field recordings of factory labor. Taken together, these artists point, in my analysis, to a shift away from music as autonomous sound and toward the possibility of music as an expanded and critical art form.

Silence and Collectivity

The first chapter, "The Limits of Performing Cage," interrogates *SILENT|LISTEN* (2005–06), a series of events in which Ultra-red present statements addressing the AIDS epidemic alongside performances of Cage's silent composition *4'33"* (1952). "AIDS is not a gay man's disease," asserts one speaker. Relevantly, while the composer spoke openly about his relationships with both men and women, Cage never fully came out as gay or bisexual. Ultra-red's intervention deliberately refigures Cage's score through activist group ACT UP's militantly antihomophobic slogan "SILENCE = DEATH," while it implicates Cage's own sexuality through the cultural politics of silence: *4'33"*'s contested status as part of the artist's historically specific strategy of queer resistance deployed during McCarthyism and the Cold War. *SILENT|LISTEN* turns on the music-formal problem of *Werktreue*, or "faithfulness" to an original score. Initiating a longer theoretical discussion of the musical score, this chapter positions Ultra-red's intervention in a complex relationship to both artistic appropriation and *Werktreue*, a concept that, in philosopher Lydia Goehr's account, begins with the solidification of the musical work-concept occurring toward the end of the 1700s.

I consider *SILENT|LISTEN* alongside the appropriation art strategies of AIDS activism and against recent theoretical attempts to bracket out sound from the historical and formal specificity of musical practice. Emblematic of the cross-disciplinary methodology employed throughout *After Sound*, this chapter reads the legacy of (primarily visual) AIDS appropriation art through the figures of Guy Debord, Chantal Mouffe, and Douglas Crimp, while analyzing the cultural relevance of Cage's sexuality through art-historical, musicological, and queer theory texts. Silence figures here as both a symbolic marker of homophobia and— as with other organizational forms and practices that Ultra-red appropriate from music (e.g., Varèse's "organized sound")—silence is reconstituted as a container for collective action. Collectivity is exhibited both through the framing of political organization and in a conception of appropriation art wherein the move away from individual creation paves the way for collective authorship and action.

Approaching the themes of collectivity and silence from a contrasting perspective, Chapter 2 examines the largely European experimental music collective Wandelweiser and their interpretations of Cage's work. "The Silent Network: The Music of Wandelweiser" analyzes Wandelweiser as a unique social and artistic formation while it considers the social import of the group's artistic works. Wandelweiser is organized as a kind of decentralized "network of affinities,"[31] which, according to cofounder Antoine Beuger, provided an alternative to the hierarchical model of collectivity that he found in Vienna Actionist artist Otto Mühl's Aktionsanalytische Organisation, the radical "free sex" commune where Beuger first met fellow Wandelweiser founder Burkhard Schlothauer. Tracing Wandelweiser's history and analyzing a selection of its musical works, this chapter considers the collective in relation to historical avant-garde movements and related theorists (Bürger, Poggioli, Mann), along with contemporary network theorists such as Bruno Latour.

As a horizontally assembled group of musicians, Wandelweiser have sought, unlike Ultra-red, to avoid statements of political or artistic intent. Yet while they lack an official manifesto, Wandelweiser's aesthetic program can be located in their interpretations of Cage's *4'33"*, expressed in the various interviews, writings, and musical works of Wandelweiser members. This chapter contrasts these readings of Cage's work—largely consonant with Beuger's consideration of "silence as an autonomous musical phenomenon"[32]—with existing and original interpretations of *4'33"* as a conceptual and socially engaged musical work. Importantly, *4'33"*'s score can be understood as a kind of proposal, a set of instructions presented in language, which links the work to the broader turn to language and conceptual art in the 1960s.

Language and Authority

Intervening into recent debates around conceptual art, language, and materialist philosophy, Chapter 3, "'IDEAS MATTER': Žižek Sings Pussy Riot," proposes two points of departure for theorizing a conceptual music. The first, "IDEAS MATTER," refers to Slavoj Žižek's description of contemporary Russian art collective Pussy Riot, while the second, "Žižek Sings Pussy Riot," plays on the title of John Baldessari's 1972 video *Baldessari Sings LeWitt*, a work in which the artist sings Sol LeWitt's well-known *Sentences on Conceptual Art* (1969). In a recent statement, Žižek hailed Pussy Riot as "conceptual artists in the noblest sense of the word," calling the group "artists who embody an Idea."[33] Žižek's characterization followed Pussy Riot's 2012 performance *Punk Prayer: Virgin Mary, Put Putin Away*, the group's infamously thwarted demonstration staged in Moscow's Cathedral of Christ the Savior, which resulted in a two-year prison sentence for three of the group's members—a consequence which, according to Anya Bernstein, paradoxically revealed both "the brutality and ultimate impotence of the Russian state."[34] With direct references to anti-LGBT violence, sexism, and state oppression linked to Russian Orthodoxy, *Punk Prayer* notably parodies the form of a religious musical text setting and thus invokes the era of preabsolute liturgical music. Returning to the premodern *harmonia, rhythmos*, and *logos* trio, I suggest that in the wake of absolute music, *logos* is reintegrated in *Punk Prayer* both through text setting and through conceptualism.

While Pussy Riot's work is frequently situated within the contexts of performance art and activism, Žižek's comment suggests further consequences for considering the group's work as a kind of conceptual music. "Anybody can take on this image," one Pussy Riot member explained in a YouTube video, referring to the group's balaclavas, instruments, and dresses.[35] Here Žižek's Hegelian-cum-Kosuthian notion of conceptual art, *Art as Idea as Idea*, is met by a conceptual art defined as proposal, which also recalls the work of Lawrence Weiner and LeWitt. This "proposal form" of conceptual art—notably mirrored in the musical score—is expressed in LeWitt's original *Sentences*: "Ideas can be works of art," to quote sentence ten, "All ideas need not be made physical." As both a kind of musical "realization" and a text setting of LeWitt's *Sentences*, in *Baldessari Sings LeWitt* ideas *become* physical matter. Finally, conceptual art as both idea and proposal returns in a consideration of authority, wherein again ideas become material presence, this time through violent force. In his recent rejoinder to Althusser's materialist philosophy, Žižek claims that authority works strictly as threat, that it is propositional; were it enacted, like the impotent father or the Russian state as Bernstein suggests, it would cease to be genuine authority. The threat, like the conceptual proposal (and the musical score), is seen here as matter virtualized.

Chapter 4 continues the discussion of language through the work of Peter Ablinger and introduces the subjects of recording technology and musical automata. Ablinger's *Letter from Schoenberg* (2007) uses a souped-up computer-controlled player piano to transduce into piano sound a recording of Schoenberg dictating a letter to protest a 1950 Dial Records release of his compositions. Specifically, the scolding missive responds to a recording of his 1942 work *Ode to Napoleon* that contained a female voice instead of the intended male performer. Ablinger's anachronistic crossing of recording technology with musical automata implicates the musical score as the subject of Schoenberg's speech and thus completes a tripartite framing of music's historical modes of technological reproduction (scores, musical automata, recordings).

Chapter 4's title, "Music to the Letter," refers both to Ablinger's literal translation of speech into music and to Schoenberg's imperative to execute his score "correctly." In addition to situating Ablinger's *Letter from Schoenberg* within broader debates around the relationships between music, language, and representation, this chapter introduces Ablinger's extensive work with noise. The artist's *Weiss/Weisslich* (White/Whitish) series is compared to precedents found in the futurists, *musique concrète*, and Varèse. But as a departure from the avant-garde, Ablinger prompts a multivalent engagement with sensory perception. In contrast to the antagonism of artists like Luigi Russolo, Ablinger's *Weiss/Weisslich* proposes an ambivalent overturning through stasis. Through a reading of Deleuze and Guattari, I suggest that Ablinger sets into motion a type of "perceptual semiotics" that mediates between philosophical thinking and sense.

Speculation and Sense

Sense is then contrasted with speculation, a category that also implicates the registers of both finance and philosophy. Recently, New York's Manhattan School of Music students graduated with an average of $47,000 in student debt, an amount matched only by a for-profit art college. Chapter 5, "The Debt of Philosophy: Music, Speculation, and *The Sound of Debt*," discusses artist Cassie Thornton's graphic scores based on debt figures, debt choruses, and other events based on student debt. In her *Debt 2 Space Program*, for example, Thornton conducts group exercises intended to exorcise participants' debts by screaming them to outer space. While I explore latent connections between Marxism and social practice art, Thornton's participatory projects invite a broader discussion of music, philosophy, and the financialization of higher education. "What is the material of your debt?" asks Thornton in a public questionnaire found on the artist's website.[36] Thornton's work points to a kind of "debt imaginary" by underlining debt's affective, social, and material substance—thereby suggesting an engagement with philosophical materialism. This chapter links the speculation of finance to philosopher Quentin Meillassoux's speculative materialism. Meillassoux's widely cited *After Finitude*, which begins with "arche-fossils," or scientific evidence supporting the theory of the big bang, is considered alongside Thornton's own primordial debt screams. Broadly, I ask if the relationship between philosophy and political economy originally elaborated by Marx—the "short-circuiting" of philosophical speculation through economic speculation[37]—can be transposed onto the contemporary neoliberal "debt economy."

Chapter 6 introduces the subject of labor to the economic questions explored in Chapter 5, while it continues the discussion of sense and philosophy. In a collaboration with media scholar Lindsey Lodhie, Chapter 6 pursues the possibility of the moving image as a form of musical mediation in Hong-Kai Wang's participatory recordings of industrial factory labor. Wang's *Music While We Work* (2011) is a two-channel video and sound installation that follows a group of retired Taiwanese sugar factory workers and their spouses through a factory owned by Taiwan Sugar Corporation as they execute a series of listening and recording exercises devised by the artist. Wang's title is taken from BBC's "Music While You Work," an experiment in state-ideological social engineering conducted in wartime Britain wherein popular music was played in factories in order to "mask" harsh mechanical sounds.

By reversing that procedure through her industrial listening exercises, Wang invokes the metaphor of *un*masking ideology—a task that has historically turned on metaphorical connections between philosophy and the sensory. The title of Chapter 6, "The Metaphoricity of Sense," refers to the continued role of sensory perception in artistic practices following conceptual art's radical challenges to medium. Sense is seen as influencing philosophical thinking through the "sense metaphors" central to ideology critique. With their *camera obscura* metaphor, for example, Marx and Engels contended that the "material conditions" of labor appear distorted to the viewer just as the camera lens inverts its subjects. Extending this optical metaphor, then, what would a theory of ideology based on musical organization reveal? The answer to this question here is not limited to sound and turns on an interdisciplinary analysis of historical representations of labor in film and their potential relevance to music.

Music After Art

The conclusion continues the discussion of the use of the moving image in critical musical practices and returns to the subjects of queer politics and the musical score introduced in Chapter 1. Intervening into contemporary queer and feminist politics, artists Pauline Boudry and Renate Lorenz (2013) created a film/video realization of Pauline Oliveros's 1970 composition *To Valerie Solanas and Marilyn Monroe in Recognition of their Desperation----*. Written following her own reading of Solanas's controversial 1967 *SCUM Manifesto*, Oliveros's composition sought to express the manifesto's "deep structure,"[38] while framing the figures of Monroe and Solanas through Oliveros's radical feminist listening practice.

As a reply to the recent proliferation of texts like Joselit's *After Art, After Sound* ends with a consideration of propositions that call for a resolute exit from the economic and symbolic circuits of the art world. The Boudry–Lorenz project serves as a prompt to speculate on the consequences suggested by writer Suhail Malik and philosopher Reza Negarestani, who demand, through different registers, a radical withdrawal from the art world. The themes of community and collectivity engaged in Solanas's infamous manifesto, and buttressed by Oliveros's "Deep Listening," intersect with Malik's "On the Necessity of Art's Exit from Contemporary Art" and Negarestani's "The Human Centipede, A View From the Art World" (both 2013). I conclude by asking whether music can supersede such an exodus by mobilizing radical forms of collectivity.

Part One

Silence and Collectivity

The Limits of Performing Cage: Ultra-red's *SILENT|LISTEN*

At the beginning of an AIDS literacy workshop in Echo Park, Los Angeles, we announced that we would perform Cage's composition [4'33"]—"The most important piece of American 20th Century music"—proceeding to sit in restrained stillness while the workshop participants, working class Latino men living with HIV and AIDS, looked on in bemusement.

—Ultra-red[1]

Audience member to Cage: "Silence equals death."
Cage: "Everything you open yourself to is your silence."[2]

Introduction: *SILENT|LISTEN*

In a large gallery space sits a long table dressed with a white tablecloth, around which several people are seated in front of microphones. Hovering near the end of the table is a reproduction of one of Rauschenberg's famous *White Paintings*, overall completing a stripped-down, somewhat clinical interior. After a small audience settles into place, one of the seated individuals speaks into a microphone, announcing, "*Four Thirty-three*, as composed by John Cage."

"Time," the announcer says, following roughly four and a half minutes of silence.

The announcer calmly proceeds, speaking to the others seated at the table. "Good evening. What did you hear?"

"Silence," a woman responds.

At this point one may wonder why Cage's composition, a work in which no intentional sounds are to be made, is followed by a direct interrogation of its audience members. And while it is typically performed in a concert hall, Cage's composition is here presented in the absence of the traditional piano or musicians in any ordinary sense.

"Good evening."

The questioning proceeds.

"When was the last time you were in this space to talk about AIDS?"

Emerging from a larger body of work interrogating the relationship between the aesthetic and the political, art/activist collective Ultra-red[3] create unique "performances" of John Cage's well-known silent piece *4'33"* (1952). Ultra-red's work *SILENT|LISTEN* (2005–06) consists of a series of events in which statements made about the AIDS epidemic—"where it has been, where it is now, and where it is going"[4]—are recorded following a performance of Cage's composition. A set of these statements, referred to by the collective as "the minutes," is then played back as part of a subsequent event. Accumulated from eight locations over the course of two years, these statements, made by health-care professionals, community organizers, activists, and other individuals, form a network linking each successive site through the collective staging of listening and vocality.

SILENT|LISTEN can be seen to parallel the artistic strategies of appropriation central to the history of AIDS activism. Yet while utilizing the strategies of contextual specificity and tactics of dissemination found in those practices, *SILENT|LISTEN* distinctly draws upon specific concerns regarding the historical status of Cage's indeterminate composition. Crystallized in his 1952 work *4'33"*, was Cage's silence affirmative, indifferent, or a political strategy of negation employed during the homophobic oppression of McCarthyism and the Cold War era? By referring to the militantly antihomophobic slogan of activist collective ACT UP (the AIDS Coalition to Unleash Power), "SILENCE = DEATH," Ultra-red point to the possibility of a consonant historical lens through which Cage's piece can be read, while using this lens to frame their contemporary intervention into the AIDS crisis. Interpreting Ultra-red's intervention through the focal points of AIDS activism and related artistic practices, this chapter attempts to tether the appropriation art strategy introduced by *SILENT|LISTEN* to the music-historical use of Cagean silence. Ultimately, this silence becomes refigured as a symbolic marker of homophobia in concert with the slogans of ACT UP and in dialogue with the imagery of groups like Gran Fury. Importantly, *SILENT|LISTEN* turns on the formal musical problem of *Werktreue*—the issue of "faithfulness" or adherence to an original score—while mutually implicating musicological and art-historical frames of analysis. Necessitating this kind of cross-disciplinary engagement between music and visual culture, my analysis of Ultra-red's intervention challenges recent theoretical attempts to isolate "sound"—as is often found in sound art theory—from the historical and formal coordinates of musical practice.

Let us return to the opening description. The speaker continues, "It is Wednesday, August 9th, 2006. The record for the Art Gallery of Ontario is now open. Will the first speaker please approach the table and enter her statement into the record? Please note the time, your name, and any affiliation you wish to declare."

A woman approaches the table and, in a collected and somewhat somber tone, speaks into the microphone:

> The time is 7:34. My name is Zoe Dodd. I am a harm reduction outreach worker and Hepatitis C support worker at Street Health Nursing Foundation. . . . I mainly work with the homeless drug-using population. In May of 2006, Street Health received a call from a client. He's lived on the streets for fifteen years. . . . He is an active drug user. He has AIDS, and he is co-infected with Hepatitis C.

The woman proceeds to describe an incident involving her client: arriving at the client's apartment to discover that he had lost over 40 pounds in less than one week, she was unable to convince the subject to seek medical attention. "He would not go," she insists, "because he [was] like many people, especially drug users . . . discriminated within our healthcare system." She continues to report that, as a Hepatitis C worker, her position has not received funding in Canada for over four months. Finally, she concludes that after a lengthy struggle the client received the medical attention he needed and lived.

The above description recounts an iteration of Ultra-red's *SILENT|LISTEN* presented at the Art Gallery of Ontario in 2006. The collective presented similar versions throughout 2005–06 at seven major North American art institutions. Founded in Los Angeles in 1994 by AIDS activists Dont Rhine and Marco Larsen, Ultra-red now incorporate members from across North America and Europe; the collective has consistently straddled the often conflictual worlds of art, music, and activism by staging direct political interventions, creating recordings and art objects, and producing performance installations such as *SILENT|LISTEN*—as well as their *What is the Sound of Freedom?* project (Whitney Biennial 2012)—which often involve participatory and dialogical components.

Authentic Appropriation

On the surface, *SILENT|LISTEN* may be said to conform to the logic of appropriation art. With theoretical roots in the writings of Benjamin, Foucault, and Barthes, and particularly in Barthes's 1967 essay "The Death of the Author," appropriation art's emergence is usually traced from the New York art scene of the late 1970s and 1980s through to contemporary work. Douglas Crimp's influential 1977 *Pictures* exhibition, which foregrounds "processes of quotation, excerptation, framing, and staging" against essentializing notions of medium, is a touchstone.[5] Often cited as a precursor to appropriation art practices, Guy Debord, in his 1956 essay, "Directions for the Use of Détournement," defines two types of *détournement*. Through the application of "corrections," or alterations introduced in original materials, both methods rely on a new context for the generation of meaning.[6] A "minor *détournement*," according to Debord, "draws all its meaning from the new context in which it has been placed," while a "deceptive *détournement*" relies upon the significance of the element itself.[7] As much as there may be something added, or "corrected," there is also that which is *drawn out* in Debord's "deceptive" mode. When an object is cast retroactively into a context alien to its origin, a new valence is produced. "Plagiarism implies progress," begins literary theorist Paul Mann's own double plagiarism of Guy Debord and Isidore Ducasse, "which is also progress toward a death already immanent in every repetition."[8] But rehearsing the birth of the reader or repeating a critic's (unoriginal) claim about the artist's unoriginality need not take center stage. Following the unidirectionality of death, appropriation can figure as a multiplication of authors—a collectivity. The death of *the* author is the prenatal condition for the multiple. Indeed, as Crimp notes in his own work with AIDS activism, collective production emerges as authorship undergoes assault.[9]

Appropriation *frames*; it reconstitutes and refigures historical substance. Permeating the landscape of artistic production, appropriation's historical reach has indeed been vast: "not just one strategy amongst many," appropriation was, as David Evans contends, "the very 'language' in which the postmodern debate [of the 1980s and 1990s] was conducted."[10] And yet while it is generally conceived as an expansive genre, appropriation is not without its limits, however seemingly imposed. Evans, for example, excludes "re-enactment" from the purview of appropriation, refusing to admit the work of Jeremy Deller or the re-performances of Marina Abramović due to these artists' alleged emphases on "unauthorized possession."[11] While it shares characteristics of re-performance, and does not preclude the category of appropriation as such, the distinctly musical structure engaged by Ultra-red's appropriation of Cage's *4'33"*—one of writing/composing, performing, listening—mandates an extended analytical frame.

Aligned with an appropriation art conceived along collectivist lines, *SILENT|LISTEN* engages an additional set of concerns inherent to musical practice, specifically regarding the question of a performer's fidelity to the musical score. Debates around the performer's adherence to the set of instructions put forth by the composer have centered on the question of "historical authenticity," or so-called *Werktreue*.[12] The "*Werktreue* ideal" is said to have emerged, according to philosopher Lydia Goehr, in the music and performance practices of the early nineteenth century, following the solidification toward the end of the 1700s of the "work-concept," an idea governing the relationship between composition and performance (among other things) which gives shape to a unified musical "work."[13] Coterminous with the arrival of the autonomous musical work (and with the advent of copyright laws), this conception of authorship effectively forbade the promiscuous use of scores that had proliferated in Renaissance practice. A new apparent "duty" bound the allegiance of performers to works and their composers.[14] If, in Goehr's account, the music of modernity inherits a work-concept structure from Romanticism, then it has also remained committed to the *Werktreue* ideal.

This "work-concept" structure has found its most significant challenge in the crisis initiated by Cage's indeterminacy, defined as an acknowledgment of the inherent unpredictability of performance, or, more significantly, as an extension of the contingency of a performer's score interpretation. The latter category is referred to as indeterminacy with respect to a composition's performance.[15] Opening onto *interpretation* in the widest sense, this form of indeterminacy more significantly threatens the established relationship between performer and composer. Performing a score becomes an act of interpretation in the literary sense. As in Barthes, primacy is given to the reader. Consider the potential consequences, then, of a "birth of the performer" in contemporary music/art practices: rather than a mandate from the composer, the score may instead provide a kind of text to be inhabited, to be activated, to be *used*.

Interestingly, Goehr cites works like Cage's *4'33"* as offering ambivalent challenges to the work-concept: "paradoxically situated in a practice that is regulated by the very concept they want to challenge," she questions whether musicians' interventions like Cage's offer any meaningful effects on what she calls the "force" of the work-concept.[16] While Goehr does list "compliant performance" as one supposed "target" of what Cage "seems to want to challenge,"[17] I would contend that the ramifications of the rupture introduced by Cage's indeterminacy have yet to be fully charted, especially from the perspective of the less-than-allegiant performer. Although discussions of *Werktreue* have indeed occupied musicologists and critics for decades, little has been said regarding the ways in which ruptures or revolts against the historically subservient structure of the musical work may apply to contemporary artistic practice. With some notable exceptions (see, e.g., artist/musician Adam Overton's 2013 manifesto "Ripe for Embarrassment"),[18] the possibility of a disruptive use of musical scores is under-theorized if not under-practiced. In Ultra-red's work, however, the *Werktreue* problematic is furthered through an application of the logic of appropriation or *détournement*. Ultra-red engage the problematic of *Werktreue* through their appropriation of artistic and activist practices associated with AIDS. Furthermore, their collective intervention becomes a question of exercising a certain kind of agency, rather than purely an act of subversion.

"Silence Equals Death"

Near the end of his life, Cage was accosted at a public symposium by an attendee who, repeating ACT UP's well-known slogan, exclaimed, "silence equals death."[19] To the agitator's opportune *détournement* of Cage's own program of silence by the silence of AIDS activism, the composer responded, "in Zen life equals death," and added, "Everything you open yourself to is your silence."[20] While for Cage silence does not equal death, death seems to haunt his reflections on silence. "Until I die there will be sounds," Cage proclaims, following his telling of the oft-repeated Harvard anechoic chamber anecdote, "and they will continue following my death."[21] For Cage, silence is impossible outside of "the silence of death."[22]

Although Cagean silence has been contextualized as a modernist strategy of erasure through the "silencing" of social import, or, alternately, valued for its acoustic properties or conceptual implications, a generation of scholars—Caroline Jones, Philip Gentry, and Jonathan Katz—has rigorously advocated a historically specific consideration of Cage's project as intimately tied to the subject position of a gay male artist responding to the heterosexist culture of the Cold War era. For Caroline Jones, silence plays the role of a Sedgwickean "closet-in-view" for Cage, a kind of surface-level bodily absence that serves as a "muting"—indeed a critique—of the abstract expressionist ego.[23] In his analysis of the cultural politics of *4'33''*, Gentry explores three possible contexts for situating Cage's sexuality: the direct political activism and homosexual pride mobilized by the

1950s homophile movement and the Mattachine Society; the post-Stonewall identity politics implicated in a conception of the "closeting" of (presumed-to-be-stable) sexual identities; and the "queer commuter" phenomenon elaborated by Henry Abelove in which gay and lesbian artists often chose to self-exile to more tolerant locations as a strategy of resistance. Gentry argues beyond these narratives, however, in privileging a model of "anti-identitarian identification" in which "Cage's subject position was often more subtly articulated than a simple 'closeted' model of sexuality would give us."[24] Acknowledging the influence of Zen Buddhism while arguing for the primacy of Cagean silence as a queer strategy of resistance during the Cold War, Katz posits silence as part of the development of a postmodern, non-authorial voice that prefigures Barthes's "death of the author."[25] Cage would, of course, go on to become a master appropriationist, with his recombinant texts that free-mix McLuhan, Duchamp, Thoreau, Joyce, and others.[26] Coterminous with his move toward Zen, however, Cage's turn to chance and silence, as Katz intimates, was part of a complex set of responses to the composer's failed marriage and frustrations with psychoanalysis as his relationship with Merce Cunningham began to take shape.

Cage spoke openly about his relationships with men and women alike, although, according to Katz, the composer never fully came out as gay or bisexual.[27] In an interview with Thomas Hines shortly before the composer's death, Cage describes his earliest sexual experiences with Don Sample, a young American he met in Europe as a teenager. This relationship, which eventually became "promiscuous" according to Cage, overlapped with his affair with Pauline Schindler and continued through his marriage to Xenia Kashevaroff. That marriage dissolved after a ménage à trois with Cunningham during which Cage realized that he was "more attracted" to Cunningham.[28] Although one of Cage's close friends was Harry Hay, the renowned gay rights activist, Cage insisted on silence when it came to representations of homosexuality. Not only were Cage's sexuality and related political stances not generally intended expressions of his artwork, but, as I will demonstrate below, the composer was openly hostile to performances of his works that foregrounded the abject or the sexual.

As mentioned earlier, along with silence, one of Cage's crucial developments was his practice of indeterminacy. Directly related to the use of silence is the type of indeterminacy in which a composition is "indeterminate with respect to its performance"[29]; as Cage had discovered, silence would become as much a critical negation as it would serve as an *opening*. Once fully exploded, the practice of indeterminacy permitted vast differences in the interpretations of

Cage's works. But it also became clear that for Cage certain interpretations of his work were deemed acceptable while others were not—even in the cases of his most "open-ended" compositions.

As though realizing the defiant reproach of Cage's activist-cum-heckler, Ultra-red attempt to short-circuit Cagean silence through the politicized voices of AIDS activism. Yet departing from the agitprop imagery of groups like Gran Fury, while still in dialogue with the slogans of ACT UP, Ultra-red explain that they sought to explore temporal and performative forms that facilitate social processes. In their reworking of Cage, therefore, Ultra-red refer to the durational frame of the concert situation to contextualize their version of Cagean indeterminacy. In their 2005 essay subtitled "The AIDS Uncanny," Ultra-red described their intention to create "work that suspends resolution and employs duration to construct spaces in which our loss and grief can acquire a critical language directed against dehumanization."[30] "In the current proto-fascist historical moment," they contend elsewhere, "*SILENT|LISTEN* invokes affective responses other than rage as constitutive of collective action."[31]

Ultra-red's collective use of Cage's silent composition as an immanent temporal container is crossed with the iconicity of silence, a crucial concept in the fight against AIDS. Silence in this context represents the undermining of valuable information that saves lives, the negligence and unwillingness of governments to respond to the epidemic on a public and global level, and an index of the violent effects of stigmatization exacerbated by the constant threat of criminalization faced by people living with AIDS. Ultra-red's project contextualizes *4'33"* in light of the AIDS epidemic, while situating AIDS activism—metonymically invoked through reference to ACT UP's slogan SILENCE = DEATH—within the frame of Cage's silent piece.

SILENT|LISTEN should also be read in relation to the ambivalent attitudes Cage himself held regarding performances of his indeterminate, "open-ended" compositions—not simply to answer the question as to whether Cage would have approved of *SILENT|LISTEN* as a realization of *4'33"*, but, rather, in the interest of drawing out a politics of musical interpretation applicable to Cage and his broader project of indeterminacy. This task must not only chart the performative boundaries specific to Cage's composition, but also explore the historical and political implications of his artwork. Was Cage's silence emblematic of his broader turn to an "Aesthetics of Indifference" during the 1950s, or did Cage utilize a "politics of negation" by deploying silence as a "historically specific [mode of] queer resistance" during the homophobic oppression of McCarthyism and the

Cold War era?[32] An attempt to elucidate this kind of political substance (arguably already present in Cage's piece) turns on the question of *Werktreue,* or "historical authenticity" in music performance. Clearly departing from conventional realizations of Cage's composition, *SILENT|LISTEN* invites a consideration of the limits of performances of Cage's works. *SILENT|LISTEN,* while proffering a distinctive refiguring of *4'33",* can nevertheless be said to include a genuine realization of Cage's composition. While engaging the problem of "historical authenticity" and its relation to Cagean indeterminacy, however, it is also important to situate *SILENT|LISTEN* within the context of the rich and varied lineage of visual art strategies central to AIDS activism.

Before continuing a discussion of the musicality of Ultra-red's use of Cage's *4'33",* it is necessary to acknowledge the long-standing connections between AIDS activism and strategies of artistic appropriation. One notable example is Canadian art collective General Idea's series *Imagevirus,* which, beginning in 1987, consisted of a series of widely disseminated images and objects, each containing an often differently colored version of Robert Indiana's iconic *L-O-V-E* painting respelled as *A-I-D-S.* According to one commentator, the intended target of General Idea's appropriation was not originality or authorship; rather, their goal was to mimic the behavior of the HIV virus itself—its transformations, travels, and proliferations.[33] While not unequivocally consonant with the AIDS activism movement of the 1980s, *Imagevirus* shares in the emphasis on language and the contextual specificity of the strategies of ACT UP and Gran Fury.[34] Infecting "large portions of the signifying field," *Imagevirus,* Gregg Bordowitz contends, "connects gallery to museum to street to public transportation."[35]

The caustic wit and culturally parasitic attitude emblematized in *Imagevirus* become echoed in many of the artistic practices encountered throughout the history of AIDS activism. These artistic strategies appropriated a range of cultural objects and artworks and often worked in propagandistic modes. Along these lines, in their detailed description of the early graphics of ACT UP, Douglas Crimp and Adam Rolston explain that "what counts in activist art is its propaganda effect; stealing the procedures of other artists is part of the plan—if it works, we use it."[36] Reiterating similar statements made by theorists of postmodernism and the avant-garde, Crimp argues that, especially in the context of the AIDS activist movement, "assaults on authorship have led to anonymous and collective production."[37] Along with Rolston, Crimp further characterizes an appropriation art "in which the artist forgoes the claim to original creation by appropriating already-existing images and objects," by showing "that the 'unique individual' is a kind of fiction" and that the self is constructed through a series of "preexisting images, discourses, and events."[38]

ACT UP's iconic SILENCE = DEATH logo, with its white Gill sans-serif font set against a black background underneath a hot pink upward-pointing equilateral triangle, contains perhaps the most well-known instance of appropriation within AIDS activism.[39] But rather than stealing from another artist, the emblem references the badges used in Nazi concentration camps to mark gay men who were exterminated by the thousands. Adopted by the gay and lesbian movement in the 1960s, as Ultra-red's Robert Sember explains, the pink triangle used by ACT UP creates continuity between historical struggles against homophobia and contemporary mobilizations against AIDS.[40] A geometric inversion of the downward-pointing triangle badges used in the concentration camps, the pink triangle used in the SILENCE = DEATH design points to rampant governmental neglect and failure in responding effectively to the epidemic as an act of genocide.[41] The slogan also evokes mathematical equivalence, conjuring the numbers of AIDS statistics: death as numerical data. Bringing together the terms of silence and death separated by a mediating equals sign, the synchronic symmetry of SILENCE = DEATH—more emphatic and immediate than pure causality; not simply resulting in death, silence *equals* death—is counterposed by the diachronic geometry of the pink triangular emblem, which points back to a history of struggle while signaling a future in which AIDS is no longer.

Inspired by a SILENCE = DEATH poster hung on lower Broadway, New Museum curator Bill Olander, who had AIDS and was also a member of ACT UP, invited the group to create an installation for the New Museum's window space in 1987. The result was the highly influential *Let the Record Show . . .*, an artistic intervention that sought militantly to counteract public misconceptions around AIDS and to address the enormous failures of the US government to respond adequately to the epidemic. Critical of the kinds of "elegiac expressions that appeared to dominate the art world's response to the AIDS crisis,"[42] Crimp considers *Let the Record Show . . .* a participatory act in the struggle against AIDS that significantly departs from the "traditional idealist conception of art, which entirely divorces art from engagement in lived social life."[43] Adopting the trope of a trial or hearing, the work consisted of a series of life-sized cardboard cutouts of public figures, each posed behind a corresponding printed "testament": US Senator Jesse Helms ("The logical outcome of testing is a quarantine of those infected"); televangelist Jerry Falwell ("AIDS is God's judgment of a society that does not live by His rules"); and Ronald Reagan, whose testament was left blank, referring to his six-year refusal to speak about the epidemic while president; among three others. Each figure was placed directly in front of a large photomural of the Nuremburg trials, over which a scrolling LED text beginning with "Let the record show . . ." rebutted each of the figures' statements.[44] All of this was staged under a large neon sign displaying the original SILENCE = DEATH design.

Following their *Let the Record Show . . .* installation at the New Museum, members from the Silence = Death Project would go on to join Gran Fury, the group that served as "ACT UP's unofficial propaganda ministry and guerrilla graphic designers," in the words of Crimp and Rolston.[45] In their large-scale photomural ad campaign project, *Kissing Doesn't Kill* (1989), Gran Fury exhibited three couples engaged in the act of kissing displayed across a horizontal frame. Each couple formed a different combination of genders and races, and above their images a text stated: "KISSING DOESN'T KILL: GREED AND INDIFFERENCE DO." Interestingly, in a more specific indictment, the original rejoinder text read, "Corporate Greed, Government Inaction, and Public Indifference Make AIDS a Political Crisis."[46] With their vibrant and impressively polished aesthetic, Gran Fury had "simulated the glossy look and pithy language of mass-market advertising to seduce the public into dealing with issues of AIDS transmission, research, funding, and government response, issues that might otherwise be avoided or rejected out of hand."[47] As with other artistic interventions centered on the AIDS epidemic, including the work of Ultra-red, context becomes all-important: "When affixed to the side of a city bus, *Kissing Doesn't Kill* functions as a mobile advertisement, traveling through neighborhoods of the city rather than remaining within the bounds of any one community or subculture."[48] Activist art, highly circumstantial and contingent, implicates, as Crimp argues, not only the "nature of cultural production," but also the site—the context—of cultural production and dissemination.[49]

Noting the resemblance of Gran Fury's work to the advertisements of United Colors of Benetton—which the brand itself appropriated from artists of the time and which were also placed on the sides of buses—Chantal Mouffe describes *Kissing Doesn't Kill* as an instance of "re-*détournement.*"[50] Gran Fury reappropriated an aesthetic that Benetton had itself appropriated from artistic practice. Indeed, as Mouffe's comment suggests, there are significant resonances between Gran Fury interventions like *Kissing Doesn't Kill* or *Let the Record Show . . .* and the work of Debord. Summarizing the Situationists' theory of *détournement,* Debord explains that, rather than being concerned with the creation of the new, "critical art can be produced as of now using the existing means of cultural expression."[51] "Critical in its content," he continues, "such art must also be critical of itself in its very form."[52] According to Debord, there were no Situationist works of art, "only Situationist *uses* of works of art."[53] This notion of the *use* of artworks becomes crucial in Ultra-red's critical musical practice.

Although Mouffe abandons the avant-garde project of radical critique, her notion of "critical art" may be viewed as an extension of Debord's project. Asserting that traditional modes of artistic critique have been recuperated by neoliberalism and incorporated into the logic of post-Fordist networked production, Mouffe asks whether, in the wake of the avant-garde, current art practices have the ability to play a critical role in a contemporary society marked by the blurred difference between art and advertising and by the appropriation of formerly countercultural strategies by the dominant regulatory modes of capitalism. "Today artists cannot pretend any more to constitute an avant-garde offering a radical critique," she claims, "but this is not a reason to proclaim that their political role has ended." Rather, Mouffe contends, "they still can play an important role in the hegemonic struggle by subverting the dominant hegemony and by contributing to the construction of new subjectivities."[54] Mouffe's own term "critical art" refers to artistic practices that actively contribute to "questioning the dominant hegemony."[55] Citing it as supplemental to her broader "agonistic approach" to the political, Mouffe insists that "critical art is art that foments dissensus, that makes visible what the dominant consensus tends to obscure and obliterate. It is constituted by a manifold of artistic practices aiming at giving a voice to all those who are silenced within the framework of the existing hegemony."[56] She stresses, however, that "the aim of critical artistic practices should not consist in dissipating supposedly false consciousness in order to reveal the true reality; for this would be completely at odds with the anti-essentialist premises of the theory of hegemony, which rejects the very idea of true consciousness . . . and asserts that identities are always results of processes of identification."[57]

What is shared by the perspectives of Debord and Mouffe, and by the appropriation art strategies of AIDS activism, is the notion of immanent critique. Instead of operating at a distance from, outside, or above the target of their critiques, the strategies cited above remain wholly embedded within a social context and work through engaged practices of reconfiguring, reactivating, and politicizing existing cultural elements. Not simply an attempt to "unveil" an ideologically inflected premise, Gran Fury's critical art practice renders actual social reconfigurations. Their interventions break up and reorganize stultified hegemonic structures, working within the contextual specificity of site and through the generality—and "viral" nature—of language and images.

Appropriating Indeterminacy

Ultra-red extend the terrain of artistic intervention around AIDS—centered primarily around images, language, and direct political interventions—to include the domain of music through their appropriative use of Cage's *4'33"*. They posit an engaged musical practice not unlike the visual art practices elaborated by Crimp such as Gran Fury. Important, however, are the ways in which Ultra-red's *SILENT|LISTEN* works as both a continuation of and a departure from the appropriation art of AIDS activism. Unlike the relation between, for example, Robert Indiana's *LOVE* and General Idea's *Imagevirus*, in Ultra-red's *SILENT|LISTEN*, Cage's *4'33"* can be said—to an extent—to retain its identity as such.

What does it mean, then, to consider *SILENT|LISTEN* an "authentic" realization of *4'33"* when it so drastically departs from David Tudor's performance of the work in Woodstock, New York in 1952? Roger Hallas contends that *SILENT|LISTEN* "paradoxically resists solidification into a permanent archival object," and that despite Ultra-red's "systematic use of archival discourse—'testimony', 'statements', 'the record', and 'the minutes'," *SILENT|LISTEN* nevertheless employs the "durational process of conceptual art and the ephemeral quality of performance art."[58] Similarly, in her analysis of *SILENT|LISTEN*, Lauren Berlant insists that Ultra-red's "record" is not normalizing or dead, but is one that circulates and "engenders rhythm."[59] As with *Let the Record Show . . .* and the *ACT UP Oral History Project, SILENT|LISTEN* emphasizes recordkeeping and archiving, but departs from these earlier projects in its continually developing, "open-ended" character—its incorporation of indeterminacy. One might suggest, however, that while Cage's *4'33"* is ostensibly distinct from archival artwork and apparently closer to the "ephemeral quality of performance art," its score is also rooted in a kind of recordkeeping. Indeed, one recalls the meticulous performance note contained in Cage's 1961 version of the *4'33"* score, in which he explains:

> The title of this work is the total length in minutes and seconds of its performance. At Woodstock, N.Y., August 29, 1952, the title was *4'33"* and the three parts were 33", 2'40", and 1'20". It was performed by David Tudor, pianist, who indicated

the beginnings of parts by closing, the endings by opening, the keyboard lid. However, the work may be performed by an instrumentalist or combination of instrumentalists and last any length of time.[60]

4'33" insists upon the disparity between the absolute "openness"—a malleability—that characterizes its realizations and the unshakable precision demanded by its score. Similarly, though more broadly, indeterminacy resides in the contradiction between the command structure necessary for a score to exist—a score demands determinate action, providing it with an identity—and the potential within the score for the complete undermining of certainty, the obliteration of authority (and at times authorship) in favor of chance or the subjective will of the performer. Ultra-red's framing of Cage's *4'33"* is distinct in that it functions simultaneously as a realization of the work and an appropriation in a manner similar to the works elaborated above. Through the specificity of the musical score, *SILENT|LISTEN* figures as an impactful (re-)politicization of *4'33"*, a performance of Cage's piece that reads the work's history into its interpretation as a focal point. The problem of fidelity to Cage's score is thus redoubled, not only because of the political implications of Cagean silence, but also because of the contradictory relationship that indeterminacy posits between score and performance.

Ultra-red may be viewed as a recent addition to a history of performers whose artistic strategies have sought to re-envision the role of the performer. In certain instances involving Cage, the use of such strategies has resulted in performances deemed unacceptable by the composer. In his recent work, for example, Benjamin Piekut analyzes the series of performances Charlotte Moorman gave of Cage's *21'1.499" for a String Player* during the 1960s, which included (in response to the score's indications for non-string sounds) various references to tampons, orgasms, condoms, and Planned Parenthood, along with her use of the "human cello": Moorman's bowing of a kneeling, seminude Nam June Paik. Cage, in the end, coldly dismissed Moorman as having "murdered" his composition.[61] For Piekut, Moorman's controversial interpretations of Cage turned on the question of subjective agency: Moorman treated the score "as a set of rules to be performed, inhabited, and experienced."[62] Beyond themes of subversion or "tropes of obedience and disobedience," Piekut insists on the question, "How did Moorman *use* Cage's piece?"[63]

In 1975, at the June in Buffalo music festival, Julius Eastman and other members of the S.E.M. Ensemble performed an interpretation of Cage's *Song Books* (1970) that has remained obscure and thoroughly underappreciated.[64]

Interjected into a panoply of other sounds and activities, Eastman began his interpretation of the instruction, "In a situation with maximum amplification . . . perform a disciplined action"—a "paraphrasing" of *0'00" or 4'33" No. 2* (1962), one of the several works that make up *Song Books*—by introducing himself as "Professor Padu" and delivering an elaborate lecture to demonstrate a new "system" of erotic love. Suited, and in a mockingly off-kilter performative style, Eastman directed his sister and then-boyfriend to engage in a series of erotic acts to illustrate his "sideways-and-sensitive" approach to an unsuspecting Buffalo audience. The following day, during one of the festival's seminars, Cage responded by banging violently on a piano in the room and scolding performers who had more generally, in his view, interpreted his indeterminate instructions as an invitation to do "any *goddamned thing*" they wanted.[65] He further condemned what he characterized as the "homosexual dimension" of Eastman's performance. According to Cage, "the question of homosexuality" that he perceived as a central element of Eastman's performance was at odds with his intended premise of the work, namely that "we connect Satie with Thoreau"[66]—two influential figures for Cage. An irony arises here, not simply in relation to Cage's own sexuality (however reluctant he was to disclose), and not only in light of his contestable objection that "neither Satie nor Thoreau had any sexual connection with anyone or anything,"[67] but also regarding Cage's project of indeterminacy and its critical challenge to the authority otherwise traditionally invested in the composer. Eastman's intervention underlines a critical shortcoming of Cagean indeterminacy: its inability to extend beyond the form of the Western musical work. In contending with the *Werktreue* ideal of the score, Eastman's transgressive performance of *Song Books* effectively exhibits the resolute failure of Cage's broader project of indeterminacy.

Performing Silence

Pertinent to Ultra-red's historical reframing of *4'33"* is the question of whether Cage's silence is to be read as a modernist "end game" strategy in which meaning is erased, or as part of a more subtly elaborated political program. In his analysis of *4'33"*, for example, Douglas Kahn notes Cage's self-purported shift during the 1960s "from musical to social issues."[68] Kahn concludes, however, that for Cage, "there was no corresponding shift to reconceptualize the sociality of sounds."[69] Interestingly, Kahn attempts to question Cage's ideas "from the vantage point of sound instead of music," and more generally considers music as a site that invites "uncritical celebrations" of Cage.[70] Yet along with this fixation on "sound,"[71] there are clear drawbacks to Kahn's self-conscious overinvestment in Cage's views on his own work. For two perspectives that do not as strictly "[take] Cage at his word,"[72] we turn to the noteworthy debate between art historian Moira Roth and queer theorist Jonathan Katz.

Grouping together a handful of influential artists from the New York avant-garde scene of the 1950s—including Duchamp, Johns, Rauschenberg, Cunningham, and Cage—Roth locates an "Aesthetic of Indifference" in their work: a tendency toward critical paralysis in the face of the ardent anti-Communist fervor and political oppression of the McCarthy period. These artists, she claims, were partly responsible for the "bizarre disjunction of art and politics that emerged in the 1960s," having adopted the "cool" stances of neutrality, irony, and negation in the context of the oppressive political climate of the 1950s.[73] Cage was, in this milieu, no minor player: "If Duchamp was the fulcrum of this new movement," Roth contends, "Cage was the lever."[74] And according to Roth, Cage's chance operations, along with 4'33", exhibited an "extreme passivity."[75] Meanwhile, Katz counters that Roth's criticism of these artists' supposed non-involvement assumes that they simply could have chosen to become involved. Noting that the period was one of the most violently homophobic decades in American history, Katz contends that for Cage and company, "silence ensured survival."[76] For gay men in the 1950s, Katz argues, "It mattered how you crossed your legs, how you spoke, and which pronouns you let slip."[77] As a historically specific mode of queer resistance during McCarthyism, "this is not silence at all," but rather "the *performance* of silence"[78]; with silent music, Katz argues, Cage performed a "statement of nonstatement."[79] Consequently, Katz substitutes for Roth's pejorative "Indifference" his more positively elaborated politics of negation, which for him is coterminous with Derrida's notion of undecidability: "First, negation avoids the recolonizing force of the oppositional—that which permits the opponent to solidify and suture through recourse to the excluded other. Second, negation operates as a closeted relation, mediating between the negating and the negated in such a way as to exclude all who are not already at the very least sympathetic to its case."[80]

However speculative Katz's argument may appear, it can be viewed as positing a critical space within which Cage's political orientation can be thought beyond intentionality—as is the case with indeterminacy. Thus the political thrust of Cage's work may even be understood as running *counter* to his own stances on his work. It is also interesting to note that for Katz, Cage's enactment of this politics of negation relies on a distinctly musical context; just as Rauschenberg's *White Paintings* depend on the frame of traditional painting, silence needs the context of music for its effect. Perhaps nowhere more explicitly than in music does silence *negate* a mandate to make sound.[81] It is then through this negational act of silence—precisely *in music*—that Cage's work acquires its genuine sociopolitical force. Reading Debord alongside Mouffe's conception of critical art, Cage's silence, despite the broader failure of indeterminacy, may be understood as a kind of proto-critical music. "Critical of itself in its very form,"[82] through this situatedness as music, Cagean silence resisted the hegemony of the 1950s through the logic of negation.

If we take this view, Cagean silence may be read as a reappropriation of silence as a symbolic marker of homophobia in a manner not unlike the Silence = Death Project's subversive reworking of the pink triangle. Ultra-red's rereading of Cagean silence serves, in this sense, as a kind of alternative realization of the SILENCE = DEATH slogan—as a *performance* of SILENCE = DEATH. *SILENT|LISTEN* can be said to contain a performance of Cage's *4'33"*. But while *SILENT|LISTEN* provides a distinctive context for Cage's *4'33"*, it doesn't directly manipulate the piece in the same manner that occurs, for example, in General Idea's *Imagevirus*. Rather, it is the proximity of *4'33"* to the AIDS statements that effectively contextualizes Cage's piece. In this sense, *SILENT|LISTEN* performs a duplicitous role as both a *détournement* and an exemplary interpretation of Cage's piece by continuing the critical/negational thrust the work posited in its inception. *SILENT|LISTEN* is therefore positioned at the edge, at the limit, of an authentic realization of *4'33"*.

In addition to the question of authenticity, Ultra-red's *SILENT|LISTEN* engages historical forms of musical organization, particularly as they relate to collectivity. Not primarily concerned with subjective expression or agency, *SILENT|LISTEN* constructs a kind of social framing that relies less upon sound as such, and instead references, and uses, the concert situation as a container for collective organization. Interestingly, Ultra-red locate this kind of organization as already inherent to Cage's work. "What *4'33"* composes," they contend, "is not so much sounds but listening as an experience of collectivity in its raw potential."[83] They continue:

> *SILENT|LISTEN* began as an investigation into silence, fueled by an urgency to organize silence. Over time, the project became a practice of distinguishing between organizing the silence and collective listening—an investigation into

organized listening. This distinction focuses us on the terms by which we are organized by our politics. For us, one such term remains the commitment to reconnecting notions of revolutionary change (i.e. anti-capitalism) with organizing.[84]

Conflating the silence of Cage's *4'33"* with the muted, suppressed voices of dissent involved in the struggle against AIDS, Ultra-red posit an "organizing" that simultaneously points to the modernist conception of music as "organized sound,"[85] while also describing the tactical orchestration of activist mobilization. Similarly, "listening" resonates with the privilege given to aurality by Cage and contemporary experimental music, while it simultaneously invokes its meaning within activist groups. Ultra-red go further, uniting both terms in positing an "organized listening." Relevantly, in his discussion of *SILENT|LISTEN*, Hallas explains that Ultra-red reframe the silence in SILENCE = DEATH through Brazilian critical pedagogy philosopher Paulo Freire's "discipline of silence," in which silence is prefigured as the site for listening and in which "listening [i]s the condition for action, since it enables genuine reflection and analysis."[86] Punning across the historical vocabularies of music and AIDS activism, Ultra-red create a conceptual-linguistic short circuit between the two contexts while directly appropriating music's material organizational form—"collectivity in its raw potential"[87]—as a container for collective action. Ultra-red redeploy organizational and formal modes specific to music as critical instruments in the fight against AIDS. Ultra-red *use* Cage's *4'33"* as one element of their critical music practice.

Ultra-red's deployment of Cage's *4'33"* as a container—a "transparent" presentation of its surroundings—suggests that historical context is inseparable from a work's performance. Considering its broader relevance, Ultra-red's intervention makes explicit a *4'33"* that frames and is framed by its context, leveraging the negational power of silence while creating a temporal space for the unfolding of social process. If *4'33"* is about the opening of the musical frame onto the noise of the surrounding world, then the outside penetrates, shines through, is never neutral—whether that outside comprises McCarthyism, the first decade of the AIDS epidemic, or the dismal scene of today in which the futures of American programs like PEPFAR, HOPWA, and Ryan White are in constant danger of budget cuts that threaten the lives of thousands; in which the lack of health insurance in the United States is responsible for three deaths every hour[88]; in which there are more than three deaths from AIDS every minute globally; and in which the rate of new HIV infections is steadily rising, such that half of all men who have sex with men will be HIV positive by age 50.[89] With its indeterminate and mutable boundaries, *4'33"* opens onto that which surrounds it. Ultra-red's realization implicates both the historical frame from which the work emerges and the temporal present of its performance.

SILENT|LISTEN stages the interpenetration of temporal frames—from the McCarthy-era origins of *4'33"* to the third decade of the AIDS crisis—while it appropriates the musical frame as a collectivizing force in the political struggle against AIDS. Interestingly, while ostensibly conceived as staging an open-ended social process, *SILENT|LISTEN* can also be said to share in the confrontational character found in Cage's *4'33"*, despite Ultra-red's intentions. Along these lines, the "shocking" effect Cage's silent piece had on audiences in the 1950s,[90] echoed throughout historical avant-garde movements and experimental music traditions, may invite questioning. Perhaps this alienating quality can also be compared to the effect *4'33"* had on the participants of Ultra-red's AIDS literacy workshop held in Echo Park, Los Angeles. An unresolved tension pervades the "bemusement" experienced by the working-class Latino men implicated in the *SILENT|LISTEN* realization cited in the epigraph of this chapter. In this sense, such an "exclusionist" tendency of *SILENT|LISTEN* may ironically figure as *too* faithful to *4'33"*'s 1952 premiere, thereby failing to revise Cage's work enough.

Returning to a consideration of artistic interventions around AIDS, aside from the "open-ended" process foregrounded by *SILENT|LISTEN*, a clear value can be found in the kind of affective rage employed by Gran Fury. For not only rage, but a distinctively subversive wit, is seen in Gran Fury and ACT UP's history of political interventions, one reclaimed in demonstrations such as the 2012 "Boehner Occupation," a collaborative action by members of ACT UP New York, ACT UP Philadelphia, and Queerocracy. In response to proposed cuts to foreign and domestic AIDS programs, activists entered US Speaker of the House John Boehner's office, stripped naked, and—playing on the near-homophones "Boehner" and "boner"—chanted slogans like "Boehner, Boehner, don't be a dick, your budget cuts will make us sick." Several of the Naked Seven, as they were later dubbed, chanted and demonstrated with inverted pink equilateral triangles painted on their backs, chests, and genitals.[91] Yet while the musical value of that group's refrains was undeniable, the strength of Ultra-red's *SILENT|LISTEN* lies in a different kind of musicality.

Ultra-red's work stages a deep continuity with the politics of Cagean silence; *SILENT|LISTEN* opens *4'33"* onto a critical confrontation with the present while threading together the musical and visual activist strategies of the recent past.

SILENT|LISTEN insists on the import of both musicological and cultural framings of Cage's work while co-implicating art-historical debates central to AIDS activism and related art practices. Exceeding the concerns of sound as a medium, Ultra-red's use of Cage's *4′33″* problematizes the historical form of the musical work and the politics of (its) performance. Turning on the music-formal problem of *Werktreue*, Ultra-red's intervention precludes an attempt to recuperate the work within the frame of a "sound art" conceived apart from the formal and historical specificity of musical practice. If Cage's indeterminacy paved the way for a kind of absolute interpretive openness—anything can be done in the name of a score; silence equals the resolute death of compositional determinacy—then in Ultra-red's collective realization of *4′33″* the formal stakes are redoubled. *SILENT|LISTEN* confronts the *Werktreue* problematic through Ultra-red's performance of Cage's silent composition. In their (re)casting of Cagean silence as a historically specific mode of queer resistance, as opposed to sidestepping music, the art form becomes central to Ultra-red's strategy of critical negation. Rather than attempting to escape the formal limits imposed by the frame of musical performance, the latter is tactically appropriated as such.

The Silent Network: The Music of Wandelweiser

Introduction: *2010*[1]

You return to your seat following intermission. The once illuminated gallery space has now darkened. It is dusk, and small amounts of sunlight from the windows scatter across the bodies of three performers. As you sit down, the subtle scraping of a metallic chair leg is audible just above the rustling generated by the clothes of the performers as they settle into place. Distributed throughout the space, Manfred Werder, Normisa Pereira da Silva, and Stefan Thut sit on the concrete floor of the gallery, each holding a small, unique object and poised in a shared state of austere collectedness. Werder holds a Japanese toy harmonica, da Silva grasps a bow, and in Thut's palm sits a small music box. The performance begins in silence. After two minutes, your attention wanders to the sounds of birds chirping just outside of the gallery; inside, you notice da Silva draw her bow across a small Chinese cymbal; the brittle inharmonic sound is nearly drowned out by traffic sounds outside. Eventually, after slowly turning the handle on the music box held in his left palm, Thut softly ekes out a single clunky tone on his tiny device. Following several minutes of silence, Thut's music box sound transforms into a quiet series of muted arrhythmic clicks overlapping with the return of da Silva's scraped gong. A similar texture continues over the course of the next fifteen minutes: an occasional sound pokes out from the noises occurring inside and outside of the gallery, dotting the otherwise barren expanse of time. Shortly before the performance ends, you see Werder blowing into his toy harmonica and realize that the delicate tone he produces had been occurring all along. Finally, after looking around the space and then at one another, the performers glance toward the audience to acknowledge the end of the piece. You—and the rest of the audience—applaud.

To anyone familiar with Wandelweiser, the above description will ring an extremely soft yet distinct bell. For, as Christian Wolff has remarked, "they play very quietly, with *huge* silences."[1] Referenced with slogan-like regularity, the group's music is purported to deal with "the evaluation and integration of silence(s) rather than an ongoing carpet of never-ending sounds."[2] My description above refers to a performance of Swiss composer and pianist Werder's *2010¹*—a text score consisting entirely of a fragment quoted from Michel Foucault's *The Archaeology of Knowledge*—presented as part of the Incidental Music Series held at Galerie Mark Müller in Zürich on July 8, 2010. Werder and Thut are both current members of Edition Wandelweiser, the publishing company and record label organized and cofounded by Dutch-born composer and flutist Antoine Beuger. With its headquarters in Haan, Germany, Edition Wandelweiser currently publishes the work of twenty composers coming from seven countries and with birthdates spanning over four decades.

Edition Wandelweiser was born in 1992—the year of John Cage's death. Indeed, Cage's work has remained profoundly influential throughout the international collective's near quarter-century of development. Following the founding of Edition Wandelweiser by Beuger and German violinist and composer Burkhard Schlothauer, the company grew steadily during its first decade, adding roughly one new composer to its roster per year. During its first year of operation, Brazilian guitarist and composer Chico Mello, who remained a member of Edition Wandelweiser until 2005, joined Beuger and Schlothauer. In 1993, Swiss clarinetist and composer Jürg Frey joined, followed in 1994 by German composer Thomas Stiegler and South Korean composer Kunsu Shim, who remained until 1999. In 1995, Michael Pisaro (USA), Radu Malfatti (Austria), and Carlo Inderhees (Germany) joined, along with Japanese pianist and composer Makiko Nishikaze, who remained until 2005. The year 1997 saw the group incorporate Werder and Marcus Kaiser (Germany), followed in 1999 by American trombonist and composer Craig Shepard. In 2002, German composer and musicologist Eva-Maria Houben and French-born Greek composer Anastassis Philippakopoulos joined. Dutch clarinetist and composer Taylan Susam joined the group in 2010. Following the addition of American pianist and composer Sam Sfirri and Swiss composer and cellist Thut, New Zealand-born violinist/composer Johnny Chang, Dutch pianist Dante Boon, and Canadian composer Daniel Brandes became the newest Wandelweiser members.

Beuger explains that Wandelweiser now extends beyond the core group of composers whose scores and recordings are published by the company, forming a "lively network of cooperations and affinities, and friendships with all sorts of gradations, a kind of community that now has real definition."[3] Although Beuger runs the day-to-day operations of Edition Wandelweiser in Haan, Germany, the composer insists that the group is functionally decentralized. According to guitarist and composer Pisaro, "The 'group' as such doesn't ever come together as a whole, and includes others besides composers: musicians, artists, writers—friends."[4] While the group does not congregate in its totality, the Kunstraum in Düsseldorf, Germany regularly holds concerts, readings, exhibitions, and festivals, and provides a strong center of activity for the collective. Beuger is quick to point out that Wandelweiser has never had a manifesto as such, and he has remained opposed to the determination of the collective by reference to shared formal aesthetic goals or criteria. Rather than maintain a list of goals or statements of intent, the collective identity of Wandelweiser is forged from its variegated collection of compositions, recordings, writings, regular performances, a clearly defined group of core members, and a number of satellite groups.

In this chapter, I examine Wandelweiser as a unique social and artistic formation while considering the social import of the group's artworks. Tracing Wandelweiser's history and analyzing a selection of its musical works, I consider the group in relation to historical avant-garde movements and contemporary network theory. While Wandelweiser lack an official manifesto, I locate the group's aesthetic program in their numerous interpretations of Cage's silent composition *4'33"*. Expressed in the various interviews, writings, and musical works of Wandelweiser members, these readings of Cage's work—largely consonant with the consideration of "silence as an autonomous musical phenomenon"[5]—are contrasted with existing and original interpretations of *4'33"* which underline its potential as a conceptual, discursive, and socially engaged musical work.

Two Beginnings: A Silent Music Contest, a "Free Sex" Commune

Before founding Edition Wandelweiser, Beuger and Schlothauer met as members of the Aktionsanalytische Organisation (AAO), a radical commune started in 1970 and led by Vienna Actionist artist Otto Mühl. In Mühl's large-scale experimental art/life project, also referred to as the Friedrichshof Commune, he sought to replace an emphasis on the individual with a valorization of the collective; communal sex replaced monogamy, group ownership replaced private property, and "*Aktionsanalyse*" replaced psychoanalysis.[6] According to AAO member (and brother of Burkhard Schlothauer) Andreas Schlothauer, there were approximately 2,000 residents between 1971 and 1991, although the commune never held more than 600 members at any one time.[7] Andreas Schlothauer's generally more critical account of the commune, *Die Diktatur der freien Sexualität* (The Dictator of Free Sexuality) (1992), presents a sociological study while Robert Fleck's *Die Mühl-Kommune* (2003) takes an art-historical perspective. Interestingly, both accounts refer to the "free sex commune" as a totalitarian formation. As Andreas Schlothauer describes it:

> The move towards "free sex" was not only the realization of a year-long discussed idea or a "dream," but also the submission to the leadership of Mühl, the increasingly specific conditions under which the "liberation" from monogamy occurred.[8]

Fleck refers to the "totalitarian character" of AAO and claims that it aimed to regulate every detail of "life context" for its members; he compares AAO with the Communist regimes of the twentieth century, suggesting that AAO had replaced party-state control of the economy with the regulation of sexuality.[9] Noting the 1980 publication of *Mille Plateaux*, Fleck offers the work of French poststructuralist philosophers Gilles Deleuze and Félix Guattari as an appropriate context for analyzing the Mühl commune.[10] Yet while Deleuze and Guattari pose their concept of the "rhizome"—a root structure that "connects any point to any other point"[11]—as a counter to the "arborescence" of totalitarianism, Fleck nevertheless insists that AAO members enjoyed creative freedom and, to an extent, hierarchical mobility.[12]

Beuger's membership in AAO began shortly after finishing his studies in music composition; with an interest in alternative communities, he simply could not pass on the opportunity.[13] Beuger goes on to explain that, for him, AAO was a kind of "psychological and sociological laboratory" in which there was a focus on expression and spontaneity, on making public that which is private; composition as a private activity had no place in it.[14] Beuger was a member of AAO from 1977 until 1989. The commune was dissolved following Mühl's 1991 conviction and seven-year jail sentence for rape, sexual abuse of minors, abuse of authority, and a series of drug offenses.[15] As Beuger expressed it retrospectively, "You learn a lot about power structures."[16] Ongoing contradictions and antagonisms remained inherent to the commune's economic and political organization. In 1978, a member of the commune wrote a letter to a local Viennese magazine explaining that the group (having begun as a "hippie flophouse")[17] got a "haircut" and had become "more realistic"; the group requested to advertise drawing, history, drama, and music courses,[18] and even turned to stockbroking to help with funding. As Beuger elaborates, "In the daytime you're in a 'theater piece', in the middle of capitalism playing a stockbroker. Then, coming back home, you're in communism with no private property."[19] Counterintuitively, it was apparently money earned from Burkhard Schlothauer's work in construction that would provide the initial funding for Edition Wandelweiser.[20]

Beuger refers explicitly to his experience in AAO when speaking about his role in Wandelweiser's formation. It was Beuger's conception of community in particular that was at stake as a member of the Mühl commune: "In it we knew too well what we were, and who was a part of it, and what the rules were and the ideals. Because of that it gets too rigid and then it explodes."[21] For Fleck, "the question remain[ed] as to how a liberation movement turned into a dictatorial *Gesamtkunstwerk*."[22] Beuger explains that the rigidity of AAO had inspired him to start Wandelweiser from the premise that a community as such should not be inflexible. He describes his role in Wandelweiser as "integrating" and that without his presence the group would not be as cohesive an entity; furthermore, the group would not be the same without the knowledge he had gained during his time in the AAO commune.

Beuger first encountered Frey at the 1991 *Internationales Kompositions-Seminar "Stille Musik,"* a "silent music"-themed competition that ended in a hung jury.[23] Held from September 10–14, 1991 at the Stiftung Künstlerhaus in Boswil, Switzerland, the event culminated in a reception on September 15 in which the decision was announced that all eight compositions from the contest participants had "proven to be so unique that the jury had decided to award the prize money equally among all composers."[24] Led by German composer Dieter Schnebel,[25] the jury consisted of Roland Moser, Alfred Schnittke, Marianne Schroeder, Jakob Ullmann, and Christian Wolff. Note that the latter's work has remained an important influence on Wandelweiser. A group of eight composers of various nationalities residing throughout Europe (Antoine Beuger, Jürg Frey, Dieter Jordi, Ricardas Kabelis, Hiroshi Kihara, Chico Mello, Urs Peter Schneider, and Ernstalbrecht Stiebler) was selected based on the prior submission of compositions.[26]

The idea was that each composition would be performed during the seminar and, following a discussion and second performance of each work, the jury would choose a winner. Perhaps unsurprisingly, much of the music performed during the four-day seminar was either very quiet or sparse in texture; interestingly, none of the works contained only silence. Beuger composed *lesen, hören, buch für stimme* (1991), a "book" for solo voice and two tape parts. Calling for a 56-minute performance, the score consisted of 147 pages of notated music that combined graphic symbols and traditional notation; sparse rhythmic figures appear alongside a graph that indicates volume-level changes for one of the tapes. Jürg Frey's *unbetitelt IV* (1990) for viola and piano consists of a repeated exchange between a scalar passage scored for piano and an arpeggio in the viola, altogether creating a hocket melody that is subtly elaborated toward the end of the work. At this early stage, Frey's work resonates with his later formulation of music as an "expanse" in which "memory is shaped less by the individual details than by a situation in which one has spent a certain period of time."[27] Referring to the overall quality of the music presented at the seminar, "it is 'quiet,'" Wolff recalled following the seminar, "because of qualities of rhythm and sonority."[28] He continues, "There is an overall rhythmic sense not of single-tracked momentum but of diffusion and suspension, moving out as though from various centers."[29] Although no single winner was selected from *Stille Musik*, Beuger obtained the long-term friendship and artistic partnership of Frey.[30] Wandelweiser gained two members as a direct result and planted the seeds for the future involvement of others.

Although clearly a formative experience for Beuger, Frey, Werder, and Mello, *Stille Musik* did not produce a founding doctrine or manifesto for Wandelweiser. Still, despite this lack of a formal aesthetic program, Wandelweiser have managed to sculpt a relatively refined collective identity, however heterogeneous its individual elements may be relative to the group. They are, as Christian Wolff puts it, "really a collective."[31] What, then, can be said of this "network" of affinities? If Wandelweiser is thought only in terms of the scores published by Edition Wandelweiser, then the term "network" might be misleading. Nonetheless, the label seems appropriate in referring to the web of activity surrounding the group's writings, musical works, and concert events. Unlike Mühl's AAO, Wandelweiser are not geographically bound; they unite, but on specifically aesthetic territory. But while successfully avoiding statements of intent, Wandelweiser have been nothing short of prolific in interviews and in their own publications. Along these lines, Bruno Latour argues in his recent work on social formations that "groups are not silent things, but rather the provisional product of a constant uproar made by the millions of contradictory voices about what is a group and who pertains to what."[32] For Latour, groups are not inert, but always mobilized by contestation. Group formations themselves are "performed" and, in the process, produce "new and interesting data."[33] Though reluctant to delineate "explicit" boundaries, there are distinct voices at work in Wandelweiser: the contours of the group are effectively traced by the discourse and artworks of its members.

As intrinsic as the study of music is to the field of sociology—for many of the great social thinkers (Marx, Simmel, Weber, Adorno, Bourdieu) music played a crucial role—relatively little has been theorized about collectivity in a musical context, for example, the Florentine Camerata, Les Six, or the Second Viennese School. Yet given the breadth of their work, a strictly musical context is perhaps too limited for an analysis of Wandelweiser. And since they share certain problems and characteristics of the historical avant-garde, a richer context may be drawn around Wandelweiser as an artistic movement more broadly. An obvious comparison might be made between Wandelweiser and Fluxus. Several members of Wandelweiser have cited Fluxus artists as important influences,[34] and although Wandelweiser began more than three decades after Cage's course at the New School for Social Research—attended by notable future Fluxus artists George Brecht, Dick Higgins, and Allan Kaprow—Wandelweiser and Fluxus at the very least share in the uniqueness of their respective interpretations of Cage's work. Chronological lag notwithstanding, we might think of Wandelweiser and Fluxus as parallel yet distinct branches stemming from the crisis initiated by Cage and his famous silent work, *4'33"*.

The question as to whether Fluxus was (or is) itself an avant-garde group is answered in Hannah Higgins's 2002 study. Referring to the infamous "purges" of George Maciunas, for Higgins, "dogmatism, ideological self-assertion, intolerance of nuances, occasional purges, and a linear time line" mean that Fluxus "can properly be described as avant-garde, or neo-avant-garde."[35] Though Wandelweiser have avoided some of those pitfalls (perhaps as a direct result of Beuger's self-conscious role as an organizer), there remain structural features linking Wandelweiser to the avant-garde that deserve consideration. For Renato Poggioli, as a "group manifestation," the avant-garde is "not so much of an aesthetic fact as a sociological one."[36] A tension is inherent to Poggioli's dialectic of avant-garde movements: while a movement is in its "*activistic moment . . . constituted primarily to obtain a positive result, for* a concrete end" (emphasis added), it is also "*antagonistic*" or "*against* something or someone." The something may be the academy, tradition; the someone may be a master whose teaching and example, whose prestige and authority, are considered wrong or harmful."[37] For Peter Bürger, the avant-garde revolves around the question of art's autonomy, its independence from society.[38] Bürger attempts to articulate the complexity of the concept of artistic autonomy: conceding to both art's separation from society (*l'art pour l'art*) as a given condition *and* the flat-out denial of any separateness that art may have from society based on the "correct insight that autonomy is a historically conditioned phenomenon" at once misses the logical and historical "contradictoriness inherent in the thing itself."[39] Poggioli's and Bürger's theories of the avant-garde can be seen as mirror images of one another: whereas Bürger's concern is art's relation to the social, for Poggioli the avant-garde is a social relation; while for Poggioli, the avant-garde is activistic, Bürger, as Mann contends, "validates only one form of activism— that directed against the institution (of) art."[40] The relative aesthetic radicalness of Wandelweiser and the view it has held of itself as remaining "outside of the status quo" created by European "new music" organizations[41] are by some token illustrative of the *antagonistic* moment to which Poggioli refers. Concerning the question of autonomy in Fluxus, Higgins maintains that the group has been "deeply committed to the world."[42] But where can one find a critical engagement with broader cultural or social concerns in Wandelweiser?

A decade after the group's founding, Wandelweiser trombonist and composer Radu Malfatti scornfully lamented,

> Almost all the music which mercilessly surrounds us today has the same underlying structure: never-ending gabbiness. What's the difference between MTV music and most of the classical avant-garde? They use different material, but they're both intensively talkative. We're surrounded by noises and sensory overstimulation wherever we go. For me, the true avant-garde is the critical analysis or issue-taking with our cultural surroundings. What's needed is not faster, higher, stronger, louder—I want to know about the lull in the storm.[43]

While there is an "off-the-cuff" quality to Malfatti's remark, the reader cannot help but to take its implications seriously. The initial charge of "gabbiness" that equates the "low" form of MTV music with the classical avant-garde is worthy of attention given Wandelweiser's limited engagements with other forms of popular culture.[44] More relevant to our concerns, the silence (or quiet) represented by Malfatti's "lull in the storm" here implicitly answers his call for cultural "issue-taking." But with the complexity of Bürger's understanding of autonomy in mind, perhaps we should not draw premature conclusions regarding whether or not this kind of criticality is achieved in Wandelweiser.

Nevertheless, there is a clear contradiction between Malfatti's confrontational quiet as "critical analysis" and Beuger's consideration of Cage's *4'33"* as "the beginning—not an end—of a serious involvement with silence as an *autonomous musical phenomenon*."[45]

Reconnecting Cage

Cage's influence on Wandelweiser may be hard to overstate. As Burkhard Schlothauer succinctly confessed, "The only composer I'm really interested in is Cage."[46] Beuger felt Cage's influence at age fifteen following a 1970 festival performance by Cage and Merce Cunningham in Breda, the Netherlands.[47] It is difficult to take into account the variety of views on Cage expressed in the numerous essays, interviews, blog entries, and program notes authored by members of Wandelweiser. But it is possible that no other single work has shaped the overall understanding of music for the collective as significantly as Cage's *4'33"*. Perhaps because of the work's sparseness—it presents only the "bare essentials" for a musical performance—*4'33"* has produced such a density of thought including but not limited to sound, silence, notation, and musical meaning in a broader sense. Specifically, the work is relevant here due not only to the ostensible similarities it shares with many works by Wandelweiser composers, but also to the historical and conceptual underpinnings of Cage's work. Indeed there are, as Frey has remarked, "many different silences,"[48] although there are, perhaps, also an equal number of discursive contexts that frame the phenomenon.

Having attained iconic status, *4'33"* has often been dismissed as a gag or scandal, an idea one need only encounter as anecdote in order to understand. James Pritchett has compared the popular reception of *4'33"* to the initial reception of Warhol's Campbell soup cans, noting that it has similarly served as a "punch line for jokes and cartoons; the springboard for a thousand analyses and arguments; [and] evidence of the extremity of a 'destructive avant-garde' that appeared in the 1950s and 1960s."[49] The thoroughly documented multiple origins of *4'33"* may be listed here: Cage's pivotal attempt to open the field of musical sound to the eventual inclusion of any and all sound; his proposed work *Silent Prayer* (1948) conceived as a physical silencing of Muzak[50]; the composer's encounter with the white paintings of Rauschenberg; his engagement with notions of emptiness and nothingness found in Zen Buddhism; his programmatic insistence upon non-intentionality and the removal of the ego from the process of artistic creation; his insistence, based on the music of Satie and Webern, that duration be thought of as the basic unit of both sound and silence[51]; and, lastly, Cage's visit to an anechoic chamber at Harvard in which he learned of the impossibility of experiencing true silence—instead Cage heard the sounds of his own nervous system and his blood in circulation.[52]

The actual score for *4'33"* has an obscure history. Two versions of the score were created—one using blank measures in metric time (1952) and the other using space-equals-time notation (1953)—before the more commonly known score was published in 1961.[53] The latter version, which also contained a dedication to Irwin Kremen, would serve as Cage's proto-text score notated entirely in language.[54] Rather than indicating sounds using traditional music notation, *4'33"* linguistically describes three durations in which the silence of the concert hall becomes the content of the piece. The main body of this later version of the score reads, "I / TACET / II / TACET / III / TACET," describing three sections during which the performer simply rests. The score follows with a note that describes the first performance of the work in 1952 by David Tudor in Woodstock, New York, and explains that the title of the composition, when programmed, should refer to the overall duration of the performance, which may be of any length.

4'33" insists upon the importance of the language used to prompt a performance: the means by which Cage's score instantiates and underlies the resulting silence is of interest. Accordingly, Pisaro has explained that, following Cage, "notation is not a form of communication, but an incitement to action (or at times, non-action). The character of that action comes in response to the score."[55] As Pisaro's comment suggests, *4'33"* represents the break between the musical score and its sounding result, which Cage defined as indeterminacy. Similarly, Ian Pepper has argued that, "by defining 'music' as writing on the one hand, and as sound on the other, and by erecting an absolute barrier between the two spheres, Cage initiated a crisis in music that has barely been articulated, let alone worked through."[56] Beuger expresses a similar attitude when he states that "asking someone to play an 'a' of a certain duration, a certain volume and a certain tone colour is like asking him to write the number pi: he'll do something more or less approaching something else."[57] Indeterminacy, the breakdown of the relationship between the score and the resultant performance of a work, suggests a shift in focus from the composer of a determinate musical work to the listener who witnesses the unfolding of a process. In this sense, the score is less a blueprint that mandates a preconstructed musical object and more a prompt that produces a series of contingent consequences in its realization.

Consisting of instructions presented entirely in language, *4′33″* is linked in Liz Kotz's analysis to the broader turn to language in 1960s art, which also paved the way for conceptual art and the various neo-avant-garde movements of the decade. Kim-Cohen has argued for an interpretation of *4′33″* aligned with a conceptual art defined by Peter Osborne as "art *about* the cultural act of definition paradigmatically, but by no means exclusively, the definition of 'art'."[58] Kim-Cohen proposes a *4′33″* in which "normally stable ideas about the roles of the performer, the composer, and the relationship of one to the other are unmoored from their anchorage, allowed to drift freely in the tides of conceptualization."[59] While for Kim-Cohen, *4′33″* is conceived as a legible conceptual work, for Paul Mann, it is the shuttling between the work's "performance-immediacy" and the work's discursivity—its meaning as constituting and constituted through its historical and critical accounts—that becomes important. Mann cites a comment made by Christopher Butler lamenting that, since the work had already "made its critical point"—that is, it had already been performed and the silence was no longer startling for audiences—it no longer retained any value.[60] For Mann, "representation is already inherent in its presentation; the work also performs in discourse."[61] I want to suggest that these modes are present simultaneously. The work is inscribed in language, in terms of its score and its conceptuality: both "performance-immediacy" and representation are intimately bound together in a kind of dynamic harmony.

Still another interpretation of *4′33″* considers the piece as a presentation of the concert situation itself, drawing attention to the frame of the musical setting *as* the work. Reinterpreting a term originally elaborated by Kant, Derrida defines the *parergon* as that which "separates the internal from the external," a kind of double border which "joins together what it splits"; as a frame or "a supplement to the operation," it is "neither work nor outside the work."[62] South African musicologist Martina Viljoen invokes Derrida's *parergon* (an intrinsic part of Kim-Cohen's interpretive framework as well), arguing that it is across this "dynamic field of influence" that musical meaning is situated.

> Acting on (and across) the "border," the "limit" of the musical work, the performer, the listener, and the hermeneutic analyst creatively shape musical meaning. They respond to its musical autonomy by constantly enacting it anew within novel performative frames, and renegotiate boundaries which fit new situations.[63]

Woodstock, New York, 1952: David Tudor's simple action of opening and closing the piano lid to indicate the beginning and end of each movement is to become indelibly inscribed into *4′33″*'s history, its score, performance, and subsequent discussion. The performance note in the "Tacet" versions of the score executes a role between instruction and documentation; it links the world of the symbolic to the contingent worlds of its realization, ultimately tethering both to broader discursive and cultural universes. Contrasting with Pritchett's claim that "looking for the meaning behind the piece takes us away from direct experience and into the world of ideas and stories"[64] is the very story built into the framing of *4′33″*. The marking that delimits the spatial and temporal boundaries of the musical frame—"the line [*trait*] which purports to mark its edges"[65]—is divided; music is opened to its outside. The durational frame of four minutes and thirty-three seconds opens onto the expanse of history, while the concert hall expands to include the noise of the surrounding world. The story of Tudor's opening of the piano lid unbars the fluid passage between musical performance and (its) representation. The outside floods music's proper interior.

Whereas, for Kim-Cohen, there is a cascading process of signification inherent to hearing/viewing whereby the spectator's perspective is—to an extent—given primacy, Mann's pessimistic formulation further reduces meaning purely to "circulation within the discursive economy."[66] Viljoen, meanwhile, emphasizes a "dynamic field" in which performer, listener, and analyst interact and produce meaning. Porous in its temporal and spatial bounds, *4′33″* permeates this field by virtue of its material and discursive mutability. As Kim-Cohen argues, *4′33″* does "unmoor" the roles of performer, composer, and listener; but it also connects: presence and representation; history and immediacy; contingency and record. As a variation upon Viljoen's interpretive framework, we might seek to combine with it the structural logic of a group such as Wandelweiser: a "network" of indeterminate agents, of "cooperations and affinities," all of which work in tandem, conflict, and collaboration. Such an expansive engagement with *4′33″* emerges out of the consideration of this confluence of elements—from *4′33″* performances, discourse, and criticism, to *4′33″* historical accounts, "post"- *4′33″* music, *4′33″* offshoots, parodies, and *détournements*—each thought as one interconnective node in a synchronic field of meaning-space. Contingent as indeterminate silence, and with its "network" of ever-shifting interpretive fluidity, *4′33″* can be considered the anti-autonomous artwork par excellence.

While "offshoots, parodies, and *détournements*" of *4′33″* are far removed from the work of Wandelweiser, if there is a single category appropriate for considering the work of the group, it might be something like "post-*4'33"* music," a term that designates a body of music considered to follow, while making important departures from, Cage's piece.[67] One such departure is that none of the collective's works actually consist exclusively of silence—although there may be certain exceptions. Werder's scores, for example, often exhibit a liminal space between his implicit acknowledgment that sounds must always occur (as Cage realized during his visit to the Harvard anechoic chamber) and an explicit call for sounds to be performed. For instance, Werder's *2006¹* score reads, "a place, natural light, where the performers like to be / a time / (sounds)." Addressing its relationship to *4'33"*, Werder states that *2006¹* is "not about exploring new sounds," but rather, it is about exploring "a new relation" to the sounding world.[68] Since 1998, Werder's scores have displayed a striking similarity to one another. Pisaro notes that, in considering the trajectory of Werder's work over time, "one considers the difference between the indications 'time' and 'a time' or between 'place', 'a place' . . . and 'places.'"[69] The parenthetical enclosing of sounds creates an even greater ambiguity between the call for an active realization of sounds and a passive listening or observing. While either interpretation (to perform sounds or simply to allow sounds to be present) is possible, a performer must ultimately consider the language used to notate the score—a feature Werder's scores share with Cage's *4'33"*.

Distinct from *4'33"*—in which silence constitutes the work's content in its entirety—silence often appears in Beuger's work as a compositional element that belongs to a broader musical syntax. Crucial are the hues or shades of silence that arise from different performance scenarios. His series *calme étendues* (1996/97), for example, consists of seventeen individual works, with each part scored for a single instrument while containing the same basic structure: the performer plays a three-second sound, followed by a five-second silence, alternating between the two elements until s/he stops for a longer silence. Acoustically, the five-second pause and the longer silence are, initially, virtually equivalent; but the experiences of each silence are incommensurable. Even during the first five seconds of the longer silence, one senses that something has halted; a *hole* is cut into the musical fabric. The "carpet of sounds" is jerked out from underneath the listener, who is left momentarily hovering above an imminent silent abyss.

Beuger explains that he had been interested in the silence preceding and following the performance of a piece of music for many years. He had been interested in exploring this experience of silence as a "disruption." In Beuger's words, silence is "a direct—not symbolic or imaginative—encounter with reality, which means with contingency, singularity, emptiness. Silence in my music always is [an] encounter with reality, enforced by the event of a situation being disrupted without any reason."[70] For Beuger, the sense of silence as an "interruption of what is there" is comparable to loss or death; it is "irreversible." It is commemorative.[71] As a distinct break—or "cut," to use Beuger's term adapted from Alain Badiou—this interruptive dimension of silence was his decisive departure from Cage. Beuger contends:

> In the music understood as the music after the event of *4'33"*, it is not the sound, but the cut itself which is the subject of compositional activity. The process is composed with which, out of the infinite variety of sounds, a new cut, a new opportunity for perception is obtained.[72]

Perhaps a more appropriate comparison to make with Beuger's *calme étendues* is Cage's *Waiting*, a little-discussed work for piano composed just eight months prior to *4'33"*. Nearly one minute shorter than the originally determined length of *4'33"*, *Waiting* consists of sixteen measures of silence during which the pianist and audience anticipate the forthcoming piano music; the expectation of audience and performer alike is then "interrupted" by a pair of delicate ostinato phrases that are followed by a much shorter silence. In *calme étendues*, the function of such silence is inverted: rather than permit musical sound to interrupt a period of "waiting," silence disrupts the state of musical flow. Beuger's *calme étendues* put Cage's *Waiting* "*vom Kopf auf die Füße*"; they stand waiting on its feet, turn silence into disruption.

Another noteworthy feature of the *calme étendues* is each work's indeterminate length, allowing realizations that can last anywhere between forty-five minutes and nine hours. German musicologist Volker Straebel discusses the potentially extreme duration of *calme étendues* in the context of conceptual art and what he refers to as conceptual music (or conceptual composition), proposing that "the aspect of the aesthetic imagination of real presence becomes especially vivid during long but time-limited events having the character of a performance (e.g., *calme étendues* by Wandelweiser composer Antoine Beuger, 1996/97, which lasts up to nine hours)." Straebel continues:

> A piece of music of nine hours' duration necessarily eludes perception as a whole. The knowledge of its actual performance at the moment is available to an audience member who is absent from the room solely as an aesthetic image. Here the uncertain element of truth in such a projective image is in antithetical tension to the phenomenological structure of perception and imagination.

When I leave the room, I can assume at any given time that the performance is going on, and something is happening in the performance space that follows the score (with which I'm familiar) and/or is related or similar to what I perceived at an earlier moment during the performance. This uncertainty nonetheless points to the uncertainty of any given perception, which can always deceive me. But my imagination cannot. Imagining, as a synthetic act, is always certainty, for rather than telling me something about the world, it is solely the project of my assumptions.[73]

Framed as a work of conceptual art/music, the *calme étendues* illustrate for Straebel the ability of the work to overcome its "objectification" in the "movement between the perceiving and imagining consciousness."[74] Straebel's privileging of the imaginary over direct perception (perception can always deceive me, "but my imagination cannot")[75] is provocative in the context of Beuger's *calme étendues*, considering the composer's insistence on "a direct—not symbolic or imaginative—encounter with reality."[76] Furthermore, and relevant to our discussion of artistic autonomy, the imaginary threatens to unravel the tightly wound threads of music as "pure sounding." It posits an inherent connection between music and its outside—the void that surrounds music, yet of which it is wholly composed. (There is, perhaps, an intuitive objection to Straebel's "conceptual" consideration of Beuger's *calme étendues*. One need only consider a similarly "ungraspable" activity such as watching the sun set. We cannot see the actual process of the sun setting at any given instant. But, one must ask, does the day therefore overcome objectification?) Straebel's conceptual composition, as the "movement between perceiving and imagining," by implicating the imaginary, tugs at one of the loose threads of musical autonomy. Ultimately, however, it leaves the "carpet of sounds" relatively intact.

Let us return to the problem of artistic autonomy framed as relating the poles of art and life. Mühl's AAO can be viewed as a radical solution to the problem of artistic autonomy, as the complete integration of an art practice into the "praxis of life" in which the two spheres became inseparable. AAO was exemplary as an avant-garde formation, in that it was not necessarily the content of individual artworks, but the way art functioned in society that was at stake. In AAO, the relationship between art and life was totalizing. As a totally integrated art/life practice, AAO had lost the ability to wage an adequate critique of art or life from either perspective. While novel as a social formation, Wandelweiser, I argue, move to the opposite extreme from AAO in their disengagement from broader social or political relevance. Bürger concludes that following the failure of the "total return of art to the praxis of life, the work of art entered into a new relationship to reality," which epitomized a "new type of engaged art."[77] What, then, might a truly engaged musical practice sound like? Where might one make a cut into music that allows for this kind of connection?

I want to add to the existing conceptual and discursive engagements with *4′33″* an attempt to take into account the social dimension of the work.[78] While the roles of composer, performer, and listener may be called into question, one may still point to specific relations within the situations made possible by the work. In *4′33″*, the dynamic between performer and audience, for example, rather than being destroyed, is underlined as a key component of the work. An audience member coughs. Looking around, she realizes that the cough, along with her physical and emotional responses, her body language, all become "part of the work." The performer then assumes the passive role of listening to the audience member; the two acknowledge the ostensible "equality" of their actions (they both make sounds), which overlays their ordinary hierarchical roles as performer and listener. An exchange occurs. The interplay multiplies across the rest of the audience as they take notice. The performance situation—the physical site as context—also behaves as an agent within this web of connections. Holding a guitar, a boy runs to the front of a public bus and announces that he will perform *4′33″* as passengers make their daily commute. It is not simply that passengers are suddenly audience members and the bus becomes an ambulant concert hall. *4′33″* intersects with the situation: *4′33″* absorbs the context as "content." That realization is available to view on YouTube[79]; indeed, mediation—whether an audio recording or video accessible via social media—functions as yet another framing of the work. Like David Tudor's original 1952 Woodstock version, performances of *4′33″* further open the work; its realizations "add" to *4′33″*. And this kind of "contextual indeterminacy" may allow critical readings of *4′33″* in which context plays a crucial role.

If, as Beuger contends, following *4′33″*, the cut itself constitutes a new subject for composition, then I would argue that this incision must also cut across the social. We have already seen how Ultra-red deploy Cage's composition as a container for political action in their militant AIDS activist project *SILENT|LISTEN*. Ultra-red constitute a significant departure from Waldeweiser's approach both in their organization as a collective and in their use of statements and manifestos. In contrast to Wandelweiser, Ultra-red do issue a statement of intent, explaining that they seek to reverse the existing model of activist art, in which the political content of aesthetic form "does the work of both cultural analysis and cultural action." Their project, as a result, becomes intimately folded along the axes of the aesthetic and the social.

> If we understand organizing as the formal practices that build relationships out of which people compose an analysis and strategic actions, how might art contribute to and challenge those very processes? How might those processes already constitute aesthetic forms?[80]

Ultra-red's politicized use of silence turns on the function of metaphor. Silence stands in for the disturbing, deathly silence that has surrounded the AIDS crisis. Writer and musician Terre Thaemlitz explains:

> The project uses Cage's *4'33"* as a metaphor for what they term the current "epidemic of silence" around AIDS within the US generally, as well as in relation to the increasingly inaudible noises of contemporary AIDS activism—activism that had once rallied around the slogan "Silence = Death."[81]

Fittingly, the emblem for Ultra-red's *SILENT|LISTEN* is a mesostic made in pseudo-Cagean fashion. It spells out LISTEN with each letter of SILENT, turning the self-referentiality of silence into an ouroboros-like text-image showing that "listen" is a part of "silent." To arrive at *listen*, *silent* need only to be respelled. Thaemlitz describes the project as a kind of palimpsest, "an archive of the absence of an archive. An archive of sound as memory."[82] Thaemlitz continues to explain how an Ultra-red performance led to local government action.

> In the annotations to *4'33"* (Arrest Record #1, County USC Hospital, May 22, 2004), Ultra-red members return fourteen years later to the site of a cornerstone demonstration on May 20, 1990, which forced the Los Angeles government to open an AIDS clinic at the hospital.[83]

As a "reading" and performance of Cage's *4'33"*, Ultra-red's *SILENT|LISTEN* doubtless participates as an agent of meaning production in the "*4'33"* network" alluded to earlier. Through its "misuse" of *4'33"*, *SILENT|LISTEN* deploys the logic of *détournement*. Exceeding the notion of music as autonomous sound, music becomes bound to (its) broader social concerns. Furthermore, *4'33"* and the AIDS crisis *frame one another as social contexts*. Thaemlitz concludes that Ultra-red challenge audiences "to confront their desires for witnessing and contributing to social transformation."[84] Ultra-red's work shows the real potential for both "critical analysis" and "cultural issue-taking" to take shape as central elements of a musical practice. More than simply political in the content of individual works, Ultra-red engage the relationship between the aesthetic and the political; art challenges and shapes social action. Interestingly, Ultra-red's work has been referred to as "'music performance'"[85] and is elsewhere classified as sound art.[86] But why not hear this work as music proper—more precisely, as *critical music*?

If Ultra-red render audible the silenced voices of those involved in political and social struggles, then Werder's recent work can be interpreted as a meditation on the context of enunciation itself, the artistic framing of a discursive act. Many of Werder's scores, like the "Tacet" versions of Cage's *4'33"*, are scored using only written language. As with Cage's *4'33"*, performances of Werder's recent scores remain open to the indeterminate sounds inside and outside of the performance space. Werder invokes *4'33"* and George Brecht's *Water Yam* (1963) to explain that, for him, indeterminacy occurs as a kind of "intrinsic unavailability (*Unverfügbarkeit*)"; in the score, "language oscillates between power and unavailability."[87] Yet another level of indeterminacy resides in Werder's works wherein a performer must decide just what s/he is to do with the minimal text fragments contained in each score. Just how does one realize a score that consists only of the text, "dost / rue / araucaria / ore / lewfü," as in the composer's work *2009¹*? Werder refers to this use of indeterminacy as a "refusal to prescribe the form of performance or set it down in the score."[88] It is as though these works lead a kind of double life: that which unfolds in performance and the strands of text which both prompt the performance and yet somehow speak behind it. Beuger often includes a citation in the introduction page of his scores; for example, in his *badiou tunings for eighteen* (2005), a brief statement is followed by a quote from the eponymous philosopher. Others have included Stéphane Mallarmé, Deleuze, Ad Reinhardt, Sam Peckinpah, and John Ashbery.

In Werder's recent work, however, a single quotation often constitutes the entire score. *2009⁴*, for example, consists of a fragment taken from the work of French essayist and poet Francis Ponge. Werder's *2010¹* score (a performance of which was described at the beginning of this chapter) consists solely of a fragment of text taken from Foucault's *The Archaeology of Knowledge* (1969 [2002]): "the rarity of the *énoncés* / that immediate transparency that constitutes the element of their possibility." Foucault refers to the conditions that construct, contextualize, and allow for discourse (in any field: scientific, legal, aesthetic); this scaffolding, or "field of objects," of which discourse is a part and makes possible, is, because of its all-pervasiveness, "neither hidden, nor visible."[89] Notably, Foucault does not describe the logical structures of propositions or phrases, but rather, aims at "defining the conditions in which the function that gave a series of signs . . . an existence, and a specific existence, can operate."[90] Writing of Foucault's project, Deleuze explains that "this virtual or latent content multiplies meaning and opens itself up to interpretation, creating a 'hidden discourse' that *de jure* is a source of great richness."[91]

The full sentence of the Foucault text excerpted in the second line of Werder's score states: "We shall try to render visible, and analyzable, that immediate transparency that constitutes the element of their possibility."[92] The irony is in what Werder leaves out. The fragment, "we shall try to render visible, and analyzable," is itself made invisible, removed, in Werder's *2010¹*, from its source. Does Werder intend to hide the attempt to render visible the immediate transparency? Or by leaving out the first part of Foucault's statement, does Werder point to a supposed impossibility of musical meaning? The "making visible, and analyzable" is itself left out, made invisible. With a provocative literalness, this invisibility might be understood as pointing to the hiddenness of the score in performance, its physical absence from the view of the audience—the status of the score as parergonal: "neither [the] work nor outside the work,"[93] it lies along the edges of the musical frame.[94] Beneath its sparse texture and behind its mute surface, there is perhaps something profound expressed in Werder's piece. While ostensibly invested in its physical presence, *2010¹* contemplates its expressive potential as a discursive musical work; paradoxically, it enunciates a kind of self-cancellation of its own ability to speak. *2010¹* may, therefore, be thought of as containing a meta-statement concerning the production of meaning—how does one locate a discourse "neither hidden, nor visible"?—in a musical context. Yet while there is a critical value to a work that proposes this kind of reflexivity, one still wonders whether the piece remains caught up within its own circular process of self-questioning, hermetically closed to an outside. In this interpretation, does *2010¹* ever move beyond the question of *what one can say in music* in order to actually say anything at all? Do *2010¹* and other works by Werder operate, as the composer would contend, "in relation to our complex situation of being [in] the world, and at the same time observing the world"?[95]

In some instances, Werder's scores feature a witty crossing of the profound with the banal. *2008¹*, for example, contains a fragment taken from Deleuze and Guattari's *Qu'est-ce que la philolsophie?* and appears in the same format—a "score" written in plain font, printed on an A4 page—as his work *2008²*, which consists of the text "birches / a butterfly / swifts / bats / a fox." Interestingly, Werder refers to *2008²* and *2008¹* both as containing "found sentences."[96]

Along with *2010¹*, Werder's *2008²* and *2008¹* engage broader questions of appropriation and authorship. In another seminal essay by Foucault, "What is an Author?," the philosopher states that the first rule of the "author function" is that "discourses are objects of appropriation."[97] Regarding Werder, there is a subversive edge to the notion that a composer simply stumbles across the text of an author, and, from that encounter, a piece is formed in its entirety. It becomes possible then to envision, with Foucault, a future in which "the author function will disappear," in which the author "will have to be determined or, perhaps, experienced."[98] Werder's appropriated texts suggest a critical position with respect to musical authorship that also recalls the appropriation strategies of Ultra-red: the act of composition understood as individual expression is replaced by a confrontation with something found, "out there" in the world. Commenting on Duchamp's ready-mades, Bürger claims that the avant-garde had already begun a "radical negation of the category of individual creation," thereby explicitly linking the collective to the problem of artistic autonomy.[99] Werder's use of indeterminacy, as a refusal to prescribe the parameters of performance in his scores,[100] is also pertinent in this respect. Taken together, these approaches suggest a withering away of the solitary figure of the composer, allowing the emergence of a creativity that truly belongs to the collective.

What about the future of the collective? At a time when collective action organized through social networks is widely purported to have shown emancipatory potential, questions posed by a group as unique as Wandelweiser are of utmost relevance. Thought around social and artistic group formations has gained wider import, and Latour explains that while sociologists still disagree on questions about the types of groups that constitute social amalgamations, the methods by which such formations occur are clear: "Groups are made to talk; anti-groups are mapped; new resources are fetched so as to make their boundaries more durable; and professionals with their highly specialized paraphernalia are mobilized."[101] According to Latour, the borders that demarcate the boundaries of a group are by nature discursive; they are *a priori* exclusionary. But can silence function, then, as a way to refigure this binary inside/outside mode of social mapping, by constructing—as a variation on Foucault's "new relational modes"[102]?—"new relation[s]" to the (sounding) world,[103] and new modes/nodes of connectivity within that world? Is it possible for a group such as Wandelweiser that rejects official, "durable" boundaries to allow into its confines nonautonomous, socially engaged practices—whether employing conceptual, activist, or discursive strategies? Perhaps to concentrate so heavily on the conflict between autonomy and anti-autonomy intimated in the writings and musical works of Wandelweiser's members is to ignore its potential as a social work in itself, an art/life *Gesamtkunstwerk* of considerable stature. What would it mean, though, for Wandelweiser to shift its focus to the other of autonomous musical silence? Would the future of Wandelweiser require an "official" manifesto or mission statement; or, ignoring the group's supposed "requirement to talk," would Wandelweiser's implicit discursive boundaries shrink back into invisibility, revealing a network of silence that extends into infinity? If premised on lending an ear to that which falls outside its (un)silent borders, perhaps only then might the *silent network* be rightfully respelled as the *listen network*.

Part Two

Language and Authority

"IDEAS MATTER": Žižek Sings Pussy Riot

Introduction: A Punk Prayer

On the morning of February 21, 2012, a group of five women entered central Moscow's Cathedral of Christ the Savior to execute an event that has remained a source of controversy in Russia and beyond. For many Russians, including those sympathetic to the opposition movement, the Moscow Cathedral serves as a lucid symbol of the revived collusion between state power and Russian Orthodoxy, which had come to a head in Patriarch Kirill's televised lauding of President Putin. Kirill, a former KGB officer who had recently become head clergy of the church, referred to the Putin era as a "miracle from God,"[1] a comment that came as a slap in the face for many Russians following the economic crisis of 2008 and the Putin administration's string of draconian legislative measures. Wearing brightly colored neon tights and dresses, and donning balaclava ski masks with slits to reveal their eyes and mouths, the costumed women hastily made their way to the altar, weaving past security guards and a horde of camerapersons (some of whom had been invited to film, while others were unexpected members of the press). Distributed across the head of the church, they began to bow, throw punches, shout, and launch air-kicks. "Gay-pride sent to Siberia in chains," one of them chanted. "The head of the KGB, their chief saint." Within less than a minute, the very apparatus that the group had targeted with their action had materialized as they were wrested from the altar and dragged off the premises by security.

But it was not until after the group, calling themselves Pussy Riot, posted a video of the event online (with prerecorded music replacing the unamplified live sound) that they were arrested en masse and charged with "hooliganism as part of an organized group."[2] Accused of "inciting religious hatred,"[3] the group, two of whom were young mothers, faced up to seven years in a Gulag-era prison facility in the remote region of Mordovia. The reaction was altogether shocking for the young Russian art collective. Even though the sentences were reduced to two years for two of the three members (the third was released earlier), the strident consequence had, according to writer Anya Bernstein, paradoxically revealed both "the brutality and ultimate impotence of the Russian state."[4]

Pussy Riot had clearly struck a nerve. Their intervention, which they titled *Punk Prayer: Virgin Mary, Put Putin Away*, posed a threat to the contemporary post-Soviet political order under which Kremlin policy had become sutured to the paralyzing influence of the Orthodox Church. Asked about Pussy Riot in a 2012 interview, and then pressed to comment on the fairness of the trial, Putin refused to pronounce the group's name, insisting that the interviewer translate the first word of their name ("Pussy") into Russian before proceeding. Queried about the chance for an early prison release, the Russian president feigned indifference maintaining, "I try to stay as far away from the case as possible."[5] Yet the Putin administration and its supporters in the Orthodox Church addressed the case by passing punitive legislation. In response, the Kremlin issued the widely contested "anti-blasphemy" law passed by Russian parliament in June 2013, a move that delivered a simultaneous blow to secular democracy and free speech.[6] Another display of the collusion between the Orthodox Church and the Kremlin came only a month after the *Punk Prayer* incident in the form of St. Petersburg's "homosexual propaganda" bill.[7] A year later, Putin extended a countrywide version of the law forbidding public expression and private support of "non-traditional sexual relationships," thereby officially sanctioning homophobia as national policy. Pussy Riot's action, while it might be seen as having backfired, was successful in garnering international awareness around the string of civil injustices initiated by the Russian state. Indeed, despite the severity of Pussy Riot's prison sentence and the ensuing legislative measures, the group, whose members cite influences ranging from Martha Rosler to Bikini Kill to Nietzsche to the Moscow conceptualists,[8] managed to garner the support of a global community of artists, activists, thinkers, and musicians. Pussy Riot's actions called attention to the series of homophobic, sexist, and neoliberal economic policies marshaled by the Russian state and supported by the Orthodox Church.

Cutting across these institutions, *Punk Prayer* mediates formal and historical components of Russian Orthodox music—particularly its status as a purely vocal art form within a male-dominated, patriarchal system—by politically retooling this traditional cultural form. For two outstanding features of Russian Orthodoxy are its pervasive sexism and its general organization around the singing voice. First, the Russian Orthodox Church is not unusual as a religious institution in its general subordination of women; while the participation of women has been on the rise since the fall of communism, they are by far the minority in church council positions. Referring to the male head of the Russian Church who is known as the "patriarch," along with their ban on abortion and various forms of gender inequality, historian Nadieszda Kizenko notes, "The very word 'patriarchy' applies more literally in Russia than it does in other Christian religious traditions."[9] Second, the singing voice forms the very bedrock for religious expression in the Orthodox tradition. The voice unites belief (doxa) and practice (praxis), which together compose "the conservative essence of Orthodox Christianity."[10] Furthermore, musical instruments are banned from Orthodox musical practice due to their dissociation from language; unlike the voice, instruments cannot pray and hence they're distanced from God.[11] Orthodox music denigrates instrumental music for its lack of conceptual language, while it operates within a religious tradition that subordinates women. Stated differently, in Christian Orthodoxy music remains coupled with the innate expressive capacity of language, while, as a rule, women remain effectively silenced.

Pussy Riot launch an invective challenge to the contemporary Russian state order by disrupting its historically entrenched theological ties in a violence orchestrated through specific formal coordinates of musical practice. With its focus on Orthodox music as both an object of critique and a mode of expression, *Punk Prayer* disturbs ideological and religious norms through performance and the medium of the voice. Relevantly, in his study of the Orthodox Christian singing practices of Estonia during the noughts, ethnomusicologist Jeffers Engelhardt develops the notion of "right singing," a term he borrows from religious music studies and sonic theology scholarship. Singing "right," Engelhardt contends, "registers an emergent moral order and reveals how religious ideology and musical ontology conflate in notions of musico-religious orthodoxy."[12] Indeed, "right sounds happen at the 'right time,' in the 'right place,' and in the 'right company.'"[13] Charged with playing the wrong sounds at the wrong time in the wrong company, Pussy Riot upend rightness with their heretical vocalizations and performativity. Importantly, the concept of "right singing" cuts to the core of the Orthodox religion, as the word Orthodoxy literally means "right belief" or "right worship."[14] The importance of the voice in Russian Orthodoxy is perhaps difficult to overstate, and, given its potency, *Punk Prayer* is wrong singing at its best.

This chapter turns on the status of the idea—the concept—in musical practice, especially as it is animated through the singing voice. Ultimately, I will argue that Pussy Riot compose a radical conceptual music that demands a reconsideration of the conceptual art of the 1960s and 1970s—specifically, the work of John Baldessari and Sol LeWitt—through the lens of Žižek's philosophical work on the materiality of the violent threat. Pussy Riot commit a twofold act of violence: they reclaim conceptuality in music for the purposes of secular protest, while they momentarily appropriate the altar as a feminist political space. If Pussy Riot's work is conceptual, then the historical notion of absolute music is also important here because, while it arguably still dominates our understanding of music, absolute music refers to autonomous sound that is concept*less*. In addition to the inclusion of concepts/language as lyrics, *Punk Prayer* mobilizes female bodies and interjects queer voices into an institution that effectively suppresses the voices of women.[15] To a site in which women are encouraged to be "like children, seen but not heard"[16] Pussy Riot add more than sound. Indeed, by composing a music of ideas, they integrally question the categories of music and conceptual art.

Specifically, Pussy Riot reterritorialize music as a critical art practice by reconfiguring and resignifying its materials. Against Russia's return to "traditional values" (a condition that only exacerbates the country's historically oppressive policies on gay rights and women), they leverage the musical form and political meanings of Russian Orthodoxy through their feminist-inflected art action. It is important that the collective comprises women, and, on that cold morning in February, Nadezhda Tolokonnikova, Maria Alyokhina, Yekaterina Samutsevich, and the two others who managed to avoid arrest, "took the altar." As Tolokonnikova explained, "The patriarch stands at the altar. But a woman should occupy it. [Pussy Riot] are feminists."[17]

Punk Prayer: Virgin Mary, Put Putin Away

Black robe, golden epaulettes
All parishioners crawl to bow
The phantom of liberty is in heaven
Gay-pride sent to Siberia in chains
The head of the KGB, their chief saint,
Leads protesters to prison under escort
In order not to offend His Holiness
Women must give birth and love

Shit, shit, the Lord's shit!
Shit, shit, the Lord's shit!

Virgin Mary, Mother of God, become a feminist
Become a feminist, become a feminist

The Church's praise of rotten dictators
The cross-bearer procession of black limousines
A teacher-preacher will meet you at school
Go to class—bring him money!
Patriarch Gundyaev believes in Putin
Bitch, better believe in God instead
The belt of the Virgin can't replace mass-meetings
Mary, Mother of God, is with us in protest!
Virgin Mary, Mother of God, put Putin away
Put Putin away, put Putin away

During the trial that followed Pussy Riot's arrest an insightful characterization of the event emerged in the laconic court testimony of the cathedral cleaner: the women were dancing, she insisted, to music that was "neither classical nor Orthodox."[18] Despite its adoption of the song form and its incorporation of

Figure 1 Pussy Riot performing in the Cathedral of Christ the Savior of the Russian Orthodox Church in Moscow (photo by White Night Press/ullstein bild via Getty Images).

language as lyrical content, *Punk Prayer* has yet to receive significant attention for its musical relevance. With its direct references to anti-LGBT violence, sexism, and state oppression linked to Russian Orthodoxy, *Punk Prayer* notably parodies the form of religious musical text setting and thus invokes the era of premodern religious music. In addition to this anachronistic deployment of liturgical music, Pussy Riot also invoke the aesthetics of Riot grrrl and punk, genres commonly thought to fall outside the purview of modern music. Pussy Riot's work therefore points backward to a moment prior to the conception of music as divorced from language, while it signals an overcoming of this very separation.

In what follows I want to elaborate just what kind of music, indeed if neither classical nor Orthodox, Pussy Riot were responsible for producing. Moreover, I aim to illustrate how their work configures such a musical practice as a site for a kind of counterhegemonic violence fomented through the spectral-material force of the proposal or threat. This virtual matter, I argue, implicates recent elaborations of philosophical materialism as much as it connects with the legacy of conceptual art.

"Conceptual artists in the noblest sense of the word . . ."

One response to Pussy Riot's intervention that did *not* address the relevance of music, though which was no less interesting, came from contemporary Slovenian philosopher and cultural theorist Slavoj Žižek. "Their message is: IDEAS MATTER," the philosopher contended in a 2012 statement entitled "The True Blasphemy." Emphatically hailing the group as "conceptual artists in the noblest sense of the word," Žižek went on to nominate Pussy Riot as "artists who embody an Idea."[19] Žižek's designation of Pussy Riot's work as conceptual may seem surprising given the philosopher's limited engagement with contemporary art.[20] More strikingly, this characterization may even appear anachronistic given the near-total absorption of a conceptualist logic into contemporary art occurring over the course of the past half-century. If conceptual art is defined as work in which the "idea is paramount and the material form is secondary"— to cite feminist artist and theorist Lucy Lippard's famous 1973 formulation of conceptual art's tendency to "dematerialize" the art object[21]—then there is perhaps little advanced art produced today that doesn't, in some sense, follow this criteria. Indeed, while material objects and events (as opposed to texts) doubtless constitute the majority of contemporary artworks, the reception and understanding of such works are indelibly influenced by conceptual art.

Conceptual art, beyond the historical impulse to supersede the commodity object (and hence the "de-objectification" of the art object),[22] is defined by the act of definition itself, the reflexive and iterative reformulating of art as a category. Definition, textuality, discursivity, and what we might call the "proposal form" serve as conceptualism's primary historical modes.[23] Distinct from any particular medium or style, conceptualism represents a radical rupture in art's very ontological status, a transformation of what it means to make and view a work of art. This shifted modality rests upon a layer of discursivity—the artwork's ineluctable immersion into the economies of language, criticism, history, and exchange—which, however legible or obscured, becomes constitutive of (or a kind of stand-in for) the artwork itself. This shift has been no less than totalizing. The prescient dictum of Joseph Kosuth that after Duchamp "all art is conceptual"[24] has ultimately become literalized/realized in contemporary art. Fully enveloped by the conceptual, contemporary art has become thoroughly *post*conceptual. Echoing Kosuth's notorious statement, philosopher Peter Osborne has recently contended that all "contemporary art is postconceptual art."[25] By postconceptual art, Osborne refers not to an art-historical concept at the level of medium, but, as he explains it, the term marks "the critical register of the historical destruction of the ontological significance of such categories" along with their appropriate interpretive strategies.[26] But if *all* art is (post)conceptual, then what is the value of deeming Pussy Riot's work conceptual? Does it make sense to refer to their work simultaneously as music and conceptual art?

A number of critics and theorists have attempted to answer the crisis initiated by conceptual art, especially as it relates to the problem of medium, or, to use the term popularized by Greenberg, "medium specificity." Canonical conceptual art, by one account, attempted to move beyond the constraints of particular mediums—inclusive of their material constitution, but also of their formal traditions and histories. "If one is questioning the nature of painting," Kosuth contends, "one cannot be questioning the nature of Art."[27] Yet one may immediately take issue with Kosuth's invocation of a privileged and deracinated "Art" to support his critical negation of painting, a move that metonymized his attempt to transcend the material fixity of artistic mediums.[28] The "postmedium condition" is Krauss's term for the impasse generated by formalist (medium-specific) modernism on the one hand, and the complete obliteration of medium heralded by (a certain strand of) conceptualism on the other. As a response to this impasse, Krauss proposes that artists must reinvent or rearticulate mediums through a form of "differential specificity."[29] In the process she takes issue with Kosuth's overarching category of "Art," while attempting to move beyond Greenbergian formalism.

As a rejoinder to Krauss's "postmedium condition," Osborne posits his notion of the "*trans*media condition" (elsewhere called the "transcategoriality") of postconceptual art. Developed through his critical exegesis of Robert Smithson's work of the 1960s and 1970s, while acknowledging Dick Higgins's notion of "intermedia," Osborne's "transmedia condition" stresses a particular kind of "crossing" of mediums, the ability to move unfettered by the formal restraints imposed by sculpture, painting, photography, etc. This is, in many ways, a fitting description of contemporary art practices: Rirkrit Tiravanija realizes a Stockhausen composition, while William Pope.L "crawls" sidewalks, paints, and sculpts; Paul Chan stages Beckett's *Waiting for Godot*, while Sanja Iveković makes videos, political demonstrations, and public monuments. In addition to tracing similar connections between recent and postwar twentieth-century art practices, Osborne is one of the few thinkers today who take seriously the important interconnections between philosophy and conceptual art. Like Juliane Rebentisch, Osborne bridges the more typically separate contexts of North American art criticism and continental philosophy.

According to Osborne, postconceptual transmediality marks "the transition [beginning in the 1960s] from an ontology of mediums (painting, sculpture, architecture, photography, film, video) to a postconceptual ontology of art in general, and, hence a fundamentally *transcategorial* practice" indicative of conceptual art's negation of the medium.[30] But while this conception allows for a potentially infinite number of "*possible* material forms,"[31] it does not seem to account for the lingering status of medium *within* these material forms, the complex remainder of the artistic medium in the wake of formalist modernism. Osborne's transcategoriality seems less suited for the task of addressing individual mediums since the advent of conceptual art. Indeed, although conceptual art did radically efface the privileged status of medium, as a critical problem it remains unresolved: by many accounts, medium remains "*the* problem" of contemporary art discourse.[32] Interestingly, at times Osborne actually equates his transmedia condition with postmedium, while at other moments it figures as a critique of Krauss's argument.[33] But can such a concept of art that transitions across mediums also account for the historical change and transformation inherent to individual art forms? For beyond transitioning between existing mediums, for example, music's very definition has shifted significantly over time—as seen in the advent of absolute music.[34]

If Pussy Riot's work is conceptual, can it still be considered music (as the Moscow Cathedral cleaner insisted)? If the term postconceptual art is to be retained, it should also account for the ability of individual forms to transform historically. It is not sufficient to merely transition between mediums; we must also account for their temporal mutability. Furthermore, the practices that "postconceptual art" defines must address art's broader cultural and discursive field: breaking from the axiomatic orbit of Kosuth's "art questioning art," this work questions power, geography, gender, religion, violence—and music. Here medium *re-enters* contemporary postconceptual art, albeit no longer in the same manner as formalist modernism. Rather, critical contemporary art proceeds from a notion of medium "at a distance" with itself: a decentered, de-essentialized medium that allows for historical change and transformation.

Pussy Riot's work is emblematic of a postconceptual approach to music following the reigning of discrete mediums within formalist modernism. They question an object more specific than "Art," and, beyond the "betweenness" of mediums, they reinvent music as a politically relevant and critical art form. Their work should therefore be considered both music *and* (post)conceptual art. "Conceptual artists in the noblest sense of the word,"[35] they work with both ideas and matter.

Ideas (and) Matter

Returning to the first part of Žižek's statement, "IDEAS MATTER" invokes more broadly the relationship between the conceptual and the material. Initially, the gallant-sounding all-caps dyad might conjure the kinds of audacity-in-the-face-of-oppression narratives that often characterize representations of Pussy Riot's ordeal. The two-word statement signals consequence: against cynicism, Pussy Riot's action rings true to its material actuality. But considered further, if the statement's two words are individuated (and if the second is read as a noun), the phrase produces a collision between two linguistic units, pronouncing them as independent concepts: "Ideas." "Matter."

Ideas matter: beyond the phrase's apparent optimism, we may read it as a kind of shorthand for Žižek's nonreductive materialist project. For the problem of philosophical materialism turns on the relationship between ideas and matter.

Simply put, on the one hand, idealism posits that the idea is all there is: at its furthest (and perhaps most "vulgar") extreme is the subjective idealism of eighteenth-century bishop and philosopher George Berkeley, who contended that matter does not exist outside of the mind of a solipsistically perceiving subject.[36] The world is entirely "in my head." On the other hand, materialism can be understood at a basic level as the assertion of material reality's primacy distinct from the mind of an observer—matter beyond (or prior to) its inscription as idea(s).

Matter and ideas: Žižek's nonreductive materialism maintains that the latter cannot be subsumed by the former, that ideas are irreducible to their material support. While matter gives rise to ideas and thought, the "all-there-is" must not only account for the material production of ideas, but also their immanent material consequences: ideas matter(ing).[37] At their worst, varieties of materialism are mechanistic, deterministic, or otherwise incapable of accounting for nonphysical phenomena like meaning, metaphor, abstraction, or even subjectivity; in short, they are reductive. This tendency is evident in, for example, the reduction of consciousness to the mental, the mental to the neuronal, and, finally, the neuronal to purely mechanical-physical processes. By a similar token, the "immaterial" violence of the threat is reduced to mere psychological phenomena, or to a process requisitely connected to some "piece of the real" (e.g., military might linked to possessing tanks and bombs). Such reductive thought tends to collapse the multivalent richness of reality into the immobile category of "matter" as inert substance.

The ingenuity of Žižek's approach lies in the ability to contend with the enumerated varieties of nonmaterial entities from *within* a materialist framework, while refraining from reducing such phenomena to mere illusory effects or lapsing into idealism. In his *Absolute Recoil: Towards a New Foundation of Dialectical Materialism* (2014), Žižek lists four main strands of contemporary materialist thought before going on to defend his materialist resuscitation of the speculative idealism of Hegel and German idealism: "1) reductionist 'vulgar' materialism (cognitivism, neo-Darwinism); 2) the new wave of atheism which aggressively denounces religion (Hitchens, Dawkins, et al.); 3) whatever remains of 'discursive materialism' (Foucauldian analyses of discursive material practices); 4) Deleuzian 'new materialism.'"[38] He goes on to characterize his return to German idealism in light of philosopher Frank Ruda's recent work on Alain Badiou: "True materialism," Žižek insists paradoxically, "is a 'materialism without materialism' in which substantial 'matter' disappears in a network of purely formal/ideal relations."[39] Importantly, this decentered, de-essentialized notion of a materialism "out of joint" with itself paves the way for a genuine philosophical reckoning with the kinds of "immaterial" phenomena considered above (abstraction, language, subjectivity, etc.). We might even posit that the philosophical tendency Žižek outlines endeavors to achieve in materialist thought what conceptual art attempted to do to the art object. Paralleling the shift from modernism's investment in the materiality of the medium to conceptual art's "dematerialization" of the art object, Žižek dematerializes materialism.

The import of Žižek's nonreductive materialism for this chapter lies in its potential to grasp the kinds of "immaterial" phenomena central to an understanding of the state oppression expended in reaction to Pussy Riot's *Punk Prayer* intervention—the virtual, or spectral-material violence exchanged in the form of the threat. In an important section of his 2006 book *The Parallax View*, Žižek criticizes V.I. Lenin's infamous 1909 treatise *Materialism and Emperio-Criticism* (whose argument Žižek paraphrases as "everything is matter") by asserting that "a truly radical materialism is by definition nonreductionist: far from claiming that 'everything is matter' it confers upon 'immaterial' phenomena a specific positive nonbeing."[40] Žižek's solution borrows from Lacan's sexuation formulae through an affirmative double negation of Lenin's "everything is matter" slogan, thereby turning it first into "there is nothing which is not matter" and then into "not-All is matter."[41] The latter formulation, according to Žižek, opens materialism up to a radical account of immaterial phenomena.

In his recent work on Žižek, philosopher Adrian Johnston insists that the "ideality of [these] immaterial events" comprises "something neither physical nor nonphysical, a more-than-material dimension that, despite Žižek's avowedly materialist ontology, is not without its proper ontological status (including an ability to generate 'effects in the Real')."[42] Žižek's materialism can be linked further to a series of aporiae concerning the concrete impact that abstraction exerts upon the real, as demonstrated in several important bodies of thought. Johnston, in fact, traces this strand as it runs through no less than

> three of Žižek's favorite thinkers: Hegel (in terms of his claim that the idea of a concrete reality existing apart from conceptual abstractions is itself the height of conceptual abstraction), Marx (in terms of his concept of "real abstraction" indebted to the preceding Hegelian claim), and Lacan (in terms of his rebuttals of the May 1968 slogan protesting that "structures do not march in the streets").[43]

Regarding Lacan's insistent reversal of the famous Paris graffito: structures don't just walk the streets—indeed they throw you in a former Soviet Gulag prison for speaking out against the corruption and injustice perpetrated by church-state apparatuses, much like Pussy Riot's experience in contemporary Russia.

Žižek's materialist philosophical project here provides a connective tissue between music, ideas, matter, and, ultimately, violence. Threaded through these nodes is the figure of the threat, a primary topic for Žižek that shares important features with his materialist philosophical framework. The threat is an "immaterial" phenomenon par excellence, a pure possibility with "an actuality of its own; that is, it produces real effects."[44] As a kind of violence avant la lettre, the threat constrains and encloses the coordinates of the possible; it forestalls, apprehends, and incarcerates. Through a more-than-material "virtual" force nevertheless concretely present, the threat produces veritable "effects in the Real."[45] It is an idea made material.

Conceptual Art and the Threat: (Art as) Idea as Matter

While Pussy Riot's work is frequently situated within the contexts of performance art and activism, Žižek's reference to the group as "conceptual artists" underscores the potential consequences of the group's work as a kind of conceptual music. In the same section of his statement "The True Blasphemy," Žižek describes Pussy Riot's balaclavas as "masks of de-individualization" and ties them directly to conceptualism: "The message of their balaclavas is that it doesn't matter which one[s] of them got arrested—they're not individuals, they're an Idea."[46] The "Idea" Žižek refers to here notably implicates continental philosophy and conceptual art: on the one hand, he conjures the philosophy of Hegel and German idealism, and, on the other, the canonical works of conceptual artists such as Sol LeWitt and Kosuth. The latter's *Art as Idea as Idea* series began in 1966 as an attempt to "'de-objectify' the object"[47] by construing the artwork as pure idea. Along with this simultaneous relevance to philosophy and conceptual art, Žižek's characterization of Pussy Riot suggests a consideration of their work as a kind of proposal for collective realization. Not unlike Žižek, writer Maria Chehonadskih contends that wearing the mask "conveys the impossibility of saying 'I'"[48]; the masks point to participation and collectivity.

As a process to be continued through action, the deskilled, "anyone can do it" character of Pussy Riot's work invokes artistic forms like the Fluxus event score, or even musical scores more broadly, despite the latter's typically presumed "skilled" nature. "Anybody can take on this image," one Pussy

Riot member explained in a YouTube video, referring to the group's dresses, instruments, and balaclavas.[49] Here Žižek's Hegelian-cum-Kosuthian notion of conceptual art meets a conceptual art defined as proposal, inviting a reconsideration of these historically primary organizing modes of conceptual art: *proposal* and *idea*. Writing in an art-historical context, Alexander Alberro locates this dichotomy in Kosuth and LeWitt: while the former holds that the "idea itself" *is* the work of art, LeWitt's idea prompts completion through further action. For LeWitt, "conception stands in a complementary relation to the process of realization"[50]; the artwork becomes a proposal to be realized. Related to the kinds of "immaterial" materiality found in Pussy Riot's work, LeWitt's vision of conceptual art takes the form of a proposal-in-advance of an artwork's actualization. The "idea" functions as a "machine that makes the art."[51] If we are to take Žižek's commentary seriously, then we might expect both of these modalities—idea and proposal—to emerge in Pussy Riot's artistic practice because, like LeWitt, Pussy Riot's "idea" is a matter of mobilization, of action.

My argument turns on the notion that the threat and conceptual art share a proposal-like structure: conceptual art's proposal for a yet-to-be physicalized object, or event, on the one hand, and the authorial denial of futurity in the constricting, contracting, or even extinguishing of life, on the other. In his rejoinder to Althusser, Žižek claims that authority works strictly as threat, that it is like a proposal; were it enacted, like the impotent father, or the Russian state as Bernstein suggested, it would cease to be genuine authority. As with the conceptual proposal, the threat is matter virtualized.

Importantly, the presence of this spectral substance appears in Žižek's argument as a kind of "weird ideal materiality"—which Althusser apparently misses but Lacan grasps as the "specific materiality of ideas themselves."[52] Referring further to Marx–Engel's *The German Ideology* and Althusser's *Ideological State Apparatuses*, Žižek insists that a radical materialism must maintain not only that "ideas are grounded in the material social and productive processes, and [insist] not only [upon] the material (ideological) apparatuses that sustain ideology, but also the immanent materiality of the ideal order itself."[53] Beyond mere material *support* for the production of ideality (as Marx and Engels argued), *ideas themselves* exert a physicalized force in the world. It is through this strange kind of idea(l)-substance, something of a short circuit between the ideal and material domains, that we arrive at a reformulation of Žižek's Pussy Riot slogan, namely: ideas *are (in this register)* matter.

In a different register, Žižek's nonreductive materialism problematizes recent art-theoretical positions that seek a return to "matter" in the form of raw materials, or the reductive "stuff" of objects, sounds, etc., through hasty applications of new materialist philosophies (evident in, for example, Christoph Cox's recent sound art theory, the *Blowup: Speculative Realities* exhibition [2013], and MoMA's 2013 exhibition *Soundings: A Contemporary Score*). Meanwhile, theories of conceptualism become too easily compatible with philosophical idealism.[54] These convenient couplings of materials/materialism and (conceptual) ideas/ idealism doubtless invite allegations of reductionism from either perspective. Nevertheless, Žižek's conceptualist characterization of Pussy Riot brings the meeting of "ideas" and "matter" to bear upon a nonreductive materialist consideration of conceptual art. Žižek's phrase suggests what we might call a *materialist conceptualism*: a conceptual art that acknowledges the discursivity of artistic practice—art as inherently grounded in concepts—while simultaneously taking into account the "immaterial materiality" of ideas: the inevitable concrete impact those "abstract" structures have on the real. Ideas matter; they leave material traces, carve impressions into the world. With Žižek's materialism in mind, perhaps we can revise Kosuth's *Art as Idea as Idea* to arrive at *Art as Idea as Matter*. Pussy Riot vary this formulation further to include music.

Given their feminist reinjection of conceptual language into musical performance, Pussy Riot elaborate a musical practice that draws from conceptual art while being politically efficacious; they render a deep structural relation between conceptualism and music composition. I want to argue, in fact, that they *compose* interventions like *Punk Prayer*; they stage the event as proposal and idea while realizing it through determinate action. Yet in order to fulfill this recasting of music and conceptual art, we will need to question some of the extant understandings of conceptual art—why does it seem to have precluded something like a conceptual music?—while also interrogating Western art music: Why does music consistently exclude ideas in the form of language and conceptualism?

Regarding the first question, I will discuss a musical work already seated within the canon of conceptual art in my interpretation of John Baldessari's *Baldessari Sings LeWitt* (1972). Within the historical recesses of conceptual art I find dormant embers of critical music waiting to be ignited through the socially engaged musical practices of artists like Pussy Riot.[55] As for the second question, I will explore the (re)integration of conceptuality into musical practice through a critical interrogation of the historical concept of absolute music. Although music, like conceptual art, lacks objecthood, absolute music stands for a music presumed to lack concepts. In the words of Carl Dahlhaus, absolute music is the term for an art form at once both "object- and concept-free."[56]

What would it take, then, to conceive of a music *with* concepts, a musical practice that mobilizes ideas of the kind Žižek finds in Pussy Riot's work? This chapter provides two points of departure for this intersection between music and conceptual art. The first, "IDEAS MATTER," refers to Žižek's characterization of *Punk Prayer*, while the second, "Žižek Sings Pussy Riot," plays on the title of John Baldessari's 1972 video *Baldessari Sings LeWitt*, a work in which the artist sings Sol LeWitt's well-known *Sentences on Conceptual Art* (1969).[57] Both *Baldessari Sings LeWitt* and *Punk Prayer* consist of texts set to musical performances, a feature I want to bring into contact with a notion of music informed by conceptualism, language, and the kind of proposal form found in LeWitt's work. Proceeding from my own *détournement* of Baldessari's musical appropriation of LeWitt through the figures of Žižek and Pussy Riot, I will look to these artists to seek elemental traces of critical music waiting to be unearthed and given proper framing.

Composing Conceptual Art: *Baldessari Sings LeWitt*

In 1972 visual artist John Baldessari produced one of the most important yet perhaps underappreciated works to appear in the canon of conceptual art. Seated in his studio while staring into a video camera, Baldessari proceeded to sing Sol LeWitt's *Sentences on Conceptual Art*, a work that consists of thirty-five written declarations intended to comment on the then-burgeoning movement of conceptual art. The import of Baldessari's piece for this chapter, and indeed for thinking further about Pussy Riot's *Punk Prayer*, lies in my own subtly provocative claim that beyond interpretations of the work as sound art, video, or performance art, *Baldessari Sings LeWitt* is, above all, a musical work. Or, more accurately, in my interpretation, my *listening*, it is a kind of art song. For the song form is generally understood as the marriage between a piece of writing, typically a poetic text, and musical accompaniment. Even though art songs often include instrumental accompaniment (especially piano accompaniment), and Baldessari sings *a capella*, the underlying structure of this work parallels that of the art song.

The art song consists fundamentally of the superimposition of text and musical sound, or, more broadly, the overlaying of referential language onto an aesthetically structured form. In this sense, the art song mirrors an important feature of conceptual art: the inscription of language onto a material object (if the latter is not completely supplanted by text). In *Baldessari Sings LeWitt* this "underlying" art object structure appears in the already "de-objectified" form of musical melody. Baldessari grafts onto the preexisting structure of the song (language married to musical sound) the content and, as we shall see, the form of LeWitt's text, itself an explicit reflection on conceptualism. Baldessari therefore fuses this reflexive character of conceptual art—a discursive form of artistic self-reflection—directly onto a musical surface, and therein posits a conceptual music.

In this sense, *Baldessari Sings LeWitt* overcomes music's prior conceptual muteness: like *Punk Prayer*, Baldessari radicalizes music by reinfusing it with conceptuality. The novelty of Baldessari's intervention lies in the fact that in choosing to set Sol LeWitt's *Sentences on Conceptual Art* to the American national anthem, a series of folk tunes, and various popular melodies, Baldessari opens the field of artistic practice to the possibility of a genuinely conceptual music (regardless of whether or not this direction was ever adequately taken up). But beyond a formalist reflection on "Art," *Baldessari Sings LeWitt* addresses broader questions of desire, authority, comedy, humor, and the social, while it questions music as a form and tradition.

Baldessari Sings LeWitt: an art song. LeWitt was the poet, Baldessari the singer. Prior to singing LeWitt's *Sentences*, Baldessari had to *compose* this series of musical text settings. This was the case despite the fact that Baldessari borrows each of the melodies from an existing source. As an artistic descendent of Duchamp, appropriation has been a cornerstone of Baldessari's practice. It might seem odd to discuss Baldessari's "text settings" in relation to the art song—a genre more often associated with the likes of Schubert, Webern, and Ives, composers known for their musical settings of poets ranging from Goethe to Georg to Emerson. But like other conceptual artists, LeWitt's work arises, in fact, from important precedents in poetry. In his analysis of LeWitt's *Sentences*, Osborne explores (latent) poetic dimensions of LeWitt's work, comparing the *Sentences* to Romantic-era poet and philosopher Friedrich Karl Wilhelm von Schlegel's *Anathenaeum Fragments* of 1798.[58] Furthermore, Osborne is quick to recall that LeWitt and many of his contemporaries thought of their work as emerging from the context of poetry.

Baldessari Sings LeWitt is a sequence of "songs," each set to one of LeWitt's *Sentences*, which thus forms a song cycle. Insisting on the order of the songs,

Baldessari establishes a formal continuity between the song cycle and the serial techniques found in conceptual art. Seriality, an approach influenced by mass manufacturing, commodity culture, and Eadweard Muybridge's early photographs, was a pivotal technique in 1960s and 1970s conceptual art. Defined by a concern with sequence—or "how order of a specific type is manifest," as Mel Bochner writes[59]—serial practices parallel the song cycle structure at a basic level in *Baldessari Sings LeWitt*. Order is central to LeWitt's *Sentences*. And, despite making several mistakes and self-consciously repeating certain passages, Baldessari moves *linearly* through his "cycle," careful to preserve their original form and order. Osborne discusses the serial nature of LeWitt's *Sentences*, arguing that "unlike LeWitt's three-dimensional projects, [*Sentences on Conceptual Art* is] an artisanal, quasi-poetic, philosophical or critical work—a kind of handmade meta-series."[60] The *Sentences* epitomize the meeting of poetry and the serial form and the intersection between philosophy and artistic process that is so central to conceptual art.

Emerging amid the radical formal and aesthetic innovations of the late 1960s and 1970s, *Baldessari Sings LeWitt* was an "art song" cycle worthy of the designation. A videotaped recital that featured each of LeWitt's thirty-five *Sentences*, *Baldessari Sings LeWitt* stands as both an emblem of and a critical reflection upon this conceptualist era. Already in this early moment of conceptual art—just three years following the 1969 publication of LeWitt's *Sentences* in the art magazine *0–9* (and then in the British publication *Art-Language* the same year)—*Baldessari Sings LeWitt* can be viewed as providing a subtle critique of the burgeoning movement by provisionally rooting LeWitt's statements formally and historically in the art song. Moreover, *Baldessari Sings LeWitt* emerged just as the stable, locatable, and circumscribed boundaries of traditional forms like the art song had been exploded and recomposed through Fluxus, Happenings, performance, and intermedia—all carried along by the tides of the conceptual turn of the 1960s. Despite these upheavals in artistic disciplinarity, *Baldessari Sings LeWitt* found its critical point of entry precisely through the art song's "etiolated" meeting of textual verse and vocal melody. Nevertheless, this was not the first time LeWitt's work was compared to a musical form. The same year he wrote the *Sentences*, LeWitt said of his methodology, "I think of it more like a composer who writes notes."[61]

By acknowledging a similar relation to composition, *Baldessari Sings LeWitt* is seen not only to suffuse music with the conceptual, but also to exhibit a musical logic *already* inherent to conceptual art. As the content of LeWitt's

Sentences suggests and Baldessari makes explicit, the compositional form can be seen as structurally homologous to the conceptual proposal. LeWitt is perhaps best known for his cube sculptures and his extensive series of wall drawings, each of which emerges from formal *structures*—LeWitt's title for an extensive series of his works—forms that begin, early on, with basic rules only to explode later into expansive serial works. Importantly, these projects employ a form of writing that is perhaps best described as "composition"—a prescription to be realized in material form: a recipe, a script, or a score to be interpreted through action. If the score essentially prompts a performative realization, then LeWitt's "idea," understood as a "machine that makes the art,"[62] appropriates this extant aesthetic form. In this sense, conceptualism borrows from music by abstracting and generalizing the score's *proposal form*.[63] Volker Straebel aptly reminds us that the breakthrough in conceptual art wherein author and executor had been conceived as separate individuals was a fact rather "self-evident and not very spectacular in the field of music."[64] LeWitt's articulation of this kind of conceptual composition (seen also in the work of Lawrence Weiner) is perhaps best expressed in sentence 10:

> 10. Ideas can be works of art; they are in a chain of development that may eventually find some form. All ideas need not be made physical.

Yet the relationship LeWitt outlines had already been deployed in the very structure of the musical score. Reading LeWitt in this light, music was a conceptual art long before the latter's conceptualization: "ideas" in the form of a text (the notated score) "need not be made physical" (they may remain unperformed or unrealized). As a kind of realization of LeWitt's score-text, then, *Baldessari Sings LeWitt* exhibits this similarity between music and conceptualism through both form and content.

If LeWitt rescued a latent conceptualism lying virtually dormant within the form of music composition, then Baldessari turns the gesture back in on itself, exploding it through ironic self-reference and performance. The video begins with an empty shot of a whitewashed brick wall with a microphone peering out of the bottom left hand side of the screen. A chair sits in the middle of the frame. Generally, the setup recalls other video works from the late 1960s and 1970s by artists such as Bruce Nauman, Vito Acconci, and Adrian Piper characterized by a single, long take of the artist, often alone, "doing stuff" in her/ his studio, executing activities in an almost ritualistic manner. Baldessari walks briefly across the frame and sits down while holding a somewhat disheveled notepad. Addressing the viewer, he explains the premise of the work and refers to his singing of LeWitt's *Sentences* as a "tribute" to the artist. The rationale is that the *Sentences* have been "hidden too long" in exhibition catalogues, and Baldessari intends to introduce them to a broader public. In the final note of his introductory disclaimer, he explains that he may have to repeat sentences due to mistakes in phrasing.

Baldessari's concentration then centers on the notepad, which seems to function as a kind of score, and, before singing each sentence, he announces each of LeWitt's "numbers" in order. Seemingly unexcited yet serious, he proceeds: "Number one: Conceptual artists are mystics rather than rationalists. They leap to conclusions that logic cannot reach." Some of the melodies are recognizable as popular tunes like "Heaven" or the American national anthem. His voice is dull, mumbly, somewhat nasal. His intonation is off. And he doesn't hold a tune by any standard. Most of the melodies are rhythmically disjointed in relation to the text's phrasing. Sentence 9 is supposed to be sung to "Camptown Races": "The concept and idea are different, DOO DA, DOO DA . . ." But in the course of singing, he messes up, twice. And after each mistake, he returns to the beginning of the sentence to repeat. During each repetition of the botched sentence 9, he begins to stomp rhythmically: reinforcing the repeated phrase "DOO DA," the stamping appears momentarily as a subtle backing beat, an effect audible only as a series of half-muted thuds without visual cue (he's framed from the torso up). In these instances, as with the introduction, he appears to break character from his singing persona, shifting his attention from the notepad to the camera to again address the viewer: "Maybe that wasn't too clear, and I should do it over."

An understated sense of humor weaves throughout Baldessari's work, some of it overt, seemingly orchestrated, while other aspects seem incidental. Broadly there is, for instance, the gesture of crossing LeWitt's "lofty" conceptual art statements with a series of lowly children's tunes and popular melodies. Or on a more formal level, there is the crossing of conceptual art—with its ambition to become art-as-theory-about-art[65]—with music, the more often presumed "abstract" (or nonlinguistic) art form. Then there is Baldessari's deadpan casualness felt in his wry camera address, generally unkempt appearance (the pseudo-Hunter S. Thompson glasses, stringy shoulder-length hair that partially covers his left eye, daft button-up thermal undershirt, his inconsistently gray burly beard)[66]; the way he half-slouches, his slightly hokey sounding West Coast accent (in sentence 32, he pronounces "banal" as the less favorable "BAY-nal," a quip that also recalls his 1971 video *Some Words I Mispronounce*), all wedged against the ostensible rigor of the endeavor, his expressed compulsion to "get it right." Despite the seeming casualness of his attitude, he is steadfast, unwavering in his determination. This is conceptual art after all. He appears to be ventriloquized by LeWitt's text; like the score in a traditional musical performance, the *Sentences* command Baldessari from afar.

There is the fact that, even though he *fails* to get it right, Baldessari simply repeats each sentence in question and keeps singing. It is as though, recalling the cartoon portrayal of a self-confident baron who falls into a puddle and gets up each time with confidence restored, when Baldessari falls he simply picks back up and keeps going, singing along. This recalls the example philosopher Alenka Zupančič uses to illustrate one of the paradoxes of comedy in *The Odd One In* (2008). The paradox concerns the relationship between comedy's emphasis on human fallibility and limitation and the way this "material" dimension of comedy often appears to undermine the universal. Not unrelated to Žižek's materialist project, Zupančič articulates what she calls a "materialism of comedy," referring to the "'failed finitude,' especially in its object form, that comedy thrives on."[67]

Like the genre of punk, *Baldessari Sings LeWitt* relies upon established musical codes precisely in order to break them. *Baldessari Sings LeWitt* illuminates the frame of music through the work's failed (comic) finitude, its shortcomings, its failure to live up to traditional measures of musical competency. In the case of a comically portrayed aristocrat who falls in the mud, the foible appears to bring His Highness down to the level of ordinary human corporeality. Likewise, with *Baldessari Sings LeWitt* the artist's deficient singing may appear to subvert music's status as a noble or "universal" art form. But comedy does not simply undermine the universal, as Zupančič argues, it stands for its very *movement*. As Zupančič insists, it "is not simply the empirical body [of the baron] that lies flat in the mud, but much more the belief in his baronage, his 'baronness.'"[68] It is not that Baldessari's comic gesture somehow "deconstructs" music as a category, unveiling the "elitism" of avant-garde music as a preconceptual construct to be superseded by a conceptual sound art. Rather, in its failure *Baldessari Sings LeWitt* points to the very movement of the categories of music and conceptual art: on the side of conceptual art, an acknowledgment of its formal debt to music; on the side of music, the (yet-to-be-fulfilled incorporation of the) radical implications that conceptualism forces upon it and other art forms.

Of course, as Baldessari's intervention affirms, neither the composed score nor the conceptual prompt has to be performed "correctly" despite the authoritative measures each tradition (music, visual art) leverages to prevent such "subversive" interpretations. Here we recall the *Werktreue* problematic explored in Ultra-red's *SILENT|LISTEN*. We can add to this the carefully written "Certificates" LeWitt issued: "This is to certify that the Sol LeWitt wall drawing number _____ evidenced by this certificate is authentic." We can also compare sentence 10 to Lawrence Weiner's 1968 *Statement of Intent*:

1. The artist may construct the piece
2. The piece may be fabricated
3. The piece need not be built

Each being equal and consistent with the intent of the artist the decision as to condition rests with the receiver upon the occasion of receivership[69]

Despite his *Statement's* prescriptive form, Weiner went so far as to compare the imperative to fascism: "The tone of the command is the tone of tyranny."[70] By the same token, the "marriage" between score/text and musical performance may not always remain a happy one. *Baldessari Sings LeWitt* can therefore be seen to extend such practices of against-the-grain musical performances to LeWitt's seminal conceptual work.[71]

Interestingly, LeWitt actually admired Baldessari's gesture and expressed his approval on a number of occasions.[72] It is also interesting to recall that in his opening address to the camera, Baldessari refers his work as a "tribute" to LeWitt. Musically, this kind of overture conjures the popular notion of a "tribute band," signaling an overt desire to emulate through homage. Formally, it can be read as underscoring the (libidinal-)artistic roles ascribed in Baldessari's work. Less a space for criticism or debate, singing LeWitt functions as a platform for admiration. In the opening dedication, Baldessari alludes to the overwhelmingly predominant male-male relationships that figure throughout art song literature and Western art music more generally. In doing so, *Baldessari Sings LeWitt* affirms, however implicitly or unwittingly, the historically prevalent "male homosocial desire" that relates poet to composer, especially within postwar American art circles.[73]

Baldessari Sings LeWitt: the title refers of course to Baldessari singing LeWitt's text; but to sing some*one* may also suggest either singing to the object of one's desire, as in a serenade, or metaphorically, to sing someone's praises in the form of compliments. Given LeWitt's amicable reception and Baldessari's intimate camera address, both characterizations seem fitting. There is nevertheless a tension between the kind of intimacy offered in Baldessari's performative delivery and his acknowledged intention of turning his video performance into public address. Working in video, the medium that Krauss once famously equated with narcissism,[74] Baldessari closes the tripartite poet-composer-singer loop by singing his own composition—in his studio, alone. Like Bruce Nauman's *Violin Tuned D.E.A.D.* (1969) and Vito Acconci's *Theme Song* (1973), *Baldessari Sings LeWitt* creates a short circuit between the solipsistic interiority of the artist's studio (through its technological mediation) and the public space of the music concert situation. Baldessari sings LeWitt—"for" LeWitt, but also *to* a public.

In addition to its social implications, *Baldessari Sings LeWitt* also implies specific relations to the self. Considering again the work's title, one notes its conspicuous reference to the artist in the third person: "Baldessari," not "I," sings LeWitt.[75] This odd self-reference conjures the artistic ("self-")reference to medium that occurs within a particular medium, a ubiquitous artistic strategy of the era. Baldessari's self-conscious title can thus be read as literalizing this "self" encountered in the much-rehearsed trope of conceptual art's self-referentiality. Along these lines, one recalls the ironic tone of Baldessari's 1966–68 paintings. The work *Everything is purged from this painting but art, no ideas have entered this work*, for example, consists of a white canvas with the work's title painted in black in all capital letters. The obvious reference is to the modernist inclination toward excavation, evacuation, and negation, the striving toward the material purity of the medium evinced by the black canvases of post-painterly abstractionists like Ad Reinhardt. Through hyperbolic overidentification, Baldessari's painting enunciates precisely, as it were, the program of formalist modernism tout court. The irony is the fact that Baldessari makes this linguistic pronouncement in painting, a medium from which, as his statement implies, discursivity was itself supposed to have been purged. As with *Baldessari Sings LeWitt*, *Everything is purged* deploys reflexive-conceptual language in a medium in which referential language was, by definition, suppressed. *Everything is purged* should not be regarded as a materialist conceptual artwork because it deploys the "raw materials" of painting (canvas, stretcher, paint), but, rather, through its reference to the history of *ideas* about painting: the matter(ing) of the medium as a concept—the discursive construction of the medium which also constructs its material/ideal forms. For if painting has a specificity, it is not to be found in flatness or in paint but rather in the social and historical context in which the debate over such a status has played out. In this light, we may consider the implications of sentence 27:

27. The concept of a work of art may involve the matter of the piece or the process in which it is made.

It is striking that LeWitt suggests here that the concept may involve a work's "matter." As with *Everything is purged*, *Baldessari Sings LeWitt* is a musical work not because it relies upon concrete "materials" found in music (sound, performance, a "score"), but rather, due to the fact that it makes meaningful reference to—and intervenes in—music *as a tradition*: it "involves the matter[ing]" of music's formal bounds, its historical (in)ability to produce meaning.

Finally, we arrive at the last sentence of Baldessari's song cycle. Interestingly, sentence 35 presents a similar effect of self-reference—and self-cancellation—as found in *Everything is purged*:

35. These sentences comment on art, but are not art.

When read in the context of LeWitt's *Sentences*, sentence 35 seems to all but nullify the preceding text, especially, for example, sentence 17 ("All ideas are art if they are concerned with art and fall within the conventions of art."). On the verge of completing his sandcastle, LeWitt knocks the whole structure down. Yet when one hears sentence 35 within the context of Baldessari's art song, the level of paradox is on par with *Everything is purged*. When sung as lyrics, it is as though Baldessari (re)cites a transformed version of the text in the *Everything is purged* painting, but he replaces references to painting with music: "Everything is purged from these songs but music, no ideas have entered this work."

With these moments of aporiatic self-contradiction, *Baldessari Sings LeWitt* and *Everything is purged* embody what Groys calls "paradox-objects," art objects that appear simultaneously to contain thesis and antithesis.[76] Not unlike Zupančič's materialist mechanics of comedy, the contradiction inherent to the paradox-art object points to transformation, to *movement* in the real.[77] In both *Everything is purged* and *Baldessari Sings LeWitt* the movement of contradiction occurs *across* material and ideal domains: in *Everything is purged*, the contradiction happens between the meaning of the statement and its material referent, a referent whose "ideal" content ("no ideas have entered this work") contradicts the very fact that the statement exists. Likewise, it is clear that in *Baldessari Sings LeWitt*—contrary to the assertion in sentence 35 ("These sentences comment on art, but are not art")—that the sentences do "comment on art" *and* they are art: specifically, in *Baldessari Sings LeWitt*, they are music.

In its recontextualized musical form, sentence 35 presents the twofold contradiction of declaring within an existing artwork the contents of such statements as nonart, while commenting on art from within the supposedly conceptually mute art form of music. It is precisely in this moment of contradiction that *Baldessari Sings LeWitt* becomes not just a musical work but, through its self-reflexive commentary on music, it inaugurates a conceptual music.

Nevertheless, it is important to add that the seeming "impossibility" of conceptual reflection (on music) within music is a contention that should itself be historically contextualized. Indeed, while *Baldessari Sings LeWitt*'s conceptual dimension is novel for music, the incorporation of language is not. In this sense, Baldessari's intervention turns on the relation between music and language historically rooted in the problem of absolute music. For if *Baldessari Sings LeWitt* stands for the formal reinscription of (reflexive) conceptual language in music, then absolute music is the term that marks language's initial exclusion.

The *Matter(ing)* of Absolute Music

Like conceptual art, absolute music was written into being. The concept of absolute music, the aesthetic category defined by the expulsion of language from music, was initially formulated, ironically, entirely in language. At the turn of the nineteenth century, through their writings published over the course of a decade, a group of Romantic writers and poets in Germany (Wackenroder, Tieck, Novalis, Jean Paul, Schlegel, and E. T. A. Hoffmann) had effectively elevated instrumental music from being one of the lowest regarded types of music not only to the highest musical form, but, indeed, to the highest form of art as such.[78] The actual term "absolute music," to be sure, did not appear until the middle of the nineteenth century; but the insistence upon autonomous instrumental sound (or "pure music," the term Schlegel used in one of his *Anathenaeum Fragments*)[79] as the privileged art form first appeared in the idealist philosophy-influenced journal articles and concert reviews of these thinkers. Their insistence on the new aesthetic, while emphatic, did not go uncontested. Kant, for example, famously associated instrumental music with the "free beauty" found in wallpaper, famously declaring it "more pleasure than culture."[80] And Hegel was, according to Dahlhaus, one of several nineteenth-century aesthetic philosophers who renounced untexted music as "artificial," "unnatural," and "conceptless."[81] Nevertheless, the concept of absolute music was profoundly influential.

Absolute music represented a radical epistemological shift in aesthetic thought during the nineteenth century wherein music's concept was thoroughly revised:

music as a multivalent category *inclusive* of language was replaced by a construct of pure sound fully exceeding linguistic representation. The category of absolute music is important to our study because this privileging of instrumental sound still dominates musical thinking today, and its continued acceptance prevents an adequate contextualization of artists like Baldessari and Pussy Riot. To achieve a genuinely conceptual music, we must move *historically* beyond absolute music.

As Dahlhaus noted in his well-known text *The Idea of Absolute Music*, the premodern notion of music as *harmonia*, *rhythmos*, and *logos* gave way in the nineteenth century to pure instrumental sound as the dominant paradigm. *Logos*—as extended to language and conceptualism—I want to argue, receives a new valence in the wake of absolute music, as seen in the work of Pussy Riot. Tracing the origins of absolute music, Dahlhaus explains that at the turn of the nineteenth century, "instrumental music, previously viewed as a deficient form of vocal music, a mere shadow of the real thing, was exalted as a music-[a] esthetic paradigm in the name of autonomy—made into the epitome of music, its essence."[82] Like other art forms near the dawn of modernity, absolute music sought aesthetic autonomy through formal purity, here in the form of deracinated instrumental sound.

But absolute music, like capitalism, has a historical origin and therefore a conceivable point of closure. Dahlhaus elaborates this point in an elegant formulation: "Understanding the historical character of the idea [of absolute music] serves," he argues, "to prepare for the insight that what has come about historically can also be changed again."[83] Music is often characterized as nonrepresentational, abstract, ineffable, or otherwise disconnected from language—in short, in terms that also separate formalist modernism from conceptual art. But critics of the essentialist tendencies of formalism (along with champions of conceptualism) often fail to recognize the essentialism of equating music with pure instrumental sound. Both musicologists and sound art theorists often proceed with a concept of music that fixes it as absolute. In order to think beyond absolute music, we must interrogate its origins.

The actual phrase "absolute music" first appeared in 1846 when Richard Wagner authored a program note for Beethoven's Ninth Symphony. Referring to the fourth movement's instrumental recitative, Wagner wrote: "Already almost breaking the bounds of absolute music, it stems the tumult of the other instruments with its virile eloquence, pressing toward decision, and passes at last into a song-like theme."[84] A glowing if particularly masculinist appraisal of Beethoven accompanied Wagner's introduction of "absolute music" alongside a thinly veiled criticism of the idea. As Wagner later made clear in his *Art of the Future* (1849), absolute music was to him a deficient musical form by itself; it was both "partial" and "detached": detached because it had been literally torn away from the trio formerly constitutive of music (*harmonia, rhythmos,* and *logos*). Each of the "absolute" arts was "partial," in Wagner's schema, insofar as it formed but one component of the total artwork: the *Gesamtkunstwerk* emblematized by the Wagnerian opera. Responsible for both naming the concept of absolute music and providing its nascent critique, Wagner would later receive his most strident opposition in the pro-absolute music polemics of Eduard Hanslick.

Hanslick's task was to transform absolute music, a concept that had arrived historically, into a permanent distinction to solidify the notion of music as sound. His *Vom Musikalisch-Schönen* (1854) began by privileging autonomous sound over the formerly multivalent concept of music. Then, anticipating Greenberg's equivalent visual art polemic by nearly a century, Hanslick argued for a kind of "medium specificity" in music: the "specifically musical," he contended, "inheres in the combinations of musical sounds and is independent of all alien, extra-musical notions."[85] Hanslick's most original contribution to the notion of absolute music can be seen in the latter part of the quotation, namely the distinction between the musical and the "extra-musical." This distinction was significant because what had begun diachronically, as a revolutionary *change* in musical thought, could now be posed as an accepted synchronic distinction: what "inheres" in (absolute) music, as opposed to that which is supposedly "extraneous." Through the adoption of this discourse, the scandal of absolute music had now been cauterized at the level of ordinary language (tacitly accepted every time someone says, "I didn't care for the lyrics, but *the music* was great"). Music had, consequently, become historically flattened, misapprehended as a one-dimensional aesthetic object: music became synonymous with (instrumental) sound. Yet, regardless of how adamantly one protested the idea of absolute music, by simply adopting Hanslick's distinction, one had "terminologically lost" the argument before it even began.[86]

This kind of synchronic flattening of music to equal sound continues to pervade many of the most incisive critiques of music. In addition to the criticism of instrumental music proffered by Kant, Hegel, and Wagner, absolute music has received criticism from the so-called new musicology movement beginning in the late 1980s, followed more recently by sound art theory. New musicology centers on the task of locating meaning within instrumental music, typically common practice-era classical music—as opposed to challenging the construction of the category of absolute music. Instead of seeking instances where the latter ceases to operate, new musicology has attempted to locate latent cultural meanings within music that abides by the conventions of instrumental music. It is difficult to summarize the contributions that musicologists such as Lawrence Kramer, Rose Subotnik, and Susan McClary have made to the practice of reading music's formal structures through a cultural lens. Yet short of radically refiguring music, these accounts more often construe "music" as pure instrumental sound.

In her iconoclastic reading of Beethoven's Ninth, for example, McClary recalls the violent homosocial-masculinist overtones of Wagner's remarks ("breaking," "pressing," "virile," "stems") when she notoriously refers to the frustrated cadence in the symphony's first movement as embodying the "murderous rage of a rapist."[87] Although McClary has been criticized from a number of perspectives,[88] her work has been crucial in bringing feminist thought to musicology. And, like Kramer, she has been instrumental in musicology's large-scale shift from formal analysis and composer biography toward a concern for music's ability to "do cultural work."[89] Yet regarding language and music, McClary has consistently sought musical meaning and signification *within* (absolute) music's formal structures instead of examining art with explicit discursive content. To be sure, McClary looks at popular music alongside contemporary concert music and genres like opera. But her work, and new musicology more broadly, generally turns on the problem of locating meaning within instrumental textures or, as in the work of Kramer, the context in which instrumental music appears. It has not, however, sought an object of study that would genuinely exceed the "bounds of absolute music" any more than Wagner's Beethoven did. Overall, in accepting "the music itself" as nothing more than instrumental sound, new musicology terminologically forfeited the argument against absolute music before it began.[90]

Sound art falls short for different yet related reasons. Sound art theory posits a novel artistic context, "sound art," because the existing context, music—here construed as an ahistorical caricature of (absolute) music spelled as "Music"— is deemed acritical or, indeed, too weighed down by historical, technical, or institutional baggage. Sound art then sees this de-historicized isolation of sound as a subversive move. In its attempt to distance itself from "Music," sound art theory ironically commits a move strictly homologous to the construction of absolute music: it extracts from a historically multivalent music the single medium of sound (and then wonders why sound art cannot move beyond the tenets of medium specificity). Indeed, sound art theory will remain incapable of providing an adequate critique of music if its scope remains limited to sound.

(As noted earlier, nowhere within the premodern trio of *harmonia*, *rhythmos*, and *logos* is there any explicit reference to sound.) Sound art theory's reduction of music from an "intermedial" (and potentially conceptual) art form to a transhistorical version of absolute music—followed by the subsequent elevation of the *further reduced* medium of "sound"—only exacerbates the original problem of absolute music. Music, construed *as* absolute music, is left unperturbed.

Perhaps more than any other critic Kim-Cohen has provided some of the most significant inroads linking music to conceptualism. But his critique of music, too, can be seen to rest upon a transhistorical version of absolute music. In a section of his widely influential book *In the Blink of an Ear: Toward a Non-Cochlear Sonic Art* contrasting music and visual art, Kim-Cohen locates a set of "values" inherent to music wherein it has supposedly "always functioned according to Greenbergian precepts."[91] The comparison equates music's separation from language and signification with a formalist modernist aesthetic here represented by Greenberg. But this would mean that even preabsolute music (he goes as far back as "since at least the advent of notation")[92] would also be deemed "Greenbergian," presumably encompassing art songs, liturgical music, and opera as well. More importantly, an acceptance of this kind of critique could limit what music could turn into.[93]

Additionally, it may preclude a clearer understanding of music's relationship to conceptualism by ignoring the prior *inclusion* of conceptual language as constitutive of music. While my approach differs from new musicology and sound art theory, it shares the historical specificity of Dahlhaus's critique wherein absolute music is recognized as a temporal rupture in the organization of music as a concept. The task is then to move beyond music's reduction from a previously multivalent form to the monodimensional medium (or, more accurately, the *sense*) of sound, while ultimately exceeding either paradigm. Indeed, if a group of German writers could so thoroughly alter the concept of music, why cannot music undergo another equally significant change?

One of the earliest known musical artifacts is a "song" dated from between 200 BC and 100 AD known as the epitaph of Seikilos. Originally discovered in what is present-day Turkey, the Seikilos epitaph consists of a score indicating a text to be sung to the tune of a notated melody, all carved into the surface of a tall, somewhat cylindrical tombstone. It is a music composition *Urtext* that marks the birth of a music inclusive of melodic and linguistic content—inaugurating music as an art form capable of both sensible and conceptual expression. In 1972 American artist John Baldessari, drawing upon the extant form of the art song, imparted conceptually reflexive language to music by singing Sol LeWitt's *Sentences on Conceptual Art*. Music had, once again, incorporated (conceptual) language and was now capable of self-reflection. In 2012, Pussy Riot instrumentalized this kind of musical conceptualism in their *Punk Prayer* intervention.

In the wake of absolute music, then, Pussy Riot reintegrate a musical *logos* both through text setting and through conceptualism. If we follow Žižek, the "Idea" forms no less than the core of Pussy Riot's work. Yet, according to the Moscow Cathedral cleaner, Pussy Riot were unambiguously responsible for making music—however nonclassical or unorthodox. For both Baldessari and Pussy Riot, the voice is crucial: *Baldessari Sings LeWitt* just as Pussy Riot overturn Russian Orthodoxy's principle of "right singing." After absolute music, Pussy Riot sing a music that is both critical and (post)conceptual.

Žižek Sings Pussy Riot

One can, of course, sing not only musically, but also rhetorically. And that Žižek is found singing the praises of Pussy Riot is not surprising, considering the philosopher's extended *Guardian*-published letters with Pussy Riot's Tolokonnikova during her prison sentence. Instigated by philosopher Michel Eltchaninoff, their prison letter correspondence, together with Žižek's above-cited "The True Blasphemy" and Tolokonnikova's "Why I am Going on Hunger Strike," was published as *Comradely Greetings* in 2014 on Verso. Dated between August 23, 2012 and March 18, 2014, the tone of their correspondence is one of thoughtful encouragement, mutual admiration, and respect. The two exchange various references to leftist figures (Marx, Trotsky, Lenin, Franco Berardi, Hardt and Negri), "information age" dissenters (Julian Assange, Chelsea Manning, Edward Snowden), twentieth-century artists (Malevich, Vertov, Kandinsky), and philosophers (Kant, Hegel, Nietzsche, Badiou). They broadly share a criticism of contemporary capitalism and the specific situation in Russia. Žižek goes so far as to hail Pussy Riot's work as exposing an unlikely line of continuity between Stalinism and today's global capitalism.[94] But when their mutual harmony turns to momentary dissonance, Žižek admits to the way he handled a debate with his interlocutor as evidence of a "deeply entrenched male chauvinism."[95]

This patriarchal quip is interesting in light of Žižek's broader philosophical project because many of the examples of "spectral-material" violence invoked earlier turn on the figure of the father. Patriarchal violence, violence enacted under the symbolic order of the father, is a prominent theme that figures throughout Žižek's work. For Žižek, as an astute Lacanian, the father is the very embodiment of authority yet exercises such a position, paradoxically, by *withholding* force: a "father who truly *is* an authority, doesn't have to beat you or to shout at you, and so on. It's just this *look*, a threatening look, and you obey."[96] Žižek contends that there is no need to exercise brute force since such a display ultimately renders the father impotent. Like the violence of the state, patriarchal authority is purely virtual; it is homologous to the threat, which says, "this will happen." It is future-oriented, albeit given to a future constructed (and constricted) entirely through language. This purely discursive and hence virtualized force, the "conceptual matter" of such a statement—"this will happen"—*is* the site of (patriarchal) violence.

Language itself, according to Žižek, is the ultimate form of violence. Exceeding the brute physicality of direct force, the violence of language is more fundamental, Žižek argues, because it imposes a "universe of meaning."[97] Language—the word, *logos*, the idea—makes a cut (to invoke Badiou). It tears into the real. As an artistic parallel, the conceptual prompt, as a text to be carried out or "executed," literalizes this cut. The conceptual proposal promises, imposes, and threatens to be. Returning to a musical register, conceptual violence is a violence that is *composed*. (One recalls here the ill-fated comments Karlheinz Stockhausen made following the 9/11 attacks wherein the composer infamously hailed the event as the "greatest work of art imaginable for the whole cosmos.")[98] In a lucid passage from *Absolute Recoil*, Žižek criticizes Marx for remaining *too much* of a materialist to adequately grasp the thoroughly conceptual violence of capitalism, its systemic obdurateness. More uncanny than precapitalist forms of direct violence, the violence of capitalism, Žižek insists, is "no longer attributable to concrete individuals with their 'evil' intentions, but is purely 'objective,' systemic, anonymous—quite literally a conceptual violence, the violence of a Concept whose self-deployment rules and regulates social reality."[99] This conceptual violence is the violence of unemployment, of not being emailed back. Due in no part to "socio-ideological" differences, you were simply not "a fit"—it was an "objective" decision, simply the result of the imposition of a concept ("we hire who we like," etc.). Shouldn't we nevertheless extend this analysis beyond a critique of capitalism? Is it not true that, in addition to the market, a similar systemic or conceptual violence applies to patriarchy, sexism, and homophobia—especially in post-Soviet Russia?

Violence as the immanent virtuality of the threat is a theme that echoes throughout Žižek's oeuvre. Perhaps nowhere is the idea more clearly demonstrated than in "Towards a Materialist Theory of Subjectivity," the first chapter of *Absolute Recoil* (and the title of the related lecture Žižek gave in 2013 at the Birkbeck Institute). Žižek begins the chapter with a discussion of an extended quotation from Althusser's "Marx in his Limits," an essay that itself began as a lecture presented to far-Left French group *Il Manifesto* in 1977 (and published posthumously in 1994). Inciting a scandal when he delivered the speech, Althusser declared Marxism to be "in a state of crisis" for its lack of a "theory of the state, state power or the state apparatus."[100] In his reading, Žižek concludes that Althusser is ultimately a "vulgar materialist" because he does not grasp the "*immanent* gap" between knowledge and belief so crucial to Žižek's thinking.[101] Žižek criticizes Althusser for maintaining that the state apparatus and its violent enforcement must always retain a connection to a "piece of the real"—here in the form of military might, tanks, riot police, etc. Althusser insists, however, that these apparatuses need not actually be actually deployed, that they can function via implication, through sheer threat. But this, for Žižek, is precisely where Althusser remains a "vulgar materialist": indeed, Žižek insists that it is *only* through this withholding of force that state violence actually works. Otherwise, excessive force is received as a kind of impotence.

Is it possible that Žižek goes too far in privileging nonphysical, conceptual violence over brute physical force? In practice, real and virtual violence are often effectively deployed coterminously, seen, as Bernstein argued, in the "impotent" use of force by the Russian state.

Interestingly, Žižek's critique of Althusser and the related anecdote constitute one of the few sections of *Absolute Recoil*'s first chapter *not* taken directly from the prison letter correspondence with Pussy Riot's Tolokonnikova. Ideas are perhaps, before anything else, copies of other ideas. And although this "copy 'n' paste" approach is not unfamiliar to Žižek,[102] it is striking that the philosopher omitted this material in his correspondence with Tolokonnikova. Then again, it's hard to tell a new mother pushed to the brink of a hunger strike in a former Gulag facility in Mordovia that "the true authority has to remain virtual."[103] Not that Žižek is wrong in claiming that authority works as threat and that real material violence renders authority impotent. But is it not evident that state power simply retains its hegemonic position *despite remaining utterly "impotent"*? For not only does authority continue to function, but, in cases like the violent suppression of the Occupy movement in the United States and the Russian government's reaction to Pussy Riot, it is clear that the state apparatus remains all the more effective despite its "impotent" acting out.[104]

Materialist Conceptualism: Composing Ideas that Matter

Against the simultaneous expenditure of state violence and patriarchal oppression, Pussy Riot "took the altar" in their Moscow Cathedral intervention. Pussy Riot sing *Punk Prayer*, and, in response, Žižek sings Pussy Riot: "Their message is: IDEAS MATTER"—they are conceptual artists. Tolokonnikova and her father have both confirmed her interest in conceptual art.[105] But the genuine conceptual valence of their work is found in Pussy Riot's feminist reintegration of conceptual language in music. Not only their use of language as lyrics, but the *context* of their intervention—as women appropriating Orthodox music for the purpose of secular protest—demands a radical reconsideration of music and its relation to conceptual art.

Throughout this chapter I have attempted to make a case for the materiality of ideas, the mattering of concepts in artistic practice through the figures of Žižek, Pussy Riot, and Baldessari. In light of Žižek's "dematerialized materialism," conceptual art is considered further in relation to what I have suggested calling a *materialist conceptualism*: the notion of a conceptual art that recognizes the kinds of "immaterial materiality" that Žižek works to articulate, while resisting a reading of conceptualism through a purely textual or idealist framework. Against the art world's recent turn to inert objects (roughly inspired by recent materialist/realist trends in continental philosophy), Žižek's singing of Pussy Riot insists upon the material impact of ideas, the "immanent materiality" of concepts.[106] The implications for music are equally significant: a musical practice is seen to incorporate the radical implications of conceptualism while exceeding the "conceptless" bounds of absolute music. Beyond sound, this is a music composed of ideas.

I want to conclude by insisting that Pussy Riot *compose* their *Punk Prayer* intervention. Drawing together writing and conceptual art's proposal form, composition becomes the counterpart of the threat: it *draws up* a future consequence, a (counter-)violence-to-come. Pussy Riot draft *Punk Prayer* as a composition; they deploy singing, staging, and musical performativity by tactically orchestrating actors across space and time. This is not to advocate a continuation of the kinds of music composition uncritically inherited from the high modernist tradition. For that notion of composition, which continues to dominate the majority of "new music" institutions, proceeds, by and large, from an unreconstructed notion of absolute music.[107] The manipulation of sound, instrumental or otherwise, goes largely unchallenged, leaving less room for the kind of conceptual and politically engaged practice found in Pussy Riot. Against these tendencies, I want to recuperate a music beyond sound, to salvage what in composition works like a plan, a proposal. For in composition (as LeWitt and new music practitioners will concur), "All ideas need not be made physical."

Composition speculates, anticipates, listens, and coordinates; it combines and assembles. As Latour has contended, composition insists that "things have to be put together," while simultaneously "retaining their heterogeneity."[108] Pussy Riot assemble a collective identity through a "de-individualized" yet heterogeneous grouping of bodies. By "taking the altar," they challenge the sexist hegemony of the Russian Orthodox Church; they sing their *Punk Prayer* and mobilize the word in a context where the voices of women remain explicitly silenced. As a group, they compose a collective force that exceeds the individual act. Proliferating, multiplying in an infinite potentiality, Pussy Riot's Idea is that of composition: they compose and make real ideas that matter.

Music to the Letter: Noise, Language, and the *Letter from Schoenberg*

Introduction: Music Without Sounds

Although the Berlin-based Austrian artist and composer Peter Ablinger has received significant exposure in European contexts ranging from music performances to gallery installations and discussions in various German language music publications, save for a few notable exceptions, discussions of his work in a broader art-theoretical context have remained limited. I will not be so ambitious as to attempt to discuss the composer's entire career, an oeuvre, which, for over four decades of consistent artistic output, might be considered staggering. Rather, I want to address the interrelated problematics of language and noise within the composer's expanded musical practice: how is authority exercised, asserted, rehearsed, and instituted through musical form? And what are the delimitations of language and the limits of noise in a musical practice? Considering my broader project to reconceive a music beyond the confines of sound, the common notion of noise as an *excess* of sound may appear counterintuitive. But Ablinger's engagement with noise, as evidenced by his extensive and ongoing *Weiss/Weisslich* (White/Whitish)[1] series, is not limited to any singular medium and includes installations, objects, texts, performances, video, and works that exist only in concept or title.

Ablinger notably brings methodologies found in postwar visual art (minimalism, site specificity, seriality, conceptualism, institutional critique) into contact with musical practice. Paralleling conceptual art's intent to "'de-objectify' the object,"[2] Ablinger proposes a kind of "de-sonified" music. The artist identifies a subsection of his noise series as *Musik ohne Klänge* (Music Without Sounds), which includes, for example, *24 Stühle* (24 Chairs), a work that consists of twenty-four chairs placed in a typical concert seating arrangement in various locations. Beyond an interest in the multiplication of sonic resources, as is often the case with practitioners of new music, Ablinger intervenes into the "conditions for making music"—music's expanded contextual and historical conventions that extend from the concert hall to ticket salespeople, instrument makers, and music critics.[3] Referring to his overall approach, the composer states summarily, "The sounds do not interest me."[4] Ablinger's work deprivileges sound to address music in its expanded situation.

Music is left, at this extreme, without sound. Sound as a material substrate of music becomes deprioritized in favor of the wider methodological scope necessary to interrogate music as a critical artistic practice. Yet while this "post-sound" approach departs significantly from the predominant attitudes found in new music circles—for much of that world, "the sounds" are of primary, if not exclusive interest—Ablinger's work remains intimately tied to musical forms and their histories. Importantly, Ablinger's musical practice does not simply resort to synesthesia (although his work often embraces its consequences)[5] in an attempt to replace one sense or medium with another, as is often the case, for example, in so-called "visual music." Rather, Ablinger's "music without sounds" illuminates a whole series of material, social, and formal apparatuses—sounding or not—that provide music with material support. The concert situation, recording technology, the score, listening: Ablinger's work interrogates music's sites of representation and modes of technological reproduction, while it draws lines of relation to historical figures, artistic conventions, and cultural practices.

Ablinger's work does of course involve actual acoustic sound, but the latter remains secondary to the formal, historical, and sensorial relations his musical practice elucidates. Nowhere more clearly is Ablinger's interrogation of music's expanded conditions exhibited than in his watershed 2007 work *A Letter from Schoenberg – reading piece with player piano.*[6] For that work is not concerned with sounds as such, but rather explores a novel perceptual phenomenon wherein ordinary musical tones, through technological extension, become recognizable as speech. The work, moreover, becomes fixated upon a set of "*parergonal*" objects of musical reproduction (scores, recordings, musical automata)[7] and instances of authoritative language deployed to ensure normative modes of musical performance and dissemination. Presented as an installation, *Letter from Schoenberg* uses a computer-controlled player piano to transduce into piano sound a recording of Arnold Schoenberg dictating a letter written to protest a 1950 Dial Records release of his compositions.[8] Schoenberg wrote the scolding missive in response to a recording of his 1942 work *Ode to Napoleon* that contained the voice of a woman instead of the intended male performer.

Ablinger's crossing of recording technology with musical automata implicates the musical score as the subject of Schoenberg's letter and therefore completes a tripartite framing of music's historical modes of technological reproduction (scores, musical automata, recordings).

Letter from Schoenberg takes as its point of departure the letter Schoenberg drafted to assert control over a performance of his composition. His letter functions as both a document and a command that sought to enforce the performer's gender identity. Thus, while sound is a distinct component in *Letter from Schoenberg*, of greater importance are the registers of language and authority that Ablinger's intervention highlights. This chapter's title, "Music to the Letter," refers first to Ablinger's literal translation of speech into music, his enacting of a kind of categorical cut wherein music is recoded through the letter of spoken language. Meanwhile, my title also thematizes Schoenberg's expressed imperative to execute his score "correctly," to perform his composition "to the letter." As with Ultra-red's *SILENT|LISTEN*, *Letter from Schoenberg* asks the question *what does it mean to perform a piece of music*? To what kinds of authority must a performer submit to execute a musical score? These questions cut to the heart of the form of music composition, and here they implicate, in different capacities, the registers of perception and identity. Ablinger's *Letter from Schoenberg* returns to the *Werktreue* problematic, or the notion of "faithfulness" to the musical score explored in Chapter 1, while it sets up questions concerning gender identity explored briefly in this book's conclusion.

Ablinger's *Letter from Schoenberg* dramatizes the historical expulsion of language from music that began with the advent of absolute music—the conceptual shift that occurred in the early nineteenth century wherein instrumental music replaced the notion of music as a multivalent art form inclusive of language. Ablinger's work creates a short circuit between the domains of language and (instrumental) music, reuniting these strata through recourse to their respective material constitutions. It is because of this kind of taxonomic reworking that I will turn in my analysis to Deleuze and Guattari's notion of the rhizome, a root structure that "connects any point to any other point" and opposes restricted categorical hierarchies.[9] In listening to Ablinger's installation, which consists strictly of (player) piano tones, we access a legible rendering of Schoenberg's own voice, effectively reconstituted through musical sound. Language is returned to music, on the one hand, in the contractual character of the musical score that Schoenberg articulates in his letter: as a kind of Deleuzian "order-word," the score forms a linguistic command structure to be violated or followed. On the other, Ablinger's work demonstrates the potential for musical tones to resemble speech. Beyond providing a superficial similarity, however, musical tones take on the function of a sound playback device. An ordinary piano is re-engineered to replay/relay, and potentially undermine Schoenberg's authorial voice.

A perceptual border zone emerges for a listener/viewer of *Letter from Schoenberg* that allows an oscillation between the poles of noise and language: the decoherence and illegibility of speech on one end, and the signifying status of Schoenberg's letter on the other. Indeed, without knowledge of the piece (or prior to reading along with the original letter), one hears only a series of loud and seemingly disjointed aggregates of piano sound that take on fleeting speech-like qualities. Conversely, while reading along with Schoenberg's letter, one recognizes the voice of the composer lucidly reconstituted through ordinary piano tones. Through this shift, this vacillation between the registers of noise and language, *Letter from Schoenberg* demands a special attention to listening and perception. And this characteristic, I contend, is also present in Ablinger's noise works.

In addition to situating Ablinger's *Letter from Schoenberg* within broader discussions around the relationships between music, language, and representation, this chapter also engages with Ablinger's ongoing noise series. Throughout his career Ablinger has focused extensively on noise in several capacities: noise as totality; as phenomenon, in lived duration, in action, as pure concept; ways of obtaining noise, ways of recording noise, ways of listening to noise—a kind of listening, I should add, that need not include sound at all. To Ablinger, listening represents "any type of perception, the ways in which we react to the world." He continues, "Listening is thus the means of observing perception."[10] Not only is music left without sounds, but here listening itself becomes unhinged from the aural.

Ablinger posits listening as a broader perceptual mode that is at once porous, permeable, reflective, and reflexive. The composer's *Weiss/Weisslich* series charts the development of this decentered listening practice while it iteratively continues the composer's investigation of noise. Both the *Weiss/Weisslich* series and *Letter from Schoenberg* occupied central roles in *Hören hören* (Hearing Listening), Ablinger's 2008 solo exhibition at Berlin's *Haus am Waldsee*, a private mansion-turned art space built in the interwar period that has exhibited contemporary art since 1946.

The prospect of hosting Ablinger's musical works in such a space ostensibly geared toward visual art may appear somewhat unlikely for a composer emerging from the tradition of European concert music. However, the works from *Hören hören*, as is typical with Ablinger's practice, took the form of sound recordings, objects, video, text, photography, site-specific interventions, installations, and performances with interactive components. (The *Haus am Waldsee* has also maintained a long-standing tradition of hosting art events including music and theater performances and literature readings alongside visual art exhibitions.) Broadly speaking, visual art has remained a critical influence for Ablinger. For although the musician studied with modern European composers such as Gösta Neuwirth and Roman Haubenstock-Ramati, Ablinger explains that he has "learned a great deal more from visual art than [he] did from new classical music," citing Gerhard Richter, Barnett Newman, and Antoni Tàpies as primary influences.[11] Not only does Ablinger incorporate visual media, but his work includes strategies central to postwar art more broadly. Nevertheless, despite this broader relevance, I wish to frame Ablinger's works not as instances of multimedia, or even intermedia, but in the context of music conceived as an art form expanded beyond the confines of sound as a medium.

I will begin by contextualizing Ablinger's *Weiss/Weisslich* noise series with respect to historical precedents such as Russolo's futurist noise, Pierre Schaeffer's *musique concrète*, and the percussion works of Varèse. Ablinger's noise is conceived here as a departure from the gestures of anti-traditionalism associated with avant-garde noise and instead prompts a multivalent stance centered around sensory perception. As opposed to the down-with-the-past tropes central to the dynamics of the avant-garde, the *Weiss/Weisslich* series proposes a paradoxical upending through stasis. Through an interpretation of Deleuze and Guattari, furthermore, I suggest that Ablinger sets into motion a type of "perceptual semiotics" that mediates between sense and philosophical thinking.[12] Perception, pivotal to an engagement with Ablinger's noise, also proves beneficial in discussing Ablinger's work that explores the materiality of speech, including *Letter from Schoenberg*.

Between Noise and Language

Like language, noise has not always been conceived as separate from music. As early as the ancient Greeks, according to Jacques Attali, music and noise were bound up with sacrifice and ritual and, taken together, were parts of a broader sacrificial economy.[13] Music is conceived in this constellation as the channeling of violence, the gradual imposition of codes, constraints, and norms. Ablinger's noise, alternatively, is concerned with a focusing and refraction of perception. Irreducible to a *passage à l'acte*, though not fully outside of the rubric of resistance, Ablinger's noise, like his *Letter from Schoenberg*, is marked by distinct forms of oscillation: between the conceptual and the sensory, legibility and decoherence, tradition and iconoclasm. Ablinger's noise is central to an understanding of *Letter from Schoenberg*. For not only does *Letter from Schoenberg* dramatize music's expulsion of language, but, through its vacillations between noise and language, *Letter from Schoenberg* rehearses noise's exclusion from music.

The story of noise's reintegration in music is perhaps better understood than its initial banishment. One need look no further than the proliferating dissonances that developed in the Western art music canon throughout the twentieth century: Schoenberg's twelve-tone music, Henry Cowell's clusters, Stravinsky's *Rite of Spring*, Varèse's *Poème électronique*, Cage's *Imaginary Landscapes*, James Tenney's computer music of the 1960s, and so on. Modernism can be seen as an extended tale charting the gradual incorporation of noise into (art) music. Extended further, we can include the ongoing developments in punk's aftermath, the sprawling work of Japanese noise artist Merzbow, Taku Unami's reductionist improvisation textures, and the recent emergence of the so-called "noise band."[14]

Yet beyond its acoustic qualities, or its gradual acceptance in the context of high modernist composition, noise is characterized by a kind of opposition. As resistance to organization, the eschewing of tradition, or subversion of norms, noise is understood as negativity. As Paul Hegarty contends,

> Noise is negative; it is unwanted, other, not something ordered. It is negativity defined—i.e. by what it is not (not acceptable sound, not music, not a message or a meaning), but it is also a negativity. In other words, it does not exist independently, as it exists only in relation to what it is not. . . . Noise is something like a process, and whether it creates a result (positive in the form of avant-garde transformation, negative in the form of social restrictions) or remains process is one of the major issues of how music and noise relate.[15]

The negative and antagonistic character of noise that Hegarty cites is found perhaps most clearly in the noise of the avant-garde. Luigi Russolo, for example, allied with the avant-garde group of Italian futurists, began his impassioned call for the use of noise in his *Art of Noises* manifesto of 1913. Concerning the general project of the futurists, described lucidly as "the matrix of an attempt to forge a total homology between the physics of the art object, the physics of the street, and the cultural physics of the vangarde,"[16] it is clear why Russolo chose noise in his effort to capture the dynamism of modernity and the cacophony of urban existence. In the opening remarks of his manifesto, Russolo insists that premodern life unfolded quietly.[17] But that would change with the onset of war, industry, and the bustle of urban life. The artist goes on to describe an evolution of music of increasing dissonance in parallel with the development of the modern city. Dissonance had increased, according to Russolo, in tandem with the multiplication of machines. "Pure sound," according to Russolo, "no longer provokes emotion."[18] Music needed to be noisy because life had become clamorous.

Yet however close for Russolo the connection was between the sounds of life and noise, he did not limit noise to imitation. Noise was not meant simply to depict life; rather, it was to serve as an element within a composition, a component to be regulated "harmonically and rhythmically," to be given pitches.[19] Russolo accomplished this via his array of *intonarumori* or "noise intoners," which consisted of what Russolo referred to as drone-machines, crash-machines, din-machines, whistle machines, shrilling machines, snort-machines, etc. Many of these instruments had the ability to produce elegant glissandi, to glide smoothly between pitches. Although such glissandi were readily available on traditional instruments such as the violin, Russolo nevertheless criticizes musical sound as being "too limited" in terms of timbre.[20] At this point, a certain hint of antagonism, even something of the "anti-traditionalism" or the down-with-the-past attitude "so dear to the Italian futurists,"[21] is apparent in Russolo's manifesto. That antagonism becomes clear when he turns to Wagner and Beethoven, proclaiming a preference for the noises of trains and crowds over the *Eroica* or the *Pastorale*.[22]

But even the avant-garde, with its incessant pursuit of the new, never truly abandoned tradition; rather, artists such as Russolo approached music (and other forms) through a kind of dialectical interplay. The new was achieved through a critical confrontation with the past. Recall Russolo's violently anti-traditionalist call for "resounding slaps and stamping with both feet on violins, pianos, contrabasses, and organs," while simultaneously claiming to have "divined" music's "great renewal."[23] The destructive impulse of the avant-garde is coterminous with the creative drive to rejuvenate tradition, to reinvent known forms. Despite his adamant striving toward renewal, Russolo situates his iconoclastic gesture in relation to the canonical figures of Beethoven and Wagner. Likewise, the *intonaurumori,* as with futurist noise more generally, can be seen as both a departure from and a continuation of musical tradition. Accordingly, the futurists celebrated of the concept of "continuity," a fact not only related to Russolo's fascination with glissando. As Luciano Chessa explains, the notion of continuity took on both musical and philosophical significance for Russolo and the futurists.[24]

Alongside the proliferation of machines, recording technology—with its consequent shifts in perception and philosophical thinking—was also a factor in noise's rise to saturation. Russolo's conception of noise was closely linked to the work of the French *musique concrète* composers for whom, beginning in the 1950s, Russolo was a precursor and clear influence. Much of the theory of early *musique concrète* derives from the writings and compositions of Pierre Schaeffer, one of the movement's most influential pioneers. First, facilitated by the new ability to conceal sounds from their sources via the technological advancement of the tape recorder, Schaeffer contemplated a corresponding mode of listening defined as *écoute réduite* (reduced listening), in which a sound's causality was to be removed or ignored. Causality was ignored if the recorded material was unaltered; it was a matter of listening practice. The removal of traces of causality occurred as a result of various tape manipulation procedures, editing, etc. Schaeffer invokes the trope of Pythagoras's curtain, according to which the philosopher's disciples listened to his lectures behind a curtain so as not to be distracted by his appearance or gesticulations. Noting that *acousmatic* refers to "a noise one hears without seeing what causes it," Schaeffer insists that the kind of listening the term inaugurates "marks the perceptive reality of sound as such, as distinguished from the modes of its production and transmission."[25] But as Schaeffer illustrates in his *Etudes de bruit* (Noise Studies), noise—encapsulated by *l'objet sonore* (the sound object), the fundamental and temporally brief perceptual unit Schaeffer defines for working with recorded sound—is *material* for composition. Noise must be placed within a structured, syntactic musical context. Rather than concentrating on the work, as Nattiez contends, Schaeffer concentrates solely on the material itself.[26]

Noise is in constant danger of legibility, of becoming domesticated or being downed out; it can also lose its noisiness through organization. Aside from the work of the Italian futurists, noise was also found in the "organized sound" of Varèse, for instance, *Ionization* (1929–31), perhaps the earliest percussion-only work of the Western art music canon. Discussing a performance of *Ionization*, Varèse noted, "People call them instruments for making noise. I call them instruments for making sounds."[27] As with Russolo, Varèse placed an emphasis on integrating noise into a composition. It was, according to Nattiez, "still the composer who decided what he wishe[d] to retain in his work."[28]

For Ablinger, noise is not returned to music as an element for manipulation, but rather becomes constitutive *of* music. An important precursor to the *Weiss/Weisslich* works was Ablinger's series of so-called one-note works. These instrumental compositions, such as *Anfangen (:Aufhören)* (1991) for violin, displayed a provocative phenomenon in which a single tone, when struck over and over, would, through enough repetition, appear to cross over into the territory of noise.[29] Not a feat of trickery and not exactly a psychoacoustic illusion, these works revealed a latent noise already inherent to musical sound. The scratching of bow hair required to produce the violin tone; the breath that belongs to woodwind embouchure: these ordinarily "secondary" aural phenomena—noises—become foregrounded over musical tones. Ablinger's single-note pieces thus allow a listener to perceive a noise *inherent* to musical experience by opening listeners to subterranean perceptual phenomena. Ablinger's noise invokes, in this sense, what Deleuze and Guattari refer to as "perceptual semiotics," a linguistic equivalent of their concept of the rhizome.[30] If, according to Deleuze and Guattari, it is "not easy to see the grass in things,"[31] then it is perhaps no less difficult to hear.

Ablinger's noise departs from the approaches of the avant-garde: not simply disruptive, it resists the kind of integration into the composition as material as was the case with Varèse and Schaeffer. Ablinger insists,

> Noise is different [from] other sounds. To me it is almost the opposite. Noise is certainly one of the oldest sounds of which humans have become aware. A waterfall, the sea or a forest rushing can involve an experience comparable to the sight of a mountain range, the desert or the stars at night. Such experiences are as far as possible devoid of meaningful information yet they act like a mirror, they throw something back upon ourselves insofar as we read something into them, turn them into something which is anchored only in ourselves. Hence, in such situations we experience ourselves.[32]

Ablinger's *Weiss/Weisslich* works are not to be reduced to the kind of antagonistic impulse found in futurist noise. And while he may possess trace amounts of the "anti-" inherent to the avant-garde, Ablinger is not caught up in the process of repeating such gestures. Nor does his noise function as a syntactical musical unit; as opposed to "composing with noise," Ablinger's noise *is* the composition. Through various material and conceptual instantiations—its physical and phenomenal presentation, its existence across media, its sheer potential for emergence in places or situations, its existence in thought—noise itself becomes the work.

This integral approach to noise was embodied in the *Weiss/Weisslich* works included in the *Hören hören* exhibition. *Weiss/Weisslich 18, für Robert Ranke-Graves, CD*, for example, was one of the works set up for CD playback at a listening station in the *Haus am Waldsee*. The CD tracks comprised twelve field recordings, including one made in a corn field east of Vienna, near the Hungarian border. In *Weiss/Weisslich 29 b, 24 Stühle/24 Chairs*, twenty-four chairs were arranged in rows in a dedicated area of the courtyard in front of the *Haus am Waldsee*. *Weiss/Weisslich 36, Kopfhörer* (Headphones) acted as a kind of acoustic magnifying glass that subtly distorts the concept of headphones by bringing closer to the listener sounds already present. *Weiss/Weisslich 15, Installation und Hinweis/Installation and Reference* occupied the entire second floor of the *Haus am Waldsee*. Yet other than a small music stand containing a diagram and the title of the piece, there appeared to be nothing to hear *or* see in the gallery. Each of the five gallery rooms was filled with a unique "colored silence," or filtered noise, each approximating one of the German vowels, A, O, U, E, I, and each of which was sustained extremely quietly over hidden loudspeakers. The listener was able to test the threshold of audibility of each vowel and, walking from room to room, various possible in-betweens.

In *Letter from Schoenberg*, a different kind of phenomenalization of language occurs in which a perceptual boundary is approached and placed upon a delicate

Figure 2 *A Letter From Schoenberg – reading piece with player piano.* View of computer-controlled piano player and piano. From Peter Ablinger, *Hören hören* (Hearing Listening), *Haus am Waldsee*, Berlin, 2008.

brink of intelligibility. Music itself is deployed as a kind of temporal copying machine, a recording device that reproduces language's material substance. Recorded speech becomes scrutinized, in this sense, by ordinary musical tones. But before going into further detail, I will return briefly to the relationship between music and language.

Music to the Letter

Music has held a complex and historically shifting relationship to language. In the preceding chapter, I discussed consequences of the historical conception of absolute music. Beginning in the early nineteenth century, music underwent a totalizing epistemological rupture: the concept of music as a multivalent art form *inclusive* of language (found in the premodern trio *harmonia*, *rhythmos*, and *logos*) was replaced with a notion of music as instrumental sound beyond language's grasp. Music had severed its ties to conceptual thinking and became equated with sound that, while formally complex, lacked intentional linguistic signification. Despite numerous critiques waged by musicologists and sound art theorists, music has, by and large, retained this designation as asignifying instrumental sound. But while widely accepted, this concept of music need not remain permanent. Recall Dahlhaus's commentary on the historical specificity of absolute music: since the concept has a determinate beginning, it can be challenged and may even come to an end.[33] As though realizing the transformation implicit in Dahlhaus's statement, the critical and conceptual music practices outlined in this book point to a subsequent reconception of music beyond the limits of sound.

Paradoxically, Ablinger's *Letter from Schoenberg* reinscribes language into music by *limiting* itself to instrumental sound, the category historically conceived in opposition to language. Nevertheless, musical thinkers have often disagreed about the opposition between music and language. Adorno, for example, discusses the subject in his essay "Music, Language, and Composition" in a manner that departs from his earlier assertions that refer to music's "aconceptual and nonrepresentational aspect," or his and Hanns Eisler's characterization of music as the "abstract art *par excellence* . . . farthest removed from the world of practical things."[34] Although Adorno begins "Music, Language, and Composition" by writing that music "does not form a system of signs," he asserts that music, in some sense, must rely on signification. He posits music somewhere between "non-signification" and language: "Music without any signification, the mere phenomenological coherence of the tones, would resemble an acoustical kaleidoscope. As pure signification, on the other hand, it would cease to be music and pass, falsely, into language."[35] Adorno's contention is interesting because it sets up such a movement between language and music as a kind of transgression. Considering *Letter from Schoenberg,* if such a passage represents a "false passage," then Ablinger's "rhizomatic" gesture completes the crossing.

Deleuze and Guattari, originators of the concept of the rhizome, view music as an aconceptual art form despite its historically variant forms. They consistently privilege music not for any signifying or "communicational value," but for its temporality, its substantive materiality. "Music molecularizes sound matter and in so doing becomes capable of harnessing the nonsonorous forces such as Duration and Intensity."[36] Music, they say, is *of the refrain.* As they explain, "The refrain fabricates time (*du temps*). The refrain is the 'implied sense'"—or *temps,* a word that, as translator of *A Thousand Plateaus* Brian Massumi notes, also connotes "meters" and "tempos."[37] Through its rhythmic organization, music *creates* temporality. "Time is not an a priori form; rather, the refrain is the a priori form of time, which in each case fabricates different times."[38] This fabrication of duration, or marking of time, has less to do with the signified, or the nonmaterial, than it does with immanent sound matter: "Certain modern musicians oppose the transcendent plan(e) of organization, which is said to have dominated Western classical music, to the immanent sound plane, which is always given along with that to which it gives rise, brings the imperceptible into perception, and carries only differential speeds and slowness in a kind of molecular lapping."[39] For Deleuze and Guattari, music resists ossification by virtue of this radical immanence; by harnessing pure intensity and duration, music allows us to hear "the grass in things."[40]

Deleuze and Guattari position music as a nonrepresentational art form resistant to categorical hierarchies, although they leave open, to an extent, the question of music's relation to language.[41] I want to argue, then, that such a hierarchical undermining may allow a different integration of language into music, one that is also suggested in Ablinger's *Letter from Schoenberg.* Eric Prieto writes about Deleuze and Guattari's conception of music, specifically noting their privileging of music as radically antihierarchical:

> For Deleuze and Guattari, music is an exemplary art, providing the clearest practical example of the kind of nomadic thought they seek to promote. A

temporal art, it puts the emphasis on the Bergsonian dynamics of flux and becoming; a non-representational art, it puts our perceptual faculties in touch with our intellectual faculties in a way that does not require the mediation of concepts and representation. But above all, they argue, it is nomadic, it brings together different levels of analysis, enabling them to be contained within a single thought. By liberating us from the limitations of representational thought in the Aristotelian tradition, which requires that we work on one conceptual plane at a time, music helps us to understand how, from the interstellar to the sub-atomic level, everything is in touch with everything else.[42]

Prieto touches upon a feature of Deleuze and Guattari's thought that is particularly relevant to Ablinger's *Letter from Schoenberg*, a category they introduce centered on the abolition of categories themselves, namely, the rhizome. In counterdistinction to the tree (*arbor*), the rhizome is a root structure; it allows unrestricted movement between fields, categories, distinctions, media, and disciplines. Although music is nomadic, for Deleuze and Guattari music is the rhizomatic art form par excellence. They insist, "Music has always sent out lines of flight, like so many 'transformational multiplicities,' even overturning the very codes that structure or arborify it; that is why musical form, right down to its ruptures and proliferations, is comparable to a weed, a rhizome."[43] Music's potential for "overturning the very codes that structure or arborify it,"[44] whether these codes figure as its existence as non-noise or nonlanguage, is realized in Ablinger's work. With Ablinger, music may also exist as noise or language. Or, as with his *Letter from Schoenberg*, music oscillates between these poles.

The presentation of *Letter from Schoenberg* in the *Haus am Waldsee* exhibition consisted of a grand piano with a large apparatus placed on top of its keyboard installed in one of the main rooms of the gallery. Every hour upon the hour a gallery visitor witnessed the piano keys, aided by the contraption hovering directly above, move in a rapid, seemingly sporadic manner. Dozens of small, felt-tipped prongs, each assigned to a single key, activated the piano to produce an animated, somewhat unpredictable sound texture that pulsated in a speech-like manner. The resulting aggregates of piano sound were exceedingly loud (one could hear the piano within a half-kilometer radius of the *Haus* itself). In front of the piano, the text from Schoenberg's original letter was printed on a sheet of paper propped up on a music stand.

Mister:

You. . . . In spite of my protest,

you have published

Leibowitz' performance
of my *Ode to Napoleon*
with a woman voice,
which I find
terrible.
(. . . behind the orchestra . . .)
I can only tell you now,
that you will
hear from me.
You will, I can tell you,
you will regret this act
severely.
I will
be busy to help you
to be ruined
by this
what I will do. . . .
(Some of the instruments . . . in small. . . .)
You are not only a bugger . . .
You are not only a man who disregards an artist's wishes,
his artistic beliefs,
you are also a man
who does not care
to keep a contract.
You know that you signed a contract,
according to which
you have
to account to me regularly.
You must have sold
quite
a number of records
of my *Violin Phantasy*,
of the *Trio*,
and other things which you . . .
but which you issued without my consent.
I tell you,
you will hear from me also about these things,
and I hope it will cost you very much money

Yours . . .

Upon listening closely to the piano, and reading along with the provided text, one realizes that Schoenberg's original speech becomes discernible entirely through the sound of the piano. The text is required to comprehend Schoenberg's letter; without it, the sound folds back into abstraction. Legibility itself then undergoes a kind of undulation: one moment the mass of piano tones appears as purely abstract; then, upon recognition of a word or phrase, the sound immediately shifts to register as intelligible speech. This vacillation between (musical) noise and language, alongside the fact that one can will it into being (a reader/listener may choose not to read along), suggests the constructedness of both language and music, their status as perceptual *acts*. Musician and writer Chico Mello notes a similar kind of perceptual ambiguity in *Letter from Schoenberg*: "In this reduplication which links two differing symbolic worlds (music and language) various cognitive perceptions are questioned. Thus the occasional intelligibility of the spoken, or rather 'played' texts [is] perceived musically as recurring irritations or even hallucinations—the decoding of words encumbers the purely musical reception pushing it into the background."[45] The presence of speech becomes a kind of apparition, the voice of a phantom character that emerges from the sonic texture; when decoding words, the instrumental character of the piano sound all but evaporates.

This shifting presence found in *Letter from Schoenberg* is closely related to the concept of the *acousmêtre*, sound-film theorist Michel Chion's notion of invisible, "offscreen" speech. Chion's *acousmêtre* is the filmic version of Schaeffer's *acousmatic*; it describes "a character whose relationship to the screen involves a specific kind of ambiguity and oscillation," as Chion explains. He continues, "We may define [the *acousmêtre*] as neither inside nor outside the image."[46] This master voice constantly shifts between appearing "on-screen" and off and in film typically takes the form of robots, computers, ghosts, and others who are granted special powers of omniscience and omnipotence.[47] Although without image per se, *Letter from Schoenberg* contains a peculiar ambiguity with respect to the origin of Schoenberg's voice. And while there is no screen, a listener becomes caught up in the process of locating the source of this ghostly character: if not the piano, from where does Schoenberg speak? And by what mechanism are we able to hear Schoenberg's voice?

Letter from Schoenberg invites a reconsideration of the relationships between music's historical modes of technological mediation: the musical score, recorded sound, and musical automata. While Schoenberg's score (and its transgressive performance) is the subject of Schoenberg's letter, Ablinger's installation stages an anachronistic crossing of the subsequent inventions of musical automata and the phonograph. Typically, the latter is conceived as having replaced the former.[48] As for musical automata, *Letter from Schoenberg* deploys a custom-designed player piano, enhanced by the precision of the computer and the dexterity of augmented mechanical elements. Historically, the components of automata have been: first, the sounding instrument (the hammers and strings in the case of the player piano); second, that which touches the instrument, for example, a fitted player; and third, a description of what and how the musical automaton should play. Pitch, duration, dynamic levels, and other attributes appear as inscriptions on paper rolls, cylinders, or, as with *Letter from Schoenberg*, an external storage device.[49] This third component, rather than defining a new composition (as is more often the case with musical automata), contains a reproduction of Schoenberg's voice.

Ablinger refers to the resulting process, in which recorded sound is reproduced through musical tones, as *phonorealism*. Using spectral analysis (a technique in which a sound is broken down into its basic component frequencies), each piano tone is derived from a corresponding tone extracted from the original Schoenberg voice recording. One can think of each note played by the piano as a kind of sonic analog of the pixel in digital art: a composite sound image is formed, similarly, by combining many individual elements, in this case piano tones activated across the range of the keyboard.[50] Mello writes that the player piano used in *Letter from Schoenberg* becomes "an oversized phonograph" for reproducing speech.[51] Thomas Edison's invention of the phonograph in 1877 was a by-product of experiments designed to reproduce the human singing voice[52] and was a culmination of a desire to "fuse speech and writing" and communicate with the dead.[53] Before his breakthrough invention, Edison had intended to convert the "phonautographic signatures of vocal sounds" into writing by ascribing to each the appropriate alphabetic letter.[54] Ablinger's machine, the player piano in *Letter from Schoenberg*, encodes into piano tones the "phonautographic signatures" of Schoenberg's letter; it fuses speech to music and binds music to the letter of language.

Ablinger's player piano musically rerenders Schoenberg's recorded letter, a document that itself refers to another recording, an LP of the composer's 1942 score *Ode to Napoleon*. Interestingly, Ablinger splits up the unbroken prose of Schoenberg's original letter into individual lines in his printed reproduction shown above: "Mister: / You . . . in spite of my protest / you have published / Leibowitz' performance / of my *Ode to Napoleon* / with a woman voice, / which

I find / terrible." Ablinger's reframing of Schoenberg's original letter here closely resembles a poetic text, thereby implicitly acknowledging a relation to texted music (art song, opera, etc.).

Music to the letter: Ablinger's work points backward to this prior inclusion of language in music, while it underscores another form of language found in the very structure of the musical score. So far we've discussed language as speech in the material incarnation of Schoenberg's voice. But we can also understand the score as being constructed by the basic linguistic form of the imperative, or the command structure. The imperative lies at the intersection of violence and signification; it sets up expectations, rules, norms, and repercussions that recall the homology between the threat and the score proposed in the previous chapter. "You will regret this act / severely," Schoenberg warns his letter's addressee. Signaling consequence, the imperative carries with it "a little death sentence"; it is a form of Deleuze and Guattari's "order-word." Language, in this sense, is an exercise of power, and power, as authority, is codified in the musical score. *Werktreue* refers to a performer's "fidelity" to the score, her adherence to the order-word. In Chapter 1 we saw how Ultra-red's AIDS activist interpretations of Cage's *4'33"* were exemplary realizations even though they went against the grain of typical *4'33"* performances. In realizing a composition, a performer may, on the one hand, seek to uphold the composer's intentions (presuming the composer knows what they are), or, on the other, try to deliberately undermine the score to produce a new text. To perform a work of music, then, is to negotiate these poles of agency and adherence, autonomy and fidelity. Inviting realizations of a potentially infinite variety, the score represents the continued accrual of meaning beyond intentionality.

But contrasting with this interpretive indeterminacy, the score also brings with it the authority of the command structure, here made explicit in Schoenberg's letter. Writing on March 3, 1951, Schoenberg expresses his discontent with the publication of a 1950 vinyl record of his 1942 *Ode to Napoleon*, a composition based on Lord Byron's 1814 poem set for string quartet, piano, and voice. Schoenberg's letter notably implicates the gender identity of the performer of his score, citing Los Angeles record producer Ross Russell as responsible for the unacceptable female recording. Despite Russell's stated reasons for choosing Ellen Adler as the vocalist—the liner notes describe her as the "most successful" to use Schoenberg's well-known *Sprechgesang* (spoken singing) technique[55]— Schoenberg decries the recording. But the composer goes further; in addition to referring to Russell as a "bugger" (a homophobic slur that holds particular weight during the McCarthy era),[56] Schoenberg also speaks of Russell's failure to keep a "contract." And this recourse to the contractual character of the score—here the score becomes a kind of legal document—provides the basis from which Schoenberg issues more threats: "I will be busy to help you to be ruined by this." Returning to concerns raised in the previous chapter, if "ideas matter" in Žižek's account of Pussy Riot, then Schoenberg's letter concretizes such a dynamic through the score's "order-word." Considering his authoritative insistence, furthermore, it is interesting that Schoenberg describes his impetus to write *Ode to Napoleon* as an explicit statement against fascism during the Second World War.[57]

Schoenberg is unmistakable in his disapproval of the recording, even though the *Ode to Napoleon* score doesn't actually stipulate a gender for the voice. While, surprisingly, Schoenberg seemed to have none other than Orson Welles in mind for the part of the speaker, the score provides no indication of such a preference. Schoenberg's reasoning seems to be that the voice of politics, justice, and war, which is echoed by Lord Byron's "voice of history," unquestionably represents a masculine voice.[58] The voice forms, then, the locus of this dispute over gender and presents an additional set of problems with respect to recording technology. One may cite related instances in the history of recorded music in which gender is a subject of scrutiny.[59] Judith Halberstam, for example, discusses the late Little Jimmy Scott, a male jazz vocalist whose voice (affected by a rare hormonal dysfunction) is often misapprehended as female, ultimately suggesting transgender as an operative category for understanding Scott's gender identification.[60] Schoenberg's *Ode to Napoleon* predates the modern notion of transgender by roughly half of a century,[61] yet a consideration in this context may prove to be fruitful. Indeed, while Scott's gender identity is received perhaps differently between visual and sonic representations, Adler's gender identity seems to go unquestioned. In each case, the conflict between expectation and identification becomes the source of contention. Hearing the voice of Scott, one expects a cisgender woman and learns that sounds can be deceiving. Hearing Adler's recitation of his *Ode to Napoleon*, Schoenberg is likewise greeted with an outcome he didn't expect. If Adler's recording is to disregard "an artist's wishes," what would it mean for a transgender performer to realize Schoenberg's *Ode to Napoleon*?[62]

Interestingly, it is through the record—a technology that purportedly removes sound from its source and thereby cloaks its identity—that Schoenberg is able to affirm the gender of the performer upon which his objection is based. Schaeffer's *acousmatic* mode of listening, wherein sounds are severed from their sources, is thus inverted in the confrontation between Schoenberg and Russell. Here it is precisely recorded sound that allows the performer's identity to be encoded, fixed, transmitted, and hence contested. It is as though the performer, the "cause" of the sound, achieves a kind of visibility, paradoxically, through the medium of sound alone.[63] Adler becomes, to cite Mladen Dolar, *A Voice and Nothing More*.[64] Composing the "offscreen" image of the performer—the *acousmêtre*—Adler's out-of-view body here is at one with the *acousmatic*: "a noise one hears without seeing what causes it."[65] Adler is, in other words, effectively "seen" while being stripped of a proper image. Her voice is noise because it embodies, in Schoenberg's view, undesirable sound: her voice is "negative," "unwanted, other."[66] Recording technology, we may conclude, does not conceal identity, or even visibility for that matter, but rather channels it—often more potently than any other medium. (Why else would popular music appear so positively obsessed with identity?)

Over recording technology, Schoenberg's letter suggests that language remains the strictest form of representation, since language constrains and regulates identity as much as it provides its conditions of possibility. At the same time, we can attest that the rationalizing, liberating stratum of *logos* exerts the authorial pressure of overdetermination; language can fold back onto itself to produce what Foucault called "'reverse' discourses."[67] In an artistic context, while conceptualism equips the artist with the forces of discursivity, language continues to struggle with and against the registers of immanence, materiality, temporality, the sensible, and the affective. Poststructuralism represents only one strand of a broader critique of language and representation in which artistic practice also participates. How, then, does one move beyond the order-word when the imperative form seems unavoidable, when normalization and capture are all but inescapable? Deleuze and Guattari, as part of their elaboration of the rhizome, describe a "principle of asignifying rupture: against the oversignifying breaks separating structures or cutting across a single structure."[68] Illustrating this phenomenon (and also to contradict many a David Attenborough film), they write, "It could be said that the orchid imitates the wasp, reproducing its image in a signifying fashion (mimesis, mimicry, lure, etc.)."[69] They continue: "At the same time something else entirely is going on: not imitation at all but a capture of code, surplus value of code, an increase in valence, a veritable becoming, a becoming-wasp of the orchid and a becoming-orchid of the wasp."[70]

Could it be that in *Letter from Schoenberg* this kind of capturing of code is occurring? A becoming-speech of piano, a becoming-piano of speech? Or perhaps it is the becoming-Schoenberg of piano. For that matter, can we speak of a becoming-Schoenberg of Ablinger? There remains a clear gesture of iconoclasm at work in Ablinger: the violence of misinterpretation of which Schoenberg accuses Russell is redoubled in Ablinger's *Letter*. The original recording serves as fodder for another misappropriation, the grounds upon which yet another transgression is committed. But just as his noise doesn't simply recapitulate the agonism of the avant-garde, neither does Ablinger's *Letter* seek to overturn the authority reproduced in Schoenberg's letter. Rather, *Letter from Schoenberg* offers an ambivalence that (to re-invoke Groys's "paradox-object") at once embodies thesis and antithesis: object and temporality, identity and nonidentity, tradition and the new, noise and language. Schoenberg's letter sought to reassert the composer's authorial voice in light of Adler's transgressive performance. Ablinger's *Letter*, through its perpetual oscillation, shuttles between noise and legibility while it fuses music to the letter of language.

Part Three

Speculation and Sense

The Debt of Philosophy: Music, Speculation, and *The Sound of Debt*

Introduction: Music, Debt, Materialism

According to a report published in *The Wall Street Journal*, recent graduates of New York's Manhattan School of Music found themselves leaving school with sums of student debt far exceeding others in their graduating class.[1] Nearly twice the national average, the Manhattan School students' median debt load of $47,000 was second only to The Creative Center, a for-profit art college based in Nebraska. These large loan sums might be considered feasible for a small number of graduates who manage to obtain lucrative careers in the arts. But given the precarious work more commonly available to artists alongside post-recession cutbacks in public arts funding, one wonders just what recourse a graduate who majored in, say, oboe performance might have in such a situation. Do the artistic techniques and training acquired through such an education remain relevant to an artist saddled with a lifetime of crippling debt? More broadly, what faculty can music offer an attempt to transform such a condition? This chapter follows from the last chapter's considerations of music's expanded field—from the concert hall to ticket salespeople, instrument makers, and music critics—to the artist's own training, specifically the system of higher education and its recent debt-funded neoliberal restructuring.

During the past three decades an increased scrutiny has focused on student debt, rising tuition, and the broader turn to privatization and neoliberal models for higher education funding, especially in but not limited to North America. The conception of education as a publicly accessible institution has shifted to that of an economic structure in which the burden of funding is placed upon the individual, often resulting in debts on a scale that far exceeds other forms of personal debt. Student debt in the United States currently totals over $1.3 trillion with an average individual debt load of $27,000.[2] The US government, along with various private lenders, furthermore, actually *profits* from student debt, with revenue exceeding that of tech giants like Google, and even top investment banks such as Goldman Sachs and JPMorgan Chase.[3] Music and art schools serve, then, it can be concluded, as the system's most lucrative line items.

Intervening into this situation, artist Cassie Thornton, in her *Sound of Debt* series, attempts to critically frame student debt in relation to this debt economy, confirmed by scholars and activists as the primary economic basis underpinning the current system of higher education. Thornton's work points to the prevailing financialization of higher education and asks for a corresponding artistic response. How can an artist address a system in which the very training required to become an artist often means owing six figure sums for a terminal degree? Of course, one could simply refuse such a system, dropping out altogether.[4] But in reality artists, musicians, and scholars recognize the need to complete formal training for their work to be taken seriously. As a result, for many, this means a lifetime of debt repayment amid a fragile and unpredictable economy. In her recent text piece presented in the style of a donor recognition plaque, visual artist Caroline Woolard asks, "What is a work of art in the age of $120,000 art degrees?" Thornton insists that "the work" is more than simply an index of such a price tag and, moreover, may even serve as a medium through which the artist can meaningfully confront this problematic.

In her series of artistic interventions, Thornton stages processes of collectivity, enunciation, and audition that function in many ways like musical performances. Thornton trained as a visual artist; her work is, in fact, typically contextualized as "social practice," a category defined by participatory projects, social engagement, and group action (I will return to social practice art below). The present volume is about music. The point, however, is not to gloss the differences between music and visual art educational institutions, pedagogical approaches, or artistic genealogies.[5] Rather, my interest in Thornton's project concerns its relevance to a broader set of problematics—education and debt; social action and artistic practice; and philosophical thought and the political—that I want to bring into contact with a conception of music as a critical art form. I will thus leave open, to an extent, the question as to whether Thornton's work *is* music and instead offer her work as a *model* for critical music practices that immanently and reflexively engage their own productive economies through issues around education and (its) financialization.

Thornton's debt performances deploy sound as metaphor and expressive medium; sound is conceived as matter, as a material substance. Yet her project deprivileges formal and medium-specific concerns in order to attempt to trace the material economies of the human subjects implicated in her participatory projects. Students, artists, activists, the working poor, those with medical debt, consumer debt, and student debt—sound is not produced by these participants as a fully packaged aesthetic object, but rather arrives as a by-product of a series of social, political, and therapeutic processes. Constituted by sound and debt, Thornton's work also makes statements about these phenomena, reflexive observations formed through experience. For example, the work from her *Sound of Debt* series that I focus on in this chapter involves participants screaming their debts to outer space and filling out surveys that outline individual experiences of debt and precarity. While it is bound up with the materiality of the objects named by its title, Thornton's *Sound of Debt* operates through language and the discourses around those very problematics. Beyond a purely conceptual approach, her work considers the material production of the concepts that inform such practices. Concepts, her work suggests, are produced through material practices, institutions like higher education. Ideas become grounded in materiality—or, recalling Žižek's materialism, "ideas matter."

We can return, then, to the subject of materialism in the context of artistic practice, and now in relation to debt. In his well-known *Debt: The First 5,000 Years* (2011), anthropologist David Graeber notably links the premodern invention of coinage—a technology that replaced IOUs, the earliest debt records—with the coterminous advent of philosophical materialism.[6] Money and materialism, he notes, were both premised upon the ability to reduce potentially anything to something else: heterogeneous determinations of value reduced to precise numerical units, in the case of money; and, in the case of philosophy, the universe in all of its complexity reduced to water, air, atoms, or matter.[7] This kind of elemental reduction to a substance championed as early as ancient Greek philosophers such as Democritus and Epicurus did not ultimately exclude thinking the movement and change of such entities, their respective transformations over time, or indeed their embeddedness within sociality. Both money and matter, especially when viewed as elements of social practice, remain indelibly marked by perpetual movement, exchange, and circulation. Yet the nature of these kinds of transformations would not receive a thoroughgoing elaboration until the meeting of philosophy and political economy central to Marx's materialism. For Marx, the key to his critique of political economy was found not in the reduction of the real to matter or money, but rather in the social relations *behind* the production of the former and the exchange of the latter. As Marxist historian Moishe Postone has argued, "The *Materie* [matter] of Marx's 'materialist' critique, then, is social—the forms of social relations."[8] Matter, in this sense, *is* the social.

Moving to the present, and to an aesthetic context, one finds echoes of this materialist critique in the work of artists like Thornton, specifically in her collaborative and performative interventions around education, finance, and debt. "What is the material of your debt?" asks Thornton in a public questionnaire found on the artist's website.[9] Thornton's work points to a "debt imaginary" by underlining debt's affective, social, and material substance— linking it, I want to argue, to a materialist philosophical engagement. Debt is a peculiar matter. Like sound, it is substantive. It is both a material form—a set of relations defined by social consensus (and dissensus)—and a linguistic construction: debt is a "promise," Graeber concludes, "corrupted by both math and violence."[10] Debt maintains, as Graeber suggests, a virtualized link to the future through the figure of the promise, a dynamic that recalls the homology between the proposal, or score-form and the spectral violence of the threat discussed in Chapter 3. Debt becomes the iterative rehearsal of a threat in the present ("If you don't make a payment now, there will be consequences") through the withholding of a (non-)secured future ("One day, if you make it out of the red, there *may* be opportunity."). This kind of risk, as Randy Martin intimates in his *Financialization of Daily Life* (2002), turns on "a rhetoric of the future that is really about the present; a means of price setting on the promise that a future is attainable."[11] Debt is, as Ross argues, a claim made on future wages—however precarious or uncertain the latter may be.[12] If wage labor is characterized by a treadmill effect whereby monetary advancement (or a reduction in work time) appears within reach yet is practically impossible,[13] then debt only exacerbates this scenario. Debt effectively steepens the treadmill's incline.

And yet where there is a debtor, as the debtor-creditor relation makes clear, there is also a creditor. Debt forms the other side of finance, the obverse of speculation. Imbricated across both philosophical and financial registers, "speculation" derives from the Latin *specula*, a term that implies both to look around and to reflect. Sound and media theorist Frances Dyson proposes along these lines an extended homonymic relationship between the "eco" in economy and the "echo" heard in sonic reflection, altogether linking philosophy, sound, and finance.[14] The financial speculator looks toward a future by making a claim on the present— and, in effect, creates more debt. Philosophical speculation attempts to mirror the real by extending principles of thought through inference, intuition, and reflection. This is where I want to link this consideration of financial speculation to the speculative materialist philosophy of Quentin Meillassoux. For speculation is found not only alongside math and violence, as in Graeber's account of debt, but, again, within the very heart of philosophy—most interestingly, perhaps, in the work of the recently formed speculative realist movement.

Math and speculation, materialism and contingency: these relationships arise with particular weight in Meillassoux's speculative materialism.[15] In his watershed book, *After Finitude: An Essay on the Necessity of Contingency* (2008), Meillassoux argues that since Kant's so-called Copernican Revolution, philosophy has split into separate autonomous spheres of thinking and being, leaving as a remainder only the correlation between the two. This "correlationism," Meillassoux maintains, which has characterized most (non-"naive") thought since Kant, has prevented thinking from getting outside of itself, into the "great outdoors," to access the object-in-itself. But exempt from the limits of the correlation are the "mathematizable properties of the object" described by a kind of pure mathematics not unlike the set-theoretical real postulated by Alain Badiou, Meillassoux's former teacher and author of the foreword to *After Finitude*.[16] Meillassoux's path to these "outdoors," to which I will later return, involves a set of philosophical observations that derive from what he calls "arche-fossils," or data gathered from space exploration that provide evidence for the genesis of a universe that predates the emergence of humankind. We are talking, of course, about the big bang.

Already the big bang, that most primordial sound of cosmological genesis, suggests an audible link between Meillassoux's arche-fossils and Thornton's elemental debt screams. First, however, Meillassoux's speculative materialism is seen here more generally to represent one faction of the broader turn in recent continental philosophy to realism. Since the coining of the term at the widely cited 2007 Goldsmiths College conference, speculative realism has remained profoundly influential in art-theoretical discussions, science studies, and across the humanities. Of particular interest are the ways speculative realism has been taken up in contemporary art and sound art theory. American philosopher Christoph Cox, for example, in his 2011 essay "Beyond Representation and Signification," advocates a "sound art" worthy of materialist analysis.[17] But against this consideration of sound's supposed "materiality" at a remove from human language and interaction, I want to position my own notion of critical musical practices that emphasize "matter" in terms of social relations—a move that parallels comparisons between Meillassoux and Marx.

Numerous critics have compared the work of Meillassoux to Marx, some arguing that the two remain irreconcilable, while others insist upon a direct continuity from Marxist thinkers ranging from Lenin to Althusser. Philosopher Peter Hallward challenges Meillassoux's philosophy, for example, by asking if he is able to think social transformation "with and after Marx."[18] In his essay titled after Marx's well-known 1847 critique of Proudhon, "The Poverty of Philosophy: Realism and Post-Fordism" (2013), theorist Alexander R. Galloway criticizes the mathematics Meillassoux advocates as remaining fully compatible with the math found in the computer applications of contemporary capitalism's most successful digital firms.[19] Still Nathan Brown argues for a Meillassoux directly in line with Marxist "dialectical materialism."[20] Approaching the problem somewhat differently, I want to ask if the speculative realism of Meillassoux can be thought with respect to the relationship between philosophy and political economy sought by Marx: the "short-circuiting," as Žižek puts it, of philosophical speculation through economic speculation.[21] How might that relationship be thought, moreover, in relation to the contemporary neoliberal debt-education complex?

While analyzing a part of Thornton's *Sound of Debt*, this chapter considers the philosophical position advanced by Meillassoux, in which thinking attempts to access its outside—thought's "great outdoors"[22]—in light of the "indoors" of thought's institutional housing, the system of higher education that appears more and more to conform to a neoliberal debt-funded model. Is there a relationship between the advancement of this kind of knowledge capitalism and the return of philosophy's claim to a knowledge of the real? Is it possible for an artistic—or musical—practice to provide a meaningful intervention? I will begin by describing Thornton's *Debt 2 Space Program*, a project from her *Sound of Debt* series that consists of guided exercises wherein participants attempt to collectively scream their debts to outer space.

The Debt 2 Space Program

The fault lies not in our stars . . . but in our institutions and our education.
—Linda Nochlin, "Why Have There Been No Great Women Artists?"[23]

In space no one can hear you scream.
—*Alien* (1979) tagline

On July 16, 2013, following the culmination of a weekly series of reading group meetings entitled *Autonomia, Occupy, Communism: Legacies and Futures* held at the e-flux space in New York,[24] Thornton led a participatory group performance as part of her ongoing series, *The Debt 2 Space Program*. The event consisted of a group of approximately ten participants who, following Thornton's lead, stood in a circle, shoulder-to-shoulder, and proceeded to follow instructions for a guided exercise. Structured like a group meditation, participants were asked to visualize their various forms of personal financial debt before attempting to collectively transmit these debts to outer space by emitting a loud, concerted scream.

"Close your eyes and feel your feet on the floor," Thornton began slowly and deliberately. She continued, asking the group to move in so that participants were touching one another. "Imagine your feet going through the floor, into the basement, and past the subway."

"Something is enclosing you," she continued.

> Try to get as much of it in your mouth as you can. You're eating it, and you're chewing it, and you're digesting it, and it's really, really hard. Once that's happened, slowly come back up onto earth. You might have to break through this wood floor. Feel the energy [this thing] has given you. And watch it as it travels up through your body to your throat. I'm going to count to three. You're going to open your eyes and you're gonna scream out "the thing."

Lasting less than ten seconds, the group's scream was as loud as it was shrill, an irruptive shriek piercing the calm that had preceded. If there ever was a "thing," then surely no longer was it contained in this world. After the expurgatory emission had concluded, Thornton sent around a form on a clipboard that requested a signature from each participant to indicate an identification with one of several statements such as "I have a tremendous amount of healthcare debt," "I cannot afford basic necessities," and "I have to work for the rest of my life because I have student debt." Each item, according to the survey, was to have been "exported" to space through the scream.

Thornton's guided exercises can be said to invoke the various "visualization" techniques used in middle-class self-help programs, group therapy, or twelve-step programs. The screams might also be considered acts of purgation that mirror the basic structure of psychoanalysis, as the direct precursor to Freud's "talking cure" was Breuer's "cathartic method."[25] Still, another point of reference can be made to avant-garde noise, or the neo-avant-garde performance practices of Fluxus and experimental music. Yoko Ono's 1961 score *Voice Piece for Soprano*, for example, reads

VOICE PIECE FOR SOPRANO

Scream.

1. against the wind
2. against the wall
3. against the sky

1961 autumn[26]

That score's repetition of "against" redoubles the scream's singularly confrontational, antagonistic, and contrarian quality. Like Ono's *Voice Piece for Soprano*, Thornton's scream employs structures of collective sounding and enunciation particular to music, while it frames the voice as abject force. Thornton's scream condenses the three "movements" of Ono's work into a single emission. While it shares an agonistic character found in Ono's score, Thornton's *Debt 2 Space Program* replaces Ono's abyssal "sky" with the beyond of outer space. Space, Thornton's utopian repository for receiving the debts of earthly subjects, reads also as a metonym for science at large. Pointing further to space exploration and NASA missions (responsible for, among other things, data that support Meillassoux's arche-fossils), Thornton's intervention insists upon lived finitude and embodied social production in the face of financial and philosophical speculation alike. As an artistic practice, Thornton's work critically engages the conditions of its material production: as an artist who went into substantial debt while earning an MFA, Thornton's "materials" become both subject and object of her work.

Thornton's *Debt 2 Space Program* brings subjective experiences of debt into contact with a collectivization that threads experiences of neoliberal precarity and capitalist violence incurred through indebtedness. While Thornton has explained her project broadly as an attempt to "understand finance in an affective way," and, indeed, subjective experiences of debt are foregrounded in her practice, of equal importance are the dimensions of collectivity and sociality. In a statement describing the founding of her artistic collective, the Feminist Economics Department, Thornton locates a "desire for a collectivity based on [an] interest in the debt industry which promotes individual liability and denies trust and interdependence."[27] On the one hand, her interventions might be criticized as "pathologizing" debt, focusing on subjective experiences of a phenomenon more properly understood in social or political-economic terms. On the other, taking debt as inherently social, Thornton's group interventions can be read as staging a form of collectivity not unlike tactics used in activist groups formed around education, debt, and pedagogy (Occupy Student Debt Campaign, Strike Debt, the Corinthian Fifteen, the USC Seven, Edu-Factory, The Pedagogy Group)—or, indeed, the critical music collectives discussed earlier such as Ultra-red and Pussy Riot. Relevantly, in his well-known essay *The Making of the Indebted Man*, Maurizio Lazzarato has argued that debt is "a mechanism for the production and 'government' of collective and individual subjectivities"; the "logic of debt," he asserts, has come to pervade the social.[28]

The question as to the philosophical implications of Thornton's work—how is debt configured materially?—becomes complicated in considering debt as a phenomenon alongside Thornton's own statements around her project. In the short talk concluding her *Debt 2 Space* event at e-flux, Thornton spoke about the possibility of debt as an "idea-form," a structure that is therefore malleable. Citing the Tibetan Buddhist concept of the "tulpa," she proposed debt as "something that becomes real due to enough people thinking about it." But is debt real because people think of it? Certainly there is the thought that if I don't acknowledge and then never pay back my debt it might be said to have no "reality"; and indeed one might reference historical moments when one could simply move to a different city to escape debt. (In contrast to the presently ubiquitous digitalization of debt in which it is more often genuinely "inescapable," historically, personal debt was often linked to local communities.)

Considering the ways it has come to shape everything from nation-states to private enterprise to education, has not debt become *the* material force in our world?[29] Beyond the question of whether debt is purely imaginary, Thornton's work expresses a tension between debt as *real affective object* and debt as *material socioeconomic process*. Nevertheless, it is important in working through such a tension that debt does not become essentialized; instead, it should be seen alongside a myriad of factors that contribute to social and economic inequality. What commonality exists between the debt of a wealthy venture capitalist and debilitating medical debt incurred by poor people of color? Disproportionately higher amounts of student debt, as Ross notes, belong to African Americans, Latina/os, and LGBTQ students. Rather than ameliorate inequality, student debt appears only to magnify economic differences; and for these reasons, student debt is, as Ross contends, "profoundly anti-social."[30] More broadly, debt can be understood as nothing more than a symptom of an economic logic premised more and more on financialization and speculation. Debt is, again in Lazzarato's words, no less than the "strategic heart of neoliberal politics."[31]

Debt, and specifically student debt, is foregrounded in Thornton's work. She describes *The Debt 2 Space Program* as "a multifaceted effort to export the behavioral, psychological and emotional ramifications of all types of financial hardship," which uses screaming to transmit to space "feelings of limitation as inspired by student debt." While participants of *The Debt 2 Space Program* revealed difficulties arising from a variety of debt sources in the earlier-mentioned survey, other projects confirm her focus on student debt. In a component of her MFA project, *Application to London School of Economics* (2012), for example, Thornton uses a pair of Richard Serra sculptures to illustrate graphically how much the total amount of US credit card debt is exceeded by the sum of America's student loan debt. One crucial characteristic of student debt, as Leigh Claire La Berge and Dehlia Hannah note in their essay on Thornton's work, is that it is "unsecured": unlike a mortgage, there is no collateral, no "object" of investment other than the student herself: "invest in yourself," as the adage goes.[32] Another important difference is that, since 1998, the US congress has made federal loans non-dischargeable; and, since 2005, a similar status has applied to private loans.[33]

Following her event at e-flux, Thornton presented subsequent iterations of *The Debt 2 Space Program*. Occurring at scheduled times over the course of five evenings, groups of debtors gathered in person at Portland's Pioneer Square, while others "phoned in" their screams using a 1-800 number.[34] The screams were delivered, according to Thornton, "beyond the debt ceiling" when later aired on a radio station in the area. One begins to get a sense of the work's aesthetics, an approach that turns on a kind of debt logic. The nostalgia of 1-800 numbers, radio broadcast, and NASA contrasts with the beyondness of space, calling forth the sense of a seemingly never-ending deferral-into-the-future of debt and repayment. The intersection of space and debt harkens back to a time of grand ambitions and large-scale collective projects like space exploration. This contemplation moves to the present to consider the increasingly privatized domains of housing, health care, and education, and the erosion of public funding for programs like NASA.[35]

Relatedly, social practice artist Gregory Sholette notes that educational funding in the United States was vastly accelerated the same year *Sputnik 1* was launched into near-earth orbit.[36] Recalling this synergistic collision, Thornton's intervention suggests that since debt and space hail from the same historical moment, the combating of the former might be related to an engagement with the latter. If student debt and space exploration began together, so too can they (or, at least student debt) come to an end.

Materialism: Science, Education, (Social) Practice

Capitalist production is not merely the production of commodities, it is, by its very essence, the production of surplus-value. The worker produces not for himself, but for capital. . . . If we take an example from outside the sphere of material production, a school-master is a productive worker when, in addition to belabouring the heads of his pupils, he works himself into the ground to enrich the owner of the school. That the latter has laid out his capital in a teaching factory, instead of a sausage factory, makes no difference to the relation.
—Marx, *Capital*[37]

More than ever, education is a core "ideological state apparatus" through which lives are shaped and managed to dance in step with the dominant tune.
—Claire Bishop, *Artificial Hells*[38]

At this point, I want to draw a seemingly unlikely connection between philosophical materialism, education, and recent elaborations of so-called social practice art—including the latter's implications for a socially engaged music practice. Along the way, it will also be useful to interrogate the relationship between science and materialism. Materialism, the philosophical tradition into which Meillassoux intervenes, has held an important if complicated relationship to science. *After Finitude*'s point of departure, for example, comes from what Meillassoux calls "arche-fossils," forensic evidence of an existence prior to humanity[39] produced, for instance, by the Wilkinson Microwave Anisotropy Probe. The latter was part of a recently culminated research program conducted by NASA that estimated the age of the universe as roughly 13.7772 billion years (give or take 59 million).[40] Taken literally, information provided by the arche-fossil, specifically the fact that there was a reality before humans existed, proves, for Meillassoux, that the correlation between thinking and being has not always been, and need not be, because at one point the two did not coexist. "Science thinks a time," Meillassoux contends, that "cannot be reduced to any givenness which preceded it and whose emergence it allows."[41]

Meillassoux thus arrives at the following aporia: "Every materialism that would be speculative, and hence for which absolute reality is an entity without thought, must assert both that thought is not necessary (something can be independently of thought), and that thought can think what there must be when there is no thought."[42] The conflict engaged by Meillassoux, and others who have allied themselves with speculative realism, converges on what Althusser referred to as the "great debate" dominating the history of philosophy: the conflict between materialism and idealism.[43] The former, which contends that there is a hard, mind-independent reality—materialism, according to philosopher Adrian Johnston, insists that there is matter alone "nothing more, nothing less"[44]—is positioned against the latter, a label increasingly applied here to the "old guard" of continental philosophy who follow the "linguistic turn" and adopt a form of "strong correlationism."[45] But in addition to the disparities between Meillassoux and the varieties of "correlationism," there are differences between Meillassoux's and Marx's respective materialisms found in the respective interpretations of "science" and in the role of education and human action.

First, one element missing from the thinking-being dyad presupposed by Meillassoux's term "correlationism" is the less referenced category of *doing*. Practice, or "practical-critical" social activity, is the category that initiates Marx's "Theses on Feuerbach" (1845), an eleven-point list that criticizes the "old materialists" who were stuck, as Marx saw it, in a "contemplative" mode unable to intervene in the real posited by their philosophy. Against what he calls the "abstract materialism of natural science," Marx pits a materialism based on human production.[46] "The *Materie* [matter] of Marx's 'materialist' critique," Postone argues, "is social"—or, we can contend, a kind of *social practice*.[47] Next, regarding science, Meillassoux's materialism relates less to the materialism of Marx than it does to the Marx*ists* of the twentieth century who prioritize a particular interpretation of Marx's use of "science." According to Paul Thomas, Lenin and Althusser, among others, proceed from the English translation of Marx's *Wissenschaft* as "science," whereas it is perhaps more accurately translated here as "learning, scholarship, erudition, and knowledge."[48]

Finally, unlike the materialism of Meillassoux, Marx's materialism, as this translational discrepancy implies, turns on the question of education. Marx responds to the "old materialist" doctrine that since there is a determinate reality and "men are products of circumstances and upbringing," change can occur simply through education; the enlightened haves need only to teach the unenlightened have-nots and our social ills will be cured. But this forgets, Marx asserts, that "the educator must himself be educated."[49] Moreover, as a consequence of Marx's "Theses on Feuerbach," there is, as Rancière argues, an imperative for a new knowledge, "an intelligence formed in the struggle."[50] A kind of intelligence beyond pure contemplation, social action, for Marx, possesses a privileged status. Along with Engels, Marx insisted that practice is not explained "from the idea," but rather, "the formation of ideas [are explained] from material practice."[51] As Rancière remarks in one of his polemics against Althusser, the latter's *"philosophical practice"*[52]—as opposed to *practice as such*—contradicts Marx's critique of the old materialism's hierarchical value of attempting to educate the oppressed.[53]

Moving to the present, education has entered an acute state of crisis with student debt serving as one symptom of the ongoing neoliberal dismantling of the university in North America and Europe alike. From the shrinking number of tenured faculty positions and the increased reliance upon precarious adjunct labor to the expansion of what Randy Martin calls the "new management" class in academia, the university is steadily shifting from a sphere of epistemological experimentation to the marketplace for an "academic capitalism" where administrators function as waged bourgeoisie, faculty are service providers, and students are merely debt-paying customers.[54] Recently, students and graduates from Corinthian Colleges made headlines after what some have called the first successful tuition debt strike in history. Following a pledge from the group calling themselves the "Corinthian Fifteen," Corinthian Colleges, Inc., the for-profit post-secondary education company based in California, announced that it would close all of its campuses following years of government investigations of fraud and predatory lending.[55] But while the Corinthian students have been hailed as victors after garnering the support of an international group of activists and academics (Graeber, Žižek, Naomi Klein, Ross), they, like many, continue to grapple with an unjust education system in decline. As a mechanism shown to actually increase inequality,[56] while effectively stifling creativity and political imagination, education has indeed become an "Ideological State Apparatus" to an extent that would impress Althusser himself.

Returning to an aesthetic context, it is interesting to note the apparent similarities between Marx's formulations of "practical-critical" materialism and recent articulations of social practice art, a movement that shares the former's concerns with education and social action. Often incorporating pedagogical approaches to art making, social practice is a category used in recent contemporary art discourse to describe work premised upon collaboration, participation, community-based practices, and similar models of social engagement. The genealogy of social practice can be traced from the institutional critique practices of the late 1960s to the relational aesthetics work emerging in the 1990s, and, more recently, to Shannon Jackson's *Social Works* (2011) and the participatory practices Claire Bishop describes. California College of the Arts faculty member Ted Purves locates the ingredients of social practice in an expanded conception of audience and practices of exchange and gift-giving that dovetail with Nicolas Bourriaud's widely discussed 1998 text *Relational Aesthetics.*[57] But a less cited social practice precedent is the critical pedagogy movement, an initiative that has worked since the 1960s to transform the structure and policies of education through open and participatory strategies and alternative pedagogical structures.[58] Importantly, as critical pedagogy helps to demonstrate, *practice*, especially in this expanded philosophical and aesthetic conception, is not simply opposed to thinking and being, but configures the very material structures that govern their production.

Thornton's work brings social practice, along with its implicit ties to critical pedagogy, into contact with her collaborative interrogations of student debt. It is interesting that the subject of Thornton's social practice work is the debt she accrued while earning a social practice MFA. Social practice is her debt, then, as both source and subject. Thornton's *Debt 2 Space Program* is, in fact, a continuation of the work she began during her acquisition of approximately $100,000 of mostly US government-subsidized loans while a student at California College of the Arts. Her social practice (MFA) becomes the source of her debt, and her debt the subject of her social practice. Through this reflexive framing of the education institution coupled with the debt required (for her) to complete an MFA, Thornton's project mirrors the institutional critique approach found in the 1960s work of artists such as Michael Asher, Robert Smithson, and Hans Haacke. Pertinent to the present discussion is the question of whether a genuinely critical dimension of "social practice" is recuperable within the configuration of social practice art. For the target of Thornton's intervention, the institution of debt-funded (art) education, only seems to survive—is perhaps made stronger—through her immanent critique. Nevertheless, Thornton's reflexive framing of student debt opens a space for critical questioning. What kinds of pedagogical structures can function outside of dominant educational (and economic) institutions? What modes of collectivity can provide affective, aesthetic, and psychical space for epistemological or therapeutic work? What forms of collectivity are conducive to listening and enunciation?

Yet another point of departure for social practice art comes from music and the performing arts. Claire Bishop locates the earliest roots of social practice, not unlike Jackson, in theater practices—Bishop goes as far as to situate her project as "rethinking the history of twentieth-century art through the lens of theatre rather than painting (as in the Greenbergian narrative) or the ready-made"— concentrating on formative avant-garde groups such as the Italian futurists.[59] Of equal interest are the ways in which music figures in this art-historical narrative: for example, Russian music theorist Arsenii Avraamov's "Hooter Symphonies," in which entire factories were conducted from rooftops, serve as a source of early industrial noise music and collaborative performance. Bishop also cites the Russian Persimfans, conductorless orchestras that began in the 1920s, which sought to rethink the hierarchical relationships between ensemble performers established by the existing orchestral music canon.[60] One could also extend this thinking to the improvisational innovations initiated by Muhal Richard Abrams and other members of the Association for the Advancement of Creative Musicians (AACM) beginning in the mid-1960s. Or consider Christian Wolff's experiments in ensemble listening and performing, works whose very performative structures are mirrored in their linguistic content, as in *Changing the System* (1972). An important aspect of those works lies in their inherent pedagogical dimension wherein the political becomes embodied through processes of de-hierarchized learning, collective listening, and collaboration.[61]

Along with *The Debt 2 Space Program*, Thornton's work has included group performances, graphic scores based on debt figures, and what she calls "debt choruses." While deploying these structures to interrogate finance, education, and debt, Thornton alludes to a significant structural correspondence between social practice and music. For both Jackson and Bishop, the work of Fluxus artists, and to a lesser extent Cage, are cited as historical precedents for social practice art. But perhaps more interesting are the latent *formal* relationships between music and social practice. "Delegated performance," or outsourced performance, for example, is Bishop's category that often relies upon score-like (compositional?) structures that suggest a move away from the first-person standard of authenticity central to pre-2000s performance art and toward the artist as the conductor of often nonprofessional performers.[62] In Tino Sehgal's work, for example, the artist instructs academics, writers, and actors to execute semi-scripted interactions with museum- or gallery-goers as is the case with *This Progress* (2010), a work in which a visitor to the Guggenheim is engaged in conversation related to the subject of progress while led up the museum's spiral ramp by increasingly older docents. The "scored nature"[63] of a work that orchestrates such an organization of actors is hard to overlook. But a deeper engagement may arise from a further consideration of these formal congruences with music. What would it mean, for example, to extend the logic of subversive or against-the-grain performances of the score to these "delegated performances"? What might a revolt against the conditions of such outsourced labor involve?

Music, in addition to serving as a precedent for social practice art, is inherently premised upon structures of collaboration and social relationality. Again, I don't want to argue simply that Thornton's work is music (as opposed to social practice or sound art). But it is interesting to note the resonances between social practice art, work that, as Bishop contends, uses "people as a medium,"[64] and music, an art form premised on organizing and distilling configurations of performance, audition, and action. For people, or rather the social relations between individuals, over sound, constitute the authentic "matter" of music, even its "medium," if one must be determined. The social is found in music's innermost core—"Music says We directly, regardless of its intentions," writes Adorno.[65] While it is uncertain what Adorno might have made of Ultra-red, Pussy Riot, or Thornton, it becomes clear that these artists do more than simply acknowledge the existence of the social. Rather, they mobilize a practical-critical *doing* as a pillar of a socially engaged musical art practice. For after sound, music operates as an incipient form of social practice, and any genuine ("sonic") materialism must make this primary.

The Poverty of Sound Art Theory (or the Debt of Sound)

Broadly speaking, sound art theory has sought an alternative to the context of music where the latter is seen as undesirable for a number of reasons, including its inability to engage the social. Sound art becomes the preferred category because music is not conceptual enough, not representational, too representational, apolitical, acritical, too abstract, too concrete, not self-reflexive, non-interdisciplinary, score-based, nonspatial, non-sculptural, etc. Yet, in many cases, a nontrivial correlate can be found in music or related areas. Even links between sound and objects have an extensive body of literature found, for example, in organology and studies of musical automata. In certain instances, the relationship between sound art and music is conceived not oppositionally but interrelatedly; the German *Klangkunst* literature, for instance, is typically positioned within the field of musicology.[66] Nevertheless, music, in these narratives, is superseded by a more conceptual, political, and spatial sound art that arrives through a determinate historical break with music (curiously found in the music of a composer such as John Cage, Max Neuhaus, Alvin Lucier, Pierre Schaeffer, etc.). Born identifies these acts of "discovery" central to the foundation myths of sound art as a kind of disciplinary "year zero" phenomenon.[67] Furthermore, by reducing music to a straw man, sound art theory exhibits what Kane describes as "musicophobia," the construction of music as sound art's "false opponent" in order to offer a novel alternative.[68] The poverty of sound art theory lies in its consistent failure to provide an adequate justification for itself through a critique of music, or by any other means.

Materiality and concreteness are nevertheless two of the primary terms philosopher Christoph Cox offers to justify the advancement of his sound art theory. Preferring these terms to abstraction and formalism, Cox outlines what he calls a "sonic materialism," which he describes as a materialist theory of sound art premised on the speculative realism of philosophers like Graham Harman, Iain Hamilton Grant, and Meillassoux.[69] Through an application of speculative realism to sound art discourse, Cox's approach may be said to take as simultaneous points of departure the so-called "sonic turn" in the arts and the "speculative turn" in philosophy.[70] The rationale for turning to "materialism" is less related, for example, to Marxism than it is to the speculative realist philosophers. But the reasons Cox provides for choosing the context of "sound art" as opposed to music remain tinged with musicophobic bias. According to Cox, musicology, for example, "remains oriented to the formal examination of discrete sound structures and performances,"[71] a contention that seems to ignore the anti-formalist and cultural analyses of music that began in 1980s with the new musicology movement. More relevant to Cox's theoretical project is his contention that sound art is more concrete and invites, by virtue of this "materiality," a materialist analysis. Since sound art is closer to the "materiality" of sound than music, it deserves both a novel aesthetic category (sound art) and philosophical framework (speculative realism).

The more fundamental, categorical problem with sound art theory lies in its conflation of medium and materiality. Medium develops out of a complex set of historical interactions between senses, technologies, social conventions, and discourses. "Sound art" flattens the formal and historical complexity of music to a singular medium conceived in terms of the brute materiality (or, perhaps more accurately, the *sense*) of sound. "Sound art" executes a short circuit between material and medium that, in any other form, would appear nothing short of ridiculous, as Neuhaus slyly demonstrated through recourse to his hypothetical category "Steel Art."[72] First, like "Steel Art," sound art conflates artistic medium with materiality, as Neuhaus's comment suggests. Then, progressing from materiality to materialism, Cox elevates "sound art" further by attributing to it ontological status.

Cox positions his "sonic materialism" against the "sonic idealism" of Kim-Cohen.[73] Notably, Kim-Cohen reworks Duchamp's famous non-retinal formulation to arrive at "non-cochlear sonic art," a category that, in Kim-Cohen's elaboration, stands as a critique of prevailing "materialist" sound artists (e.g., Francisco López), along with music conceived as an abstract art form. Deploying a Derridian philosophical framework and working primarily through an art-theoretical lens, the strength of Kim-Cohen's argument is its ability to think a sound-related practice that is conceptual, relational, reflexive, and opens onto, while standing in a critical relationship to, a broader cultural universe— attributes often shared by contemporary art more broadly.[74] Meanwhile, Cox explicitly opposes Kim-Cohen's conceptualism with a theory of sound art based on the recent philosophical revival of realism. Although the philosophical figures Cox cites (Schopenhauer, Nietzsche, Deleuze) are not typically associated with speculative realism,[75] Cox makes reference to primary philosophers of the movement and grounds his argument in a way that mirrors the general structure of Meillassoux's anti-correlationism.

Much in line with the claims of Graham Harman, for example, Cox aims "to contribute to the general revival of realism in contemporary philosophy and its challenge to the idealism and humanism that have characterized philosophy and cultural theory since the 'linguistic turn.'"[76] Furthermore, he criticizes recent theory and philosophy, echoing charges waged by speculative realists in pointing to an alleged "chauvinistic anthropocentrism" due to the support of a divide between "culture" and "nature."[77] Cox goes on to outline his own critique of the kind of correlationism opposed by Meillassoux in referring to contemporary theory's supposedly Kantian program, which splits the world into two spheres: "a phenomenal domain of symbolic discourse that marks the limits of the knowable, and a noumenal domain of nature and materiality that excludes knowledge and intelligible discourse."[78] As opposed to abstraction, Cox argues, sound is more concrete than the visual arts and therefore requires "not a formalist analysis but a materialist one"; he distinguishes this materialist analysis of sound from what he refers to as the "neo-Kantian" theory at work in Kim-Cohen.[79]

Cox continues to provide a justification for his privileging of sound art over music, which also supports his adoption of a materialist framework. He writes,

> Music has long eluded analysis in terms of representation and signification and, as a result, has been considered to be purely formal and abstract. However, the most significant sound art work of the past half-century—the work of Max Neuhaus, Alvin Lucier, Christina Kubisch, Christian Marclay, Carsten Nicolai, Francisco Lopez, and Toshiya Tsunoda, for example—has explored the *materiality* of sound: its texture and temporal flow, its palpable effect on, and affection by the materials through and against which it is transmitted. What these works reveal, I think, is that the sonic arts are not more *abstract* than the visual but rather more *concrete*, and that they require not a *formalist* analysis but a *materialist* one.[80]

As indicated here, Cox seems to rely upon an implicit proximity between "materiality" and "materialism." Cox's philosophy is not interested, for example, in the social production of such materiality, and hence, there is no mention of Marx's materialism.[81] But neither does he explain how works that "[explore] materiality" require a materialist analysis any more than works based on ideas— or, indeed, works that *consist* entirely of ideas, for that matter. For materialism, of course, does not exclude the existence of language, signification, representation, etc.; it merely insists that those are not *all that exists*. And while he argues for a "materialist" analysis of sound, there is no indication as to what such an analysis would look (or sound) like. Nor is it apparent why sound works that lack "extra-material" substance—such as reference, metaphor, conceptual strategies, etc.— would have any deeper relevance to philosophical materialism. If the "materiality of sound" leaves out, for example, the linguistic play found in Lucier's scores, it would figure as a philosophy at once both misconceived and misapplied.

In addition to sound art theory's "forced choice" between music and sound art, there appears to be another false dilemma posed by Cox, namely between idealism and a so-called "*materiality* of sound."[82]

Contingent Speculation: Chance versus Practice in Meillassoux

When dealing with the Absolute, there can be no such thing as debt.

David Graeber[83]

Beyond pointing to the materiality of phenomena such as sound, the task put forth by Meillassoux consists in elaborating the possibility of a real in the absence of thought itself. Meillassoux's assault on "correlationism"—the "unsurpassable" relation between thinking and being—hinges on scientific evidence dating the emergence of human life.[84] Bookending his argument, Meillassoux turns human life and its extinction into generators of a philosophical system set up to challenge both idealism and "dogmatic" or naive realism. On one end, as mentioned before, the emergence of human life is posited by the arche-fossil's ability to provide "ancestral statements," facts based on evidence of a reality that existed prior to the birth of humanity.[85] For Meillassoux, the arche-fossil works as a kind of onto-epistemological prosthesis. Pointing backward to an absolute prior to the dawn of anteriority, the arche-fossil "touches" the real ontologically through the production of ontic statements concerning the origins of life and thought. On the other end, Meillassoux considers the consequences of a global catastrophe such as a meteor impact, speculating on this capacity-to-be-wholly-other in death.[86] That the correlation did not exist in the past, and may not exist in the future, conforms to a state of precariousness in which everything is bound to perish, what he calls facticity. It is, in fact, "not the correlation," for Meillassoux, "but the facticity of the correlation that constitutes the absolute."[87] This precarity of the sheer bindedness of thinking to being *is* itself being.

We move, then, from life and death to chance. For Meillassoux, facticity is a less radical form of what the philosopher terms "contingency," or the *pure possibility* found in his notion of hyper-Chaos. Hyper-Chaos is a kind of devastating uncertainty, a state in which everything is at any moment up for complete and total revision. Contingency eradicates, for Meillassoux, the need for necessity. Yet with hyper-Chaos contingency itself is paradoxically *the* absolute necessity (hence the subtitle of Meillassoux's book, *An Essay on the Necessity of Contingency*). It is paramount, in this relation, that actual contradiction is not permitted, since, "if an entity was contradictory," according to Meillassoux, "it would be necessary."[88] And doubtless, a "necessary entity," in this context, refers to the kind of supernatural entity materialism would categorically seek to refute. (The emergence of God-like forces and concepts in Meillassoux's schema, then, is problematic for several reasons.)[89] Nevertheless, Meillassoux insists that in hyper-Chaos,

> We see something akin to Time, but a time that is inconceivable for physics, since it is capable of destroying without cause or reason, every physical law, just as it is inconceivable for metaphysics, since it is capable of destroying every determinate entity, even a god, even God.[90]

When viewed critically, hyper-Chaos itself appears contradictory. It insists that everything, including the laws of nature, is open for revision at any moment. But what is more likely, according to Adrian Johnston, is that (as with Hume's criticism of the idea of miracles) what one took for a violation of a law was simply consistent with an *actual* set of laws governing it and everything else.[91]

This notion of chance can be seen to invoke the aleatory found in postwar art and political economy alike. On the one hand, hyper-Chaos conjures the emancipatory chance of Cage as Hallward's reading of Meillassoux suggests. Specifically, Hallward cites "Deleuze and Guattari's appreciation for those artists and writers who tear apart the comfortable normality or ordinary experience so as to . . . remind us of the tumultuous intensity of things."[92] One imagines, in this regard, the "tumultuous intensity" of Cage's *Music of Changes* (1951), a work for solo piano composed by deriving pitches, dynamics, durations, and other parameters from the *I Ching*. On the other hand, critical engagements with Cage's indeterminacy, and chance more broadly, may prove to be productive in reading Meillassoux. Andreas Huyssen, for example, compares Cage's "uncritical celebration of chance" to Walter Benjamin's analysis of the proximity of the assembly line and gambling, altogether linking artistic aleatory with economic risk.[93] Moreover, is it not true that hyper-Chaos can be seen as an elegant homology to the contemporary "risk society," the "speculative" basis of the neoliberal debt economy theorized by Lazzarato?

More broadly, Meillassoux's speculative materialism invites a consideration of the potential conceptual intersections between the different statuses of "speculation" inherent to philosophical and economic registers. The term is used to describe philosophy that proceeds conjecturally—working from supposition, on the basis of incomplete information, through projection—as opposed to inference, from evidence, (pure) reason.[94] As mentioned earlier, deriving from the Latin *specula*, to look around, speculation also contains a link to *speculum*, or mirror, which, since late antiquity, refers to the state in which mind and matter are seen to reflect God.[95] Whitehead defines speculative philosophy as "the endeavour to frame a coherent, logical, necessary system of general ideas in terms of which every element of our experience can be interpreted."[96] But Whitehead also points out the common criticism of speculation's "over-ambitious" nature,[97] its investments in grand, totalizing schemas. Extending the evidential given, speculative philosophy posits a wager on the real. Unfurling from Meillassoux's arche-fossil, for example, we get the real of hyper-Chaos and pure contingency.

In an economic register, speculation is no less totalizing. As with the pervasive logic of debt, speculation has represented "synecdochically," according to Urs Stäheli, "the entire economy" since the nineteenth century.[98] Furthermore, speculation is the other side of the same coin, the Janus-face twin of debt. Rhetorically, speculation privileges agency on the side of the speculator: the privileged speculator *looks around* for the best possible future returns on her investment, while minimizing associated risk. This looking around constantly demands new objects for the speculator's gaze, further horizons to submit to capital—domains like health care, space travel, and education, as we've seen. Whose precarity, then, whose "contingency," does speculation implicate? As the degree of "risk" increases for the speculator—recall the above-cited examples of the 1998 and 2005 US laws disallowing student loan bankruptcy— so too does the degree of violence deployed in the enforcement of "speculative" instruments. With this increased violence, speculation loses perhaps all genuine content as risk, dissolving its identity as contingency.[99] Under scrutiny, speculation proves to be in fact solid, certain, concretized. The group *uncertain commons* refer to this as "firmative speculation," a phenomenon that "*produces* potentialities and then *exploits* and thus *forecloses* them."[100] Power never truly leaves the side of the speculator(s)-at-the-top. The truly "contingent" are the indebted. Economic speculation, then, seems less related to Meillassouxian contingency than it does to determinacy. As the results—and conditions—of economic speculation are *produced* through human action as much as their potential negation.[101]

Yet the problem remains as to whether Meillassoux's materialism is capable of thinking social transformation of the kind this negation would require outside of the contingency of chance. "We know that the terms 'chance' . . . and 'aleatory,'" Meillassoux contends, "both refer back to related etymologies: 'to fall,' and 'falling' in the case of the former; 'dice,' 'dice-throw,' or 'game of dice' in the case of the latter." He continues,

> Thus, these terms bring together notions . . . of play and of calculation, and of the calculation of chance which is inherent in every game of dice. Every thinking in which the *identification of being with chance* is dominant foregrounds the theme of the dice-totality (which is to say, of the unalterable enclosure of the number of the possible), of the apparent gratuity of the game (the play of life and of a world whose superior artificiality is acknowledged), but also that of the cool calculation of frequencies (the world of life insurance and evaluable risks). The ontology of the enclosure of possibilities inevitably situates us within a world

whose aversion to gravity is but the obverse of the fact that it only takes counting techniques seriously.[102]

But Meillassoux contrasts his more radical notion of contingency with the chance elaborated above: whereas the latter occupies the domains of calculation and play, contingency refers to a more monumental something that happens "*to us*," outside our direct control.[103] While there is surely a risky foundational chance inherent to the political *act*, an indeterminacy governing the results of an intervention—Žižek for one insists upon the risk inherent to any "true materialism"[104]—this condition is distinguished from the more fundamental contingency conceived by Meillassoux. It is also differentiated from the uncertainty that results from the "practical-critical" activity found in Marx's materialism and social practice art/music alike.

In any case, Meillassoux's work shouldn't be considered as an "updated" Marxism for the twenty-first century, despite frequent comparisons to the work of twentieth-century Marxists such as Lenin.[105] Hallward takes issue with the philosopher's concept of contingency, asserting that through this conception of non-causal phenomenal flux, Meillassoux is deprived of the possibility of thinking the material transformation of social situations "with and after Marx."[106] Hallward, together with Žižek and Toscano, each for different reasons,[107] explicitly problematizes Meillassoux's insistence upon non-contradiction. Yet in his rejoinder to Hallward, Brown insists that Meillassoux's speculative materialism can be thought in continuity with and, indeed, as a "contribution to" Marxist "dialectical materialism": "What Meillassoux offers in *After Finitude*," according to Brown, "is not only a speculative materialism but a rigorous effort to fulfill the conditions of a properly dialectical materialism,"[108] a contentious claim considering the history of the term. The concept was, according to George Lichtheim, an "intellectual disaster."[109]

Where then does the reply to the challenge of thinking "with and after Marx" leave us in thinking the debt left by philosophy, the unfulfilled legacy of "practical-critical" social action advocated by Marx? In a different register, is it not evidence of a potentially similar "intellectual disaster" when the most strident critiques of academic capitalism become recuperated within its own debt economy of knowledge production? For this seems to remain a dynamic inescapable even by the most radical approaches to critical pedagogy. The mountains of debt invested in critique may never resolve the *need to create*: universal, open, and free education, not for the few but for all. Before moving on, I want to think briefly about the appearance of space in Thornton's student debt imaginary alongside Meillassoux's ancestral arche-fossil. Each presents the thought of a certain kind of deferral, the beyond of a "capacity-to-be-wholly-other" of the present moment; each posits a special kind of suspension of the "down here" by virtue of the "out there"; each remains underpinned by the precarious contingency of the production of human thought. (Perhaps only the polarity of the gestures is reversed: Thornton's debt is sent *to* the cosmos, whereas Meillassoux's arche-fossil sends back contingent speculation.) Not simply beyond thought, but providing its conditions of possibility is the precarious act of doing, the uncertain space of "practical-critical" activity. By tethering this outer space to the "down here" world of human action, Thornton's work proffers the materialism of a (musical) "social practice" in the place of economic and philosophical speculation alike.

It is still, after all, only philosophers who have interpreted the world; it is now up to artists, against the debilitating effects of debt, to change it.

The Metaphoricity of Sense: Hong-Kai Wang's *Music While We Work*—with Lindsey Lodhie

Introduction: From Scene to Sense

A pair of adjacent video projections displays two views of a sugar factory in Huwei, a small industrial town found in present-day Taiwan. On the left screen an initial long shot renders a mostly-cleared sugar cane field. A large harvesting vehicle drives slowly across the daylight-filled horizon extracting still-standing cane husks. The other screen shows a large factory warehouse from which a set of train tracks emerges. The scene opens with a factory transport train shuttling toward the camera; the engine crescendos as several train cars track across the screen. After the locomotive clears from view, the scene cuts to a distant shot of a Taiwanese woman standing in the field not far from the harvesting area. Facing the approaching harvesting vehicle while wearing a pair of headphones, the woman grasps a small, portable sound-recording device with an attached microphone.

This scene is from artist Hong-Kai Wang's *Music While We Work* (2011), a two-channel video and sound installation included in the 54th Venice Biennale's Taiwan Pavilion and MoMA's 2013 exhibition *Soundings: A Contemporary Score*. The 39-minute work follows a group of retired Taiwanese workers and their spouses through a factory owned by Taiwan Sugar Corporation as they execute a series of listening and recording exercises devised by the artist. Wang began initial work for the project in January 2011 by documenting a series of interviews with a group of five of the retirees and their families, assisted by her collaborator, Taiwanese musician and political organizer Bo-Wei Chen. "Are you retired?" Chen asks Kun-Shan, the husband of the woman seen during the video's opening sequence. "He used to work at the Railway Section of the department of transportation," notes the others in the group. Chen introduces himself to the families, and Wang explains to them the premise of the project. "I am interested in sound," Wang begins, "because I am drawn to the people, and to the history of the social relations behind sounds that we hear and listen to." She continues, speaking to the entire group: "This project aims," Wang asserts, "to paint a world composed by your own listening."[1] In her concise formulation, Wang brings together both active and passive modes of sound production while synaesthetically conflating the aural and visual. This irresolute "split" between the senses—Wang's formal separation of the video into two channels subtly mirrors the "stereoscopic" nature of hearing—becomes complicated in this chapter through further bifurcations of sense and metaphor, fact and ideology.

Wang's *Music While We Work* frames sound recording technology through the lens of the moving image, while it places philosophical and aesthetic precedents related to film in dialogue and conflict with those of music and sound. *Music While We Work* deploys digital video to address music as both form and subject matter through Wang's participatory recording activities. Although listening and audition are central components in this multichannel video work, Wang's critical musical practice features sound as one sense modality among many. As with Peter Ablinger's "post-sonic" music discussed in Chapter 4, Wang realizes a de-essentialized musical practice through a myriad of materials and mediums: site-specific installation, public performance, video, text, and social practice.

Wang explains that *Music While We Work* was part of a conscious shift in her practice from working with expressions of subjectivity to "exploring collective experiences."[2] Each of the retired sugar factory workers functions not only as an actor (if in a documentary mode), but also as a participant, a kind of ensemble member solicited to collectively carry out Wang's listening and recording processes. Extending the notion of social practice introduced in the previous chapter, these processes invoke what Jean-Luc Nancy refers to as the "methexic," or participatory tendencies of sound.[3] Specifically, Wang's participatory listening and recording exercises construct collective technological representations of industrial labor amid the latter's decline in global import.

This chapter moves from the consideration of music stripped of sound— in light of conceptual art, performance, and social practice strategies—to a reconsideration not only of sound as sense, but the question of sense more broadly in contemporary art practices. More than simply "in itself," sense is important because of its influence on conceptual thinking, its relation to various modes of technological mediation, and its metaphorical capacity. With this in mind, both "medium" and artistic lineage are seen here as *critical problems* rather than a set of neatly resolved determinations.

And yet, despite the work's formal complexity, it might be tempting to choose a single medium or context for *Music While We Work*. Settling perhaps on video as an "intermedial" form, this medium appears to contain both sound and the moving image while serving as a conduit for music, an overall structure that can be located in *Music While We Work*. But the question would remain as to whether video retains a link to its "parent" art forms, identified here as music and film. This chapter can be read, then, both to problematize and to clarify the status of video and sound in contemporary art. Paul Hegarty has recently argued for an understanding of video art as a medium that emerged not only from the gallery arts, including performance and conceptual art, but also from avant-garde music. Not unlike many of the exponents of "sound art" (Hegarty contends that video can be and use sound art), he argues *against* a sense of continuity or formal inheritance from music, taking issue with the recent work of Holly Rogers.[4] The latter coins the term "video art-music" and insists upon its extended historical lineage from music and visual art. "Rather than creating a new art form without a history," Rogers contends that even since its early moments, "video's intermedial capabilities allowed these two disciplines [music and visual art] to come together, acting as a conduit that enabled the fusion and manipulation of pre-existing practice."[5] Meanwhile, Hegarty views early, music-influenced video art as a distinct break from preexisting practices, hailing video art as "a new form that no longer refers back to the 'parent'" art form.[6] Despite his insistence on "formal analysis," Hegarty prefers a historical break with tradition, here characterized by a point at which "the early history of the medium has little relevance" to the present discussion.[7]

Against this divorce of video from its artistic "parents," historical forms such as music and film remain relevant to the work of contemporary artists like Wang. Specifically, Wang's project implicates crucial moments from the history of film and music while it engages broader theoretical and aesthetic concerns. *Music While We Work* depends upon an important set of references to state-ideological uses of music and historical representations of industrial labor in cinema.

Music While We Work, in addition to these historical visions of work, speaks to the emergence of a contemporary desire for mediatized depictions of bodies engaged in industrial labor processes. Themes of pastness, obsolescence, and historicity coalesce around a gesture of *return* in Wang's intervention: through her invitation to revisit the factory, Wang brings the retired workers back to the site of a subjectivizing and ritualized trauma; for viewers, she stages an encounter with an "anachronistic" form of labor in an era in which, while intrinsic to the reproduction of capital, the body of the industrial worker is increasingly made invisible, moved off-site, or placed "offscreen."[8] Wang's *Music While We Work* shares in a twofold gesture of medium self-reflexivity that implicates labor and the technics of its representation. Examples of the latter phenomenon can be traced to early silent film and Soviet avant-garde films such as Dziga Vertov's *Man with a Movie Camera* (1929). More recently, Tacita Dean's 2006 work *Kodak*, a film that consists of footage of a soon-to-close Kodak film factory in Chalon-sur-Saône, France, offered a similar meditation on technological obsolescence and its requisite material labor support.[9] What happens, then, when this kind of structure migrates from the moving image to take music as a point of departure?

Shifting from the question of ocular representation, Wang's project maps a socio-acoustic topology of laboring bodies through participatory recording exercises. *Music While We Work* stretches the notion of "field recording" from its early applications in ethnomusicology—the recordings by Alan Lomax, for instance, that link the emergence of American blues to the forced labor, segregation, and racism suffered by black Americans during the first half of the twentieth century—to the term's more recent appearance in *musique concrète* and experimental music. Beyond typical "ethnographic" field recording practices, Wang equips her subjects themselves with the empirical instruments of record and capture. As a variation on the kinds of soundscape practices found, for example, in Luc Ferrari's *Presque Rien* series that began in 1970 with field recordings of a fishing village in Yugoslavia, Wang replaces this first-person sonic perspective with "collective experiences" obtained through participatory recording. Although she draws on existing field recording practices, Wang offers a different approach.

Through these field recordings, *Music While We Work* subtly inverts the musicalized noise abatement strategies found throughout the early twentieth century and with increased frequency throughout the Taylorization of the 1920s and 1930s. *Masking* is a term used in psychoacoustics that refers to the ability of one sound to "cover up" or "mask" another. During this period, music was often used to mask the noises of industrial production experienced by workers. To counter the sounds of heavy machinery, the soothing backbeats of "light" band music, including show tunes and other popular music, were piped into factories, increasingly, on a mass scale. Music supposedly provided an ameliorating effect on workers, functioning as an ideological tool to increase productivity by decreasing noise. Wang's *Music While We Work*, rather than masking noise with music, exhibits factory sound as the object of a kind of musical listening. As opposed to drowning out the sounds of work with music, the latter constitutes a perceptual mode through which labor is interrogated. Wang's intervention suggests, furthermore, that this notion of "masking" might be extended to include, for example, one sense covering up another through a kind of sensory interference or synaesthetic cross-talk.

Masking, as metaphor and phenomenon, plays a central role in Wang's project and in this analysis. Since it describes one sound *standing in* for another, masking is seen as homologous to the linguistic operation of metaphor. For metaphor, like masking, can also be described as one sound—a word—standing in for another. Metaphor is important here because it mediates sensory experience; metaphor creates a bridge between conceptual thinking and the sensible. Masking relates more broadly to the question of sense—what is "revealed," "uncovered," or "deciphered" in thinking, seeing, or hearing beyond the "mask"?—while it simultaneously serves as a trope encountered in ideology critique: a metaphor for that which "masks" state power, etc.

It is important to note, then, that *Music While We Work* makes primary reference to a form of musical social engineering conducted at the state level in wartime Britain. Wang's *Music While We Work* takes its title from BBC's "Music While You Work," a radio program initiated in the UK in 1940 during the war with the intent to increase worker productivity. Music was conceived as a kind of "mental tonic," and therefore bright and cheerful selections including Viennese waltzes, musical comedy, and brass band music were used to boost worker morale.[10] As Karin Bijsterveld points out in her *Mechanical Sound* study (2008), music was used not only to mask the sounds of industrial manufacturing, but also as a means to make workers more efficient. Music both abated the noises heard on the factory floor and "led to an increased rate of work, fewer errors, better temperament, and less fatigue."[11] This strategy of musicalizing labor, as Bijsterveld notes, had arisen from the presumed links between the rhythmical character of work—its requisite application of repetitive physical force—and the repetition found in music. "Music While You Work" used the same Stimulus Progression models developed by the Muzak Corporation in the late 1940s wherein music was rated in terms of energy and mood, and programming was carefully orchestrated to peak at productively timed intervals. Deploying a regimen of lock-and-step affective synchrony, "Music While You Work" had harnessed a musical equivalent of Frederick Winslow Taylor's 1911 *The Principles of Scientific Management*: the rhythms of the assembly line and worker alike were now groove-locked and state-conducted.[12] Music, initially construed as a weapon for industrial noise "masking" techniques, had been effectively deployed as an Ideological State Apparatus par excellence.

The task of *un*masking ideology, then, would seem to turn on the phenomenal activity of listening, of penetrating more intently the sensible register, thus hearing through ideology's "screen." Yet the appropriate stratum for this sensory unworking, along with its efficaciousness, remains a point of contention. Žižek, for one, has argued against the notion of ideology as a veil that simply "mask[s] the real state of things," and pursues instead the Lacanian-influenced formulation of ideology as an "(unconscious) fantasy structuring our social reality itself."[13] Although he takes issue with the "visual" mask metaphor, Žižek draws on a distinctly "audible" metaphor when he refers to Robert Schumann as a "Theorist of Ideology," referring to the "silent" (or hidden) melodic lines of the *Humoresque in B-flat major* (1839).[14] Over the audible, however, ideology is conceived more often in relation to the visual, or the optical, a tendency found as early as Marx and Engel's well-known *camera obscura* passage in *The German Ideology*.[15] Importantly, this *camera obscura* metaphor would later prove to be profoundly influential for film theory and in cinematic practice beginning with the early Soviet realist films of Vertov. Still, Rancière argues for the abandoning of ideology critique altogether, replacing it with the "distribution of the sensible," a formulation that eschews ideology metaphors through ways of thinking, seeing, and hearing.

This elevation of the sensible, especially when considered from an aesthetic perspective, can be said to conflict with the discursive and conceptual approaches developed in art since the 1960s. What is the relevance of sensory perception following the radical aesthetic rupture of conceptual art? Do the "sense metaphors" found in ideology critique remain relevant to philosophy and politics following the inauguration of the postmedium condition? Sense influences conceptual thinking, channels into language as metaphor through a process at a remove from restricted notions of medium. Both music and film *frame* sense, while each form remains irreducible to a single sense. (If "theater" was Cage's term for the acknowledgment of the inseparability of the senses,[16] then this determination seems equally applicable to music and film.) As inseparable, the senses resist being neatly folded into discrete artistic mediums, while sense remains intimately tied to artistic practice and reception.

This chapter's title, "The Metaphoricity of Sense," refers to the continued role of sensory perception in artistic practices following conceptual art's radical challenges to medium. Here, and especially through technological mediation, sense is unmoored from medium; it forms a stratum for both discursive and material practice. *Music While We Work* first invites a reconsideration of Marx and Engels's *camera obscura* ideology model in which optical sense inverts a view of the "material conditions" of labor. As opposed to this metaphor of retinal inversion, what would it mean to derive a conception of ideology (or its potential displacement) based on acoustic inscription or musical organization?

Reworking Ideology: Ocular Obscura or Acoustic Lucida?

The supersession of private property is, therefore, the complete emancipation of all the human qualities and senses. It is such an emancipation because these qualities and senses have become human, from the subjective as well as the objective point of view. The eye has become a human, social object, created by man and destined for him. The senses therefore become directly theoretical in practice.

—Marx, *Third Manuscript of 1844*[17]

For the senses to become "theoretical in practice," as Marx would have it, not only private property but also ideology must be overcome; workers must view their "life-processes" for what they are, indeed, both unoccluded and undistorted. During the onset of industrialization in Europe, Marx and Engels launched their famous polemic against the Young Hegelian idealist philosophers—the German "ideologists" Ludwig Feuerbach, Max Stirner, and Bruno Bauer—in their deployment of a materialist philosophy based on human production. As already suggested by the opposition between idealism and materialism, antinomic operations such as inversion, substitution, ascension/descension, replacement, revolution, flipping, and turning form primary tropes in the Marx–Engels text. Specifically, it is the image of the *camera obscura* and its inversional function upon which their conception of ideology hinges. "If in all ideology men and their circumstances appear upside-down as in a *camera obscura*," begins the oft-cited passage, then "this phenomenon arises just as much from their historical life-process as the inversion of objects on the retina does from their physical life-process."[18] The passage notably links instrumentality and sense through the process of optical distortion. Indeed, this upside-down, flipping/turning operation alludes simultaneously, it seems, both to basic human perception—naked retinal seeing—and to technologized ocularity, scientific or artistic imaging. The sense of the visual, whether aesthetic or scientific, becomes primary.

Yet, while seeing is privileged in Marx and Engel's formulation of ideological inversion, there is nevertheless from the outset a hint of listening and the audible. The figure of *"echoes* of [the] life-process,"* for instance, imbricates across ideological reflections as a consequence of "actual" life: life includes reverberations of ideology rippled across its surface.[19] Indeed, "the metaphor of reflection," as Kofman notes, "works to convey the sense that the autonomy of ideology is illusory"[20]; the stronghold of ideology is purportedly only temporary or partial. But in Marx and Engel's account, it is not art wherein we find the possibility of piercing through the prism of ideology to reveal a clear, undistorted view. Rather, the *camera lucida* is discovered through science: "Where speculation ends," they insist, "real, positive science begins."[21] The "dark passage" marking the origins of photographic inscription[22] and ideological delusion alike has a corrective in science. In his critique of *The German Ideology*, Rancière provokingly asks, "What makes it possible for science to tear the tissue of the production of material life as well?"—what gives "science" this penetrating and incisive power?[23]

Rancière, moreover, rejects the very notion of ideology in its entirety, replacing it with his concept of the "distribution of the sensible." The philosopher defines the latter as the

> system of self-evident facts of sense perception that simultaneously discloses the existence of something in common and the delimitations that define the respective parts and positions within it. This apportionment of parts and positions is based on a distribution of spaces, times, and forms of activity that determines the very manner in which something in common lends itself to participation and in what way various individuals have a part in this distribution.[24]

For Rancière, the difference between ideology and the distribution of the sensible lies in the contention that the latter is not a matter of illusion or knowledge, but rather of consensus and dissensus. "A belief is not an illusion to be replaced by knowledge," Rancière explains, "it's a consensus: a way of seeing and saying, of being and doing in accordance with a distribution of the position that puts you at your place."[25] There is no "inversion" for Rancière because the belief in a heaven or hell is not an illusory view of a hierarchy to be overcome, but merely one component of a broader topology arranged, in a sense, horizontally.[26]

Rancière pits the distribution of the sensible, his notion of "self-evident facts" of sensory perception, against the traditional view of ideology as a distortion against which (scientific) truth is to be asserted. Rancière intends to move beyond ideology, yet he retains a link to sense, the register upon which various models of ideology have been based. Perhaps sound can provide a worthy "sense metaphor," given this privileging of the sensible. For one, sound does not seem to support the operation of "inversion" central to the *camera obscura* metaphor. Indeed, contrary to the vertical orientation of the viewer required for the flipping function of Marxian ideology—"*vom Kopf auf die Füße stellen*" requires *standing*, however oscillatory—sound is experienced as orientation-independent, largely indifferent to posture. Whether standing on one's head or not, factory noise sounds pretty much the same. *Music While We Work* follows sound's dispersion across the factory floor, tracing, in Wang's words, a "collective experience" of the retired factory workers. Is it possible that in *Music While We Work* we witness an attempt to render a "distribution" of acoustic "facts of sense perception"? Can sound offer an alternative to the sense of sight found so predominantly throughout ideology and its critique? Beyond the distortion of ideological optics, following this line of thought, the acoustic "signal" becomes a function of *noise*. The opticality of ideology critique is counterposed by the signal-to-noise ratio of the sensible.

We should then be able to simply replace the centrality of sight with sound; but the aim here is neither to resort to a privileging of sound, on the one hand, nor to repeat the sort of antivisual stance often encountered in sound studies (and sound art theory), on the other.[27] The trope of antivisuality, or "anti-ocularcentrism," defined as the criticism of vision and its supposed dominance throughout Western thought, in fact, has an extensive legacy. Martin Jay, for example, in his book *Downcast Eyes: The Denigration of Vision in Twentieth-Century French Thought* (1993), traces a broader history of these critiques of visuality with a focus on French theory. Jay's account of the Lacanian and post-Lacanian "antivisual" Marxist ideology theorists of the 1960s and 1970s, including Althusser, is particularly relevant.[28] Before Rancière had refused the concept of ideology, it was his former teacher and eventual intellectual rival, Althusser, who had, as Jay explains, "jettisoned the distinction between an occluded and a clear vision, and identified ideology with a reliance on sight of any kind."[29] Seeing had become *equated* with ideology.

But sight is not the only sense metaphor encountered in ideology critique, and the scope of these thought figures expands when we consider various references to architecture and technology. Althusser invokes the edifice metaphor found in the classical Marxist concepts of "base" and "superstructure" in his widely cited 1970 essay, "Ideology and Ideological State Apparatuses." "This metaphor,"

Althusser explains, "suggests something, makes something visible," which is the notion that the "upper floors" of this infrastructure rest upon the lower ones.[30] Importantly, these ocular and architectural registers were subsequently joined in the "apparatus theory" that dominated film scholarship throughout the 1970s. Viewing ideology critique through the lens of cinema's technological "base," apparatus theory focused on the material operations of film's moving parts. The "apparatus" therefore included the film stock, camera, projector, screen, audience, and the production processes that connected them.[31] Within this technological constellation, cinema's ideological operation was located precisely in the veiling—or *masking*—of the complex "work" behind the seamless realism of the projected image.[32]

Might the "apparatuses" employed by the field recorders in *Music While We Work* also possess their own kinds of distortion, recording artifacts that mask the "real state of things"?[33] *Music While We Work* allows a comparative refraction of questions that link technological mediation to the problem of ideology. But in order to consider these questions further, it is necessary to examine *Music While We Work*'s implicit links to cinema's historical markers that place Wang's project in an artistic lineage of engagements with industrial labor.

"Hearing Things Through Things": Music with a Movie Camera

Music While We Work not only draws upon state-ideological uses of music, but it also conjures representations of work and industry found in early cinema. The approach of the transport train described in the beginning of this chapter, for example, invokes the Lumière brothers' 1896 silent film *L'arrivée d'un train en gare de La Ciotat* (The Arrival of a Train at La Ciotat Station). One of the first films produced, *L'arrivée* achieved foundation myth status when viewers allegedly fled their seats in shock as the train veered toward an unsuspecting French audience during its premiere.[34] The literal approach of one modern machine, the locomotive, was met by the advent of another: cinema. Work and industry, recurring tropes in early cinema, were fundamental to the Lumières' first film *La Sortie de l'Usine Lumière à Lyon* (Workers Leaving The Lumière Factory in Lyon).[35] In contrast to *La Sortie*, Wang's *Music While We Work* documents the *return* of retirees to their former place of employment, whereas the Lumières depicted workers exiting the brothers' own film factory. As a foundational instance of cinematic self-reference, *Workers Leaving the Factory* underwent additional treatment in Harun Farocki's 1995 film essay of the same name, which interrogated the coevolution of industrial labor and the cinematic apparatus through recursive historical engagement.

With echoes of cinema's beginnings, *Music While We Work* allows these "anachronistic" representations of labor on screen to become re-embodied in the current moment. Pastness re-emerges when the retirees encounter current laborers, a subtle kind of "twoness" that is echoed through the work's formal demarcations. The two-channel "stereoscopic" image supports the contrast between visual documentation and sonic inscriptions of factory labor. Through a gradual progression of overlapping scenes staggered across her binocular screens, Wang's camera choreographs the technologically equipped bodies of former laborers. Her "field recorders" spread throughout the factory, patiently capturing various components of the sugar production process. With a neutral, observational gaze, the images work in a documentary mode; the participants function as witnesses. Not so much the factory workers, but the machinery occupies their attention. In one scene, for example, a participant records the sound of a woman standing in front of a large funnel; she bags sugar before placing the containers on a conveyor belt. Moving the microphone closer to the funnel, the worker becomes less a subject than the production process itself, which connects worker, funnel, bag, and sugar.

Historically, cinema's production processes have appeared on screen as a way of questioning film's status as an optical medium, especially during the silent era. Here a comparison can be drawn between Wang's *Music While We Work* and Vertov's watershed 1929 film *Man with a Movie Camera*. A canonical Soviet realist film of the 1920s, *Man with a Movie Camera* attempts to represent cinematically the totality of labor and industrial activity occurring throughout a single day in a typical Soviet city. Staged through amalgamated footage from Moscow, Kiev, and Odessa, the breadth of industry across the Soviet Union is collapsed into the length of a single film. A silent film devoid of intertitles, *Man with a Movie Camera* purportedly sought an autonomy of the image through montage. Beginning with a close-up shot of a camera that occupies the bottom two-thirds of the frame, *Man with a Movie Camera* progresses through a myriad of industrial processes interspersed with displays of the "cinematographic apparatus."

Not unlike Vertov, sound recording in *Music While We Work* is construed as a form of labor. The retirees deliberate as they travel from site to site; the

Figure 3 Dziga Vertov, *Man with a Movie Camera* (1929).

subject of the recordings is echoed in their execution. In Vertov, the cameraman, comparable to Wang's field recorders, leads the viewer through the city as the recorders move through the factory. In one segment of *Man with a Movie Camera*, the antiquated and "primitive" labor of mining with an axe is highlighted through a shot of a miner framed next to a camera operator. The repetitive manual movement of the axe-wielding miner is mirrored by the cameraman's hand-winding of the camera crank. Meanwhile, Wang's field recorder remains patiently still and, as described above, holds out her microphone while a worker continues to fill large bags with sugar.

Film theorist Annette Michelson has argued that *Man with a Movie Camera* goes so far as to stage a kind of *realization* of Marx and Engel's *The German Ideology*. Although Michelson contends that a range of "analogical and metaphorical readings" can be taken from *Man with a Movie Camera*, her evidence linking Marx and Engels to Vertov is presented through parallels between textile production and Vertov's portrayals of "film-as-production" or labor.[36] According to Michelson,

> Vertov seems to take or reinvent *The German Ideology* as his text, for he situates the production of film in direct and telling juxtaposition to that other particular sector, the textile industry, which was for Marx and Engels a status that is paradigmatic within the history of material production.[37]

Figure 4 Hong-Kai Wang, *Music While We Work* (2011).

Michelson describes Vertov's editing structure, which builds to a climax two-thirds through the film and intercuts shots of industrial labor (mason, axe grinder, miner, cigarette maker) with representations of filmmaking, including editing, processing, exhibiting, and camera work.[38] Extending Michelson's association of filmmaking with industrial production, one can go one step further to include as a primary symbolic operation Marx–Engels's *camera obscura* metaphor. Optical metaphors run throughout *Man with a Movie Camera*, seen in the insistent references to the lens and other parts of the camera. If we accept that *Man with a Movie Camera* is a translation of *The German Ideology*, it should follow that Vertov's "Camera" functions unambiguously as a *camera obscura*.

Although *Man with a Movie Camera* is a silent film, Vertov began working with film as an attempt to record or even "photograph" sounds.[39] And while the camera motif in *Man with a Movie Camera* is primary, according to Vertov, the film moves from "kino-eye to radio-eye"—a comment that expresses Vertov's formal investments in music and sound recording seen especially in his subsequent film, the first Soviet sound-film, *Enthusiasm* (1930).[40] In fact, alluding to his musical training and his practice of creating "scores" for his films, Vertov often referred to his artistic role not as filmmaker but as *composer*.[41]

By isolating principal terms from the works' respective titles ("camera" and "music"), moving from *Man with a Movie Camera* to *Music While We Work* shifts from one system of signification and philosophical metaphors to another. We proceed from the notion of the *camera obscura* to a network of philosophical thinking that links the economic to musical organization. Adorno's "forces of production" (*Produktivkräfte*) and "relations of production" (*Produktionsverhältnisse*), for example, refer not so much to the music industry, but to the relationships between distinct actors within the presentation of musical works; and rather than incidental, music is intrinsic to Adorno's materialist philosophy.[42] Another example of this musicalized representation of the economic can be found in Attali's *Noise: The Political Economy of Music* (1977), wherein the economist contends that the "constitution of the orchestra and its organization are also figures of power in the industrial economy." Attali continues:

> The musicians—who are anonymous and hierarchically ranked, and in general salaried, productive workers—execute an external algorithm, a "score" [*partition*], which does what its name implies: it allocates their parts. . . . Each of them produces only a part of the whole having no value in itself.[43]

Wang's intervention insists that the move from one sensory-philosophical register to another is neither simply a matter of negating vision, nor of privileging any other sense such as sound. Instead, *Music While We Work* is seen to mark out and cut across the formal-historical categories of music and the cinematic and provoke new philosophical thinking. This kind of provocation was already prefigured in Vertov's approach to cinema as a synaesthetic art form. Not restricted to the ocular, Vertov's "kino-eye" was conceived as a means to represent one sense *through* another (to "photograph" sound). Furthermore, by extending kino-eye to "radio-eye," Vertov sought to frame sound transmission as simultaneous and communal listening for workers—an intention that contrasts with the ideological interpellation found roughly a decade later in BBC's "Music While You Work."[44]

Of course, the comparison between Vertov and Wang can only go so far, and important distinctions should be noted regarding the types of industry referred to and their respective geopolitical and historical statuses: *Man with a Movie Camera* remains focused, optimistically, on textile manufacturing, which, in the Soviet Union of the 1920s, was a major staple of the economy. Meanwhile, *Music While We Work* stages a *return* to the sugar industry of present-day Taiwan, where the towering prominence sugar held for the Taiwanese economy for centuries has dwindled to its near obsolescence.

Returning to the question of ideology, how does one reconcile Rancière's rejection of optical ideology critique with Vertov's *camera obscura* metaphor?

Interestingly, Rancière devoted an entire chapter—or, what he calls a "scene"—of *Aisthesis: Scenes from the Aesthetic Regime of Art* (2013) to an analysis of Vertov's films, including *Man with a Movie Camera*. Rancière uses many of the tropes of "the distribution of the sensible" in championing Vertov. He describes one of the filmmaker's goals as "making community visible," a task that entails the conflicting features of showing "the relatedness of all activity to all others," on the one hand, and exhibiting their similarity, on the other. Rancière adds that "the sensible interconnection of activities is primarily the relation of their *visible* manifestations."[45] Considering his refusal of ideology, however, Rancière's interpretation of *Man with a Movie Camera* remains implicitly at odds with Michelson's equation of the film with *The German Ideology*. Indeed, is there not a contradiction between Rancière's distribution of the sensible (which eschews models of ideology critique like the *camera obscura*) and his promotion of the inherent "camera obscurity" of Vertov? Interestingly, Rancière borrows a phrase found in a text by critic Imail Urazov that accompanied the release of Vertov's *A Sixth Part of the World* to arrive at his scene's title: "Seeing Things Through Things."

Considering the foregrounding of listening encountered in Wang's intervention (and Vertov's own investments in music and recording), perhaps we can rewrite Rancière's scene as "Hearing Things Through Things."

The Mask of Metaphor

Music While We Work stages an attempt to "hear things through things," to penetrate the sounding surface of industrial work to arrive at its truth. Wang's field recorders scrutinize workplace noises that were historically subjected to musical "masking." By leveraging a musicalized listening, the recorders uncover an occluded perspective of labor through its sounding image. They listen through the "mask" of noise and beyond sight to sound's site. What is revealed, then, through these listening processes? What is "unmasked" through the metaphor of "Hearing Things Through Things"?

Shifting to a linguistic context, that very phrase describes the kind of substitution found in the notion of metaphor. A linguistic, philosophical, and aesthetic operation with profound reach, metaphor is found within the very heart of language and plays a role in the formation of meaning more broadly. Derrida has gone so far as to contend that the meaning of *all* language is "metaphoricity itself."[46] Yet the paradox he encounters is that while all language is seen as metaphor, the latter depends on literal discourse in order to function. One can't have metaphor without its opposite: a stable, literal reference. Metaphor breaks the ordinary links between meaning and sense and, according to Derrida, destroys the bond that "passes from sense to sound."[47] A listener comprehends one meaning *through* the sense of another thing; a message is substituted for the original, literal sign. One finds this kind of substitution in Lacan's succinct metaphor formula: "*one word for another*."[48] Here the "spark" of metaphor occurs not simply due to the juxtaposition of terms, but through replacement and substitution. Standing in for, covering up: in metaphor, one word *masks* another.

Masking thus becomes the operative term: in psychoacoustic masking, as in metaphor, one *sound* masks another. If masking is a metaphor, then metaphor is also a mask. Acoustically phenomenalizing metaphor, masking envelopes sonic and linguistic registers alike. A mask creates an appearance for a thing, substituting one appearance for another. Masking covers something up; it creates a facade of sensation. Marking the movement from one referent to another, masking is inherently *spatial*. "What can be at stake when you are listening," asks Wang, "in a particular architectural music-space?"[49]

Returning to the workplace, the masking techniques used by BBC radio's "Music While You Work" can be seen as precursors to those found in more recent applications developed in the field of so-called "architectural acoustics." Historically the latter, as Sterne notes, has construed noise as a nuisance, and, as with "Music While You Work," noise is seen as a problem for abatement. Citing Leslie Doelle's 1972 publication *Environmental Acoustics*, Sterne notes a similarity between early industrial masking efforts like "Music While You Work" and recent strategies employed in workplace acoustics. Metaphor is a central device in these strategies. For example, Doelle describes the introduction of artificial noises into an environment as "acoustical perfume" or "acoustical deodorant."[50] If metaphor is already a conceptual short circuit (apropos Lacan's "spark"), then Doelle's olfactory/sonic synesthesia blows a sensory fuse; masking and noise become multisensory. But what if noise is *not* a nuisance to be avoided or "covered up"? What if noise represents not a *camera obscura* but a kind of *acoustic lucida*? As opposed to occluding or obscuring focus, perhaps noise can illuminate.

One of the troubling aspects of the "mask" is that it may go unnoticed. The presence of a single mask leads to the notion that everyone might be wearing one—a phenomenon that recalls Žižek's take on Pussy Riot's balaclavas.[51] In the context of psychoacoustic masking, the presence of "acoustic deodorant" somewhere leads to smelling the fragrance everywhere. Nancy's observation that "sound has no hidden surface"[52]—the contention that sound is "all out in the open"—quickly turns into its opposite: sound contains a multiplicity of surfaces with occluded paths and planes. With a tradition stretching from *Ars subtilior* note coloring practices to Bach's musical cryptograms to the recent so-called "Black MIDI" movement, music exhibits time and again that there is always somehow "more" to what is heard. Does this mean, however, that to decode the message of one of Bach's fugue motives is to gain a "deeper" understanding of the piece?

Programmatically, Rancière refutes the notion of a "science . . . of the hidden" because he contends that such a search for the hidden, that which lies behind the mask, presumes a position of mastery.[53] And although Žižek's interpretation of Schumann's "silent" melodic lines could suggest otherwise, Žižek insists that the problem of ideology is not a matter of removing the mask that veils the "real state of things."[54] If "Hearing Things Through Things" is anything like these notions of ideology, it requires a move beyond the goal of "making sense" of an encrypted message, of hearing through the mask of metaphor.

The Scene of Sense: Time

Sense, as it turns out, is itself also a metaphor. Referring to the capacity both to make sense and to perceive sensibly, sense cuts across the intelligible—that which "*makes* sense"—and that which is made *by* the senses: sensory experience. According to Derrida, sense stands in for an indeterminate signified or "content" of sense. He describes a "double twist which opened up metaphor," thus allowing the term "sense" to apply to "that which should be foreign to the senses."[55] Sense also *stands in* for sense-making. The very act of using language to describe sensation—the process of making sense out of sense—falls under the category of metaphor; sense connects the sensible with sense-making.

Negating intelligibility turns sense into nonsense.[56] "Non-sensory," as a sense for a particular sense in its absence, might be used to describe the recent work of Christine Sun Kim, an American composer and artist who was born deaf. We may also think of the kinds of sensory deprivation depicted in Ken Russell's 1980 film *Altered States*. But there is perhaps a different connotation of "non-sense" beyond the negation of sense. "Non-sense" may be conceived as a sense for *time*—a category upon which sense depends but which is often said to resist (philosophical) conceptualization (thereby eschewing sense).[57] It seems fitting that the work Cage composed following his own sensory deprivation experience in the famous Harvard anechoic chamber episode consisted of only a (variously notated) temporal signifier: *4′33″*. If metaphor is spatial, then sense and nonsense converge as temporal phenomena.

Considering this relation to the temporal, *Music While We Work* coordinates a collective set of sensory inscriptions that *mark out the time of labor*: a time which, as an "anachronistic" form of labor, remains "outside" of its original time while central to the present workings of capital. Time is not a sense, but temporality is an element common to music, the moving image, and labor. The time of labor is subjected to technological inscription as the trace of phenomenal encounter in *Music While We Work*. Wang encodes, presents, and represents the time of labor through scenes of sense. *Music While We Work* represents a return not only to representations of industrial labor—in this case opening up the latter to sound—but also to the general question of sense in an artistic context whose relation to sense has been radically refigured through the proliferation of conceptual, performative, and intermedial practices that began in the 1960s and 1970s.

The first North American exhibition to feature *Music While We Work* was MoMA's 2013 *Soundings: A Contemporary Score*, and although Wang's work was the ostensible centerpiece of the show, it received little more than brief reviews. Art-theoretical discussions of *Soundings* foregrounded the show's grouping of art practices around sense, medium, and materiality. Branden W. Joseph, for example, rephrased Martha Rosler's indictment of the art world's treatment of video art in the 1980s, suggesting a similarly applicable "*social* history" of sound.[58] Kim-Cohen devoted much of his *Against Ambience* to a critique of the exhibition, ultimately echoing Dworkin's call for *No Medium*.[59] Nevertheless, the category of sense, while implicitly a subject of *every* exhibition and text on "sound art," often evades direct address—that is, "sound" is immediately conceived as a medium (separate from music's historical forms). Through its comparative reference to historical and philosophical uses of music and the motion image, *Music While We Work* insists upon sense: not an autonomous sense ascribed to medium-specific art forms, but a sense for the metaphoricity of sense itself.

Conclusion

Music After Art

Throughout this book I have argued for a conception of music in dialogue with contemporary art and engaged in a range of political issues and philosophical debates. The artworks, artists, and collectives discussed in this book have demanded a set of cross-disciplinary analyses that bridges musicology, art history/theory, and continental philosophy. Beginning with a comparison between the activist strategies of Ultra-red and the post-Cagean silence of Wandelweiser, listening figures as a strategy for collective organization that hinges upon the historical form of the musical score. Extending this logic to conceptual art and the material violence of the threat, Pussy Riot's feminist-conceptual interrogation of language buttresses Ablinger's iconoclastic *Letter from Schoenberg*. Next, in Cassie Thornton's group interventions around student debt, a continuity emerges between music and social practice art. Her collaborative debt screams then find a counterpart in Hong-Kai Wang's critique of state-ideological "masking" techniques. Through Wang's visual renderings of participatory field recording exercises, the moving image joins social practice as a tool for critical music. Broadly speaking, these artists point to a shift from autonomous sound to music as an expanded art form in which sound appears as one element among many.

I have insisted upon critical music as a category irreducible to sound as a medium, and these practices emerge from a breadth of different artistic forms (performance, installation, social practice, conceptual art). Beyond sound, these artists stage forms of participation and collectivity by reimagining music's historical forms; they organize bodies through processes of listening and enunciation by *composing* radical forms of commonality. Sound does appear in the practices of these artists, but its presence should not limit our consideration to the "unremarked commonality" that unites absolute music and "sound art."[1] These practices find a home in music rearticulated as a critical alternative to the existing contexts of sound art and new music. Departing from these contexts (sound art and new music), critical music maintains an important relationship with contemporary art, as the latter is a prerequisite for an adequate contextualization of critical music.

Contemporary art is a central anchoring point for the artists discussed in this book. It is the primary context for Pussy Riot, Thornton, Wang, and Ultrared, as these artists engage in a critical dialogue with contemporary practices. Still, while they are presented more often in "new music" contexts, Ablinger and Wandelweiser receive a richer analysis when contemporary art informs existing music discourse. Accordingly, deepened exchanges between music and contemporary art remain crucial to the aims of this book. Yet one may nevertheless question the degree to which contemporary art can present a viable arena for critical music—and even critical (art) practice more generally. Returning to a question raised in the introduction, *is a critical practice possible today?*, contemporary art remains problematic—especially when considering many of its recent expressions of dissatisfaction and dissent.

Can contemporary art provide a suitable context for critical music? If not, can music play a role in conceiving an alternative to contemporary art? Is it possible to imagine an alternative context not only outside of "new music" institutions, but also beyond the grasp of contemporary art? These questions follow a series of recent statements made throughout 2013 that call for a resolute break with contemporary art institutions. If we've been conceiving a music after sound throughout this book, can we now begin to imagine a *music after art*? I want to end, then, with a consideration of music in relation to these imperatives to move beyond contemporary art.

Desperate Times: To Valerie Solanas

But before concluding, I want to add to the artists analyzed so far the Berlin-based duo Pauline Boudry and Renate Lorenz. They, also in 2013, created a film/video realization of Pauline Oliveros's 1970 score, *To Valerie Solanas and Marilyn Monroe in Recognition of Their Desperation----*. Boudry and Lorenz's 18-minute film (16 mm transferred to HD video) follows six performers through Funkhaus Nalepastraße, a former GDR Radio studio in Berlin, as they execute Oliveros's score. Wearing brightly colored spandex outfits, the performers, who represent a range of different gender identities,[2] move slowly throughout the space while playing long tones on various instruments (guitar, accordion, theremin, keyboard, voice), all before congregating in a large sound-stage area where the majority of the performance takes place. Shortly, I will end by framing Boudry and Lorenz's project in relation to broader questions around criticality and collectivity and the relationship between music and contemporary art.

Speaking at a roundtable discussion at MoMA in 2014, Lorenz refers to feminism in the 1970s and queer politics in the present in explaining that their project seeks "to bring together these different political moments and to ask, with [Oliveros's] score, what's the desperation now?" Boudry and Lorenz's project implicates the musical score as a means to reanimate the past, as a way to bring together "different temporalities at the same time"[3] through performance. Not unlike Ultra-red's SILENT|LISTEN, which, as we've seen, uses Cage's score to reframe the homophobia of the 1950s in light of the AIDS crisis in the early twenty-first century, Boudry and Lorenz place Oliveros's feminist work of 1970 in dialogue with queer politics of the present. As a way of layering multiple temporalities, Boudry–Lorenz enact a kind of "chronopolitics."[4]

Oliveros composed the score in 1970 following her reading of Solanas's infamous SCUM Manifesto of 1967, seeking to express the manifesto's "deep structure"[5] while framing Monroe and Solanas through Oliveros's feminist practice of "Deep Listening." Oliveros explains that she was interested in the egalitarian principles expressed in Solanas's manifesto. In her controversial statement, Solanas, whose work received an upsurge in attention after she non-fatally shot Andy Warhol in 1968, promoted the eradication of men through "total female control of the world," a state that would lead to the ultimate extinction of humanity.[6] Yet despite such an extreme stance, Solanas's manifesto can be read as premised upon anarchist forms of collective organization. The SCUM Manifesto was, as Breanne Fahs contends, a paradoxically "utopian text."[7] Referring to Solanas's difficulties with publishers and Monroe's struggles with celebrity, Oliveros asserts that "both women seemed to be desperate and caught in the traps of inequality"[8]—a state Solanas resisted through her writing and direct violent action, but also through a call for nonhierarchical cooperation.

Oliveros cites the following passage from SCUM Manifesto as a primary point of departure for her composition:

A true community consists of individuals—not mere species members, not couples—respecting each others [sic] individuality and privacy, at the same time interacting with each other mentally and emotionally—free spirits in free relation to each other—and cooperating with each other to achieve common ends. Traditionalists say the basic unit of "society" is the family; "hippies" say the tribe; no one says the individual.[9]

Oliveros, attempting to mirror the "deep structure" of Solanas's cooperative community, describes in her text score a scenario in which performers must work to maintain a nonhierarchical relationship to one another. Each performer selects five different pitches and performs a series of long tones to which various forms of modulation may be applied. If, at any point, the volume level of a particular performer begins to dominate, the rest of the ensemble is instructed to increase their levels accordingly to maintain equality. The score also specifies changes in stage lighting, which Boudry and Lorenz accomplish via a series of large, backlit panels that surround the performers on the Funkhaus Nalepastraße sound stage.

Boudry and Lorenz bring this tightly knit historical constellation—composed of Oliveros, Solanas, Monroe, but also of feminism and queer struggles of the 1960s and 1970s—into the present. To the question *is criticality possible today?* Boudry and Lorenz answer with a reference to the past: "[We pursue] moments in the past that [look] quite queer to us." Politics is not a matter of a utopia that requires an investment in futurity, but rather lies in a special form of historical engagement. In addition to providing a contemporary reframing of queer and feminist politics, Boudry and Lorenz's project can also be seen to extend the tension between dissent and collectivity found in the various calls made throughout 2013 to exit the art world.

Exit Signs and Afterthoughts

In 2013, contemporary art fantasized about its own death—or at least it sought an exit strategy. Although it was an important year for sound art and music, 2013 also saw a proliferation of statements that contemplated an end to the art world. The monumental *Sound Art: Sound as a Medium of Art* closed at the Zentrum für Kunst und Medientechnologie Karlsruhe (ZKM). New York showcased its much-criticized "summer of sound and light" exhibitions that included MoMA's *Soundings* and the Guggenheim's *James Turrell*.[10] And a series of unrelated talks, publications, and roundtable discussions unfolded that variously appealed to contemporary art's collapse. The topics of financialization and increased inequality were central to many of these events, including London's Institute of Contemporary Arts (ICA) roundtable discussion "The

End of the Art World . . .?" Critic and art historian Joselit's book from the same year, *After Art*, posited art as a kind of "universal currency" in the wake of contemporary art's thoroughgoing monetization.[11] These statements arrived not long after critic Dave Hickey's announcement that he would leave the art world in hopes that it would be the "start of something that breaks the system,"[12] along with the publication of Pamela M. Lee's *Forgetting the Art World* (2012), and Andrea Fraser's 2012 Whitney Biennial essay that indicted contemporary art as "painfully contradictory, even as fraudulent."[13] Taken together, these statements variously exhibited the desire for a radical withdrawal from extant art world structures. They shared the perception of a certain limit point, an impasse calling for a secession from contemporary art and its institutions.

Perhaps the most interesting of these events were talks given by critic and theorist Suhail Malik and Iranian philosopher Reza Negarestani. In his talk, "The Human Centipede, A View From the Art World," delivered at e-flux, New York, Negarestani described a sequence of "mouths and rectums through which the art world bootstraps itself" as contemporary art's financialized horizon.[14] Malik's four-part inquiry into the conditions and horizons of contemporary art, "On the Necessity of Art's Exit from Contemporary Art" (to be published in book form in 2016)[15] argued that contemporary art has hitherto sought forms of *escape* through various means, including participatory art and deskilling. But if it is to have a genuine impact on "anything beyond or larger than itself," Malik contended, art must *exit* contemporary art. Negarestani similarly concluded that art must proceed through a "systematic extrication" from the contemporary art world.

Malik's talk took the form of a series of axioms that began by describing a logic inherent to contemporary art: not central to any particular artist or artwork (neither, he claimed, is "where the action is"), contemporary art is governed by an affirmation of "indeterminacy." Malik explained, "Art's contents and claims are now at best placeholders or alibis for a series of power operations to which it is now subordinated." Contemporary art's logic insists upon upholding what Malik described as an "anarcho-realist maxim," an enforced state of anarchy that allows sustained abuses of power and that prevents a realization of the kinds of collective projects that would effectively reach beyond the art world.[16] Malik's thesis was that we must abandon contemporary art's "anarcho-realist maxim" in favor of a wholly different form of social organization.

One wonders, then, what this *art beyond contemporary art* might look (or sound) like. Do these statements simply refer to an art beyond current contemporary art institutions? Would such an art require a ban on reference to existing art, operating, in a sense, outside of history? For an inclusion of art-historical reference might blow its cover and risk recuperation into the existing field of contemporary art. Is it not true that any such "post"-contemporary art would remain by definition wholly inherent to contemporary art, bound by patrilineal descent? Would not such an origin prevent contemporary art from accessing that which is "larger than itself"?

Malik and Negarestani's talks shared a resolute critique of contemporary art in their flat-out rejections of its current formation in favor of alternative forms of social organization. Yet not unlike Solanas's controversial manifesto, both speakers privilege forms of community and collectivity. Negarestani, for example, questions whether contemporary art can provide a constructive contribution to a project of the "illiberalization of freedom and collective enhancement." And Malik began his talk by describing the "dream" of Dan Graham (of what form could such an alternative take but that of a "dream"?): "All artists are alike. They dream of doing something that's more social, more collaborative, and more real than art."[17] It is interesting that, as Malik acknowledges, Graham's statement also appears as the epigraph of Bishop's social practice study, *Artificial Hells*. Malik thus indicates a link between his exit strategy and social practice art—the latter being a field that, as Bishop and Jackson note, is premised upon historical forms of participation and collaboration found in music.

Time After Time

As the art world self-destructs, and "new music" institutions continue to prove immutable to certain forms of change, the question remains as to where critical music practices are to be situated. Moreover, what forms of agency can these musicians and artists assert if they are required to move between—or, perhaps, beyond—current disciplines? Andrea Fraser noted in 2012 a profound sense of disconnect and alienation from the art world, indicating her own turn away from art theory and toward the disciplines of sociology, psychoanalysis, and economics.[18] Relatedly, artists and musicians have increasingly looked to philosophy, cultural criticism, activism, and other nonartistic disciplines as alternatives to existing institutions. Yet while contemporary art purportedly undergoes its own immanent destruction, the concomitant dismantling of public institutions and educational resources presents further obstacles for

the question remains as to where critical music practices are to be situated artists seeking to move beyond existing institutions. (Academia is perhaps no more immune to the kinds of abuses of power and financialization that permeate the art world—the homeless adjunct professor and lifelong student debt remain, as Thornton's work attests, intrinsic parts of the system.) Nevertheless, as contemporary art purportedly enters a phase of self-induced deterioration, what can a work like *To Valerie Solanas* tell us about radical forms of equality, collectivity, and resistance?

Music offers ways to frame and reframe time. As an alternative to Malik's spatial metaphor of "exit," Boudry and Lorenz's project engages a politics of temporality by recasting historical moments through a musical logic. For Oliveros—as with Boudry and Lorenz—"music is not an object but a process engaging bodies, time, and space."[19] Like the other artists in this book, their project posits a form of *composition* based on radical forms of commonality. As a process of engaging bodies, times, and spaces, these artists rearticulate a music beyond sound that stands both in dialogue with and as a challenge to contemporary art and its institutions. Not simply an escape or an exit, they compose collective forms through an iterative engagement with the past. In *After Art*, Joselit concludes, "One need not exit the art world or denigrate its capacities. Instead, we must recognize and exploit its potential power in newly creative and progressive ways."[20] Despite the persistence of the art world and new music institutions, one should not hesitate to leave behind sound as an autonomous medium. Our real work, after sound *and* art, begins by composing radical collective formations of bodies, times, and spaces.

"Music offers a way to frame and reframe time."

Acknowledgments

I wish to thank Leah Babb-Rosenfeld, Michelle Chen, Ally-Jane Grossman, and everyone at Bloomsbury for their hard work and support. At an early point in the process, Ben Piekut encouraged me to write this book and later reviewed sections of it. Lindsey Lodhie has been a wellspring of intellect and support for over a decade. Leigh Claire La Berge, who also helped with various aspects of this book, demonstrates time and again what it means to "have a thought." Thanks to Bill Dietz, James R. Currie, and Michael Gallope for reading an earlier version of this book and providing thoughtful insight and valuable feedback. I thank Eldritch Priest and Marc Couroux for providing important preparatory comments and suggestions. Thanks also to Seth Kim-Cohen, James Saunders, David Cecchetto, and Francesco Gagliardi; each of you has contributed immeasurably to this project.

This book is the result of an ongoing dialogue with an international network of artists, curators, academics, activists, and musicians including Michael Pisaro, Cort Lippe, Peter Ablinger, Philip Thomas, Travis Just, Kara Feely, Hong-Kai Wang, Jennifer Walshe, Tom Leeser, Sara Roberts, Renate Lorenz, Pauline Boudry, Adam Overton, Antoine Beuger, Manfred Werder, Petr Kotik, Ron Kuivila, Cassie Thornton, Andrew Ross, Pamela Brown, Elana Mann, Theo Baer, Zackary Drucker, Justin Luke, Devin Maxwell, Katie Porter, Robert Sember, Dont Rhine, Caroline Woolard, Christoph Migone, Michael Tikili, Tao G. Vrhovec Sambolec, Brandon LaBelle, Johnny Herbert, Tora Bjørkheim, John Lely, Joseph Kudirka, Mark So, John P. Hastings, Casey Anderson, Liz Kotz, Sari Carel, Fahad Siadat, FLUX Quartet, SEM Ensemble, Amy Ireland, Geraldine Finn, Volker Straebel, Esther Neff, Brian McCorkle, Andrew Hiller, Laurel Ptak, Che Gossett, Bjørnar Habbestad, Alwynne Pritchard, Thorolf Thuestad, Christian Kesten, Steffi Weismann, Johnny Chang, James Orsher, Kerstin Fuchs, Sara Eddleman Clute, Mike Winter, Matthieu Saladin, Magali Daniaux, Cédric Pigot, Martin Supper, and Stephen Elin.

Several academic conferences, symposia, journals, art organizations, and researchers provided pivotal resources. The Occulture's Tuning Speculation symposia allowed for an ongoing series of exchanges with a group of committed interdisciplinary thinkers. I presented early research on Ultra-red at The Future of Cage: Credo conference at the University of Toronto, thanks to Nik Cesare and the organizers. Thanks to Seth Kim-Cohen and the participants of the Singing LeWitt: Sound and Conceptualism panel at the 104th annual College Art Association conference. I thank Georgina Born for sharing her recent research on sound art and music. And thanks also go to Annie Moore from *Postmodern Culture*, Dawne McCance at *Mosaic*, Bill Dietz and Woody Sullender from *Ear|Wave|Event*, and James Saunders, Nicholas Melia and the editors of *Contemporary Music Review*. Thanks to Elisabeth Thomas (MoMA Archives), Athena Christa Holbrook (MoMA Performance Art), John Bewley (SUNY at Buffalo Music Library), and Martha Wilson and Jenny Korns (Franklin Furnace).

The USF Bergen residency in Norway and the Akademie Schloss Solitude fellowship in Germany offered me valuable time and space to work on this book. Thanks to Line Nord and Evy Sørensen from USF and to Roar Sletteland and nyMusikk Bergen for hosting my related talk in Norway. Thank you Jean-Baptiste Joly, Silke Pflüger, Lotte Thieroff, and fellow artists at the Akademie.

A personal note of thanks to my family for their support and to Maria Huffman for her valuable insights. Debra Ligorsky provided helpful commentary and editing suggestions. Taylan Susam and Sarah M. Schmidt helped with Dutch and German translations. Finally, I thank Melody Nixon for her patience, support, copyediting help, and thoughtful engagements with this project.

Early versions of material from this book have appeared in *Postmodern Culture* 23, no. 2 (2014), *Contemporary Music Review* 30, no. 6 (2011): 449–70, *Mosaic, a journal for the interdisciplinary study of literature* 42, no. 4 (2009): 147–64, and *Ear|Wave|Event* Issue One (2014): 1–6.

In memoriam Mark Trayle.

Notes

Introduction

1 This perspective, that "sound is a minimal condition of the musical fact," is cited in Jean Jacques Nattiez, *Music and Discourse: Toward a Semiology of Music*, trans. Carolyn Abbate (Princeton, NJ: Princeton University Press, 1990), 43. His similar contention, "Sound is an irreducible given of music" (ibid., 67), also appears in Seth Kim-Cohen, *In the Blink of an Ear: Toward a Non-cochlear Sonic Art* (New York: Continuum, 2009), 174.

2 My point, of course, is not that music had necessarily *excluded* sound, but rather that the latter was not, in these accounts, *essential* to music's definition. The *harmonia*, *rhythmos*, and *logos* trio, for example, is attributed to Plato and said to have "never [been] doubted until the seventeenth century," in Carl Dahlhaus, *The Idea of Absolute Music*, trans. Roger Lustig (Chicago: University of Chicago Press, 1989), 8. The comparable formulation "oration, harmony, and rhythm," or *oratione*, *harmonia*, *rhythmus*, is found in Marsilio Ficino's 1491 Latin translation of *The Republic* (cited in Mark Evan Bonds, *Absolute Music: The History of An Idea* [New York: Oxford University Press, 2014], 11). The related Greek concept of *Mousikē* was perhaps more expansive and included song, dance, word, and even philosophy (see Penelope Murray and Peter Wilson, "Introduction: *Mousikē*, not Music," in *Music and the Muses: The Culture of Mousike in the Classical Athenian City*, ed. Penelope Murray and Peter Wilson [New York: Oxford University Press, 2004], 1–8). Pythagoras's concept of music can be viewed as differently removed from sound through its deep reliance upon ratio and number. At its extreme, in fact, "Pythagoreanism rejected the senses altogether" (Bonds, *Absolute Music*, 30). For more on the subject of absolute music, see Daniel K. L. Chua, *Absolute Music and the Construction of Meaning* (Cambridge: Cambridge University Press, 1999). My discussion of the topic continues in Chapter 3.

3 Clement Greenberg seemed to have this in mind when he commented on (absolute) music's role in the development of the avant-garde and (medium-specific) artistic modernism:

> Music as an art in itself began at this time to occupy a very important position in relation to the other arts. Because of its "absolute" nature, its remoteness from imitation, its almost complete absorption in the very physical quality of its medium, as well as because of its resources of suggestion, music had come

— to replace poetry as the paragon art. ("Towards a Newer Laocoon," in *Pollock and After: The Critical Debate*, ed. Francis Frascina [New York: Routledge, 2000], 65)

That Greenberg acknowledges the category of program music (his example is Debussy) does not change his point, namely that *absolute* music served as the exemplary modernist art form.

Moreover, Greenberg's perspective had been prefigured in the early 1800s writings of the group of Romantic German thinkers that included Wackenroder, Tieck, Novalis, Jean Paul, Schlegel, and E. T. A. Hoffmann. Through their writings, instrumental music (later termed "absolute music") had been elevated "from the lowest to the highest of all musical forms, and indeed of all the arts in general" (Mark Evan Bonds, "Idealism and the Aesthetics of Instrumental Music at the Turn of the Nineteenth Century," *Journal of the American Musicological Society* 50, no. 2/3 [Summer - Autumn, 1997]: 387).

Greenberg's medium-specific artistic modernism was only one "flavor" of artistic modernism, yet it shared important ideological conceits with absolute music including the exclusion of language ("literature" in Greenberg) and an emphasis on "purity," form, and autonomy. For a philosophical comparison of the different strands of artistic modernism (aesthetic, specific, generic), see Peter Osborne, *Anywhere or Not at All: Philosophy of Contemporary Art* (London: Verso, 2013), 77–83.

4 See Rosalind Krauss, *A Voyage on the North Sea: Art in the Age of the Post-Medium Condition* (New York: Thames & Hudson, 2000), the widely cited text based on Krauss's 1999 Walter Neurath Memorial Lecture at Birkbeck College, London. Note that the "post-medium condition," which is Krauss's critical target in the book, refers to the "international spread of mixed-media installation [that had] become ubiquitous" (ibid., 20). Her corrective is "differential specificity," a concept that, according to Krauss, calls for the reinvention or rearticulation of mediums (ibid., 56). Unless specified otherwise, I will use the term "postmedium condition" to refer to her argument as a whole.

5 The view that sound is the proper "medium" of music can be found throughout both musicology and sound art theory. Writing of the Western musical score, for example, Peter Kivy insists that sound has been the medium of music since as early as the seventeenth century: "The score has . . . stood between the composer and *his* [sic] artistic medium, *sound*, as an instrument that must be mastered in order to work that medium" (Peter Kivy, *Sound and Semblance: Reflections on Musical Representation* [Princeton, NJ: Princeton University Press, 1984], 106, emphasis in original). From the perspective of a sound art theorist critical of music, Kim-Cohen expresses a similar (and tacitly Hanslickian) contention: "The

intramusical (simply referred to, in music parlance, as 'music') is captured either in inscription of notation, or in specifically quantifiable audible phenomena" (Kim-Cohen, *In the Blink of an Ear*, 40).

6 Chantal Mouffe, *Agonistics: Thinking the World Politically* (London: Verso, 2013), 91.

7 Boris Groys, *Art Power* (Cambridge, MA: MIT Press, 2008), 2.

8 Guy Debord, "The Situationists and the New Forms of Action in Politics or Art," in *Guy Debord and the Situationist International: Texts and Documents*, ed. Tom McDonough (Cambridge, MA: MIT Press, 2002), 164.

9 I recall here Theodor W. Adorno's 1962 essay "Commitment," partly a response to Jean-Paul Sartre's call for an "engaged" writing in "Qu'est-ce que la littérature?" (1949). To Sartre's gloss of the signifying potential of painting and music, "Who would dare require that the painter or musician engage himself? . . . The writer deals with meanings" (*What is Literature?: And Other Essays* [Cambridge, MA: Harvard University Press, 1988], 28), Adorno contended that the philosopher "restricts his notion of commitment to literature because of its conceptual character." Adorno went on to add, "Cultural conservatives who demand that a work of art should say something join forces with their political opponents against atelic, hermetic works of art," concluding that autonomous and *not* committed artworks "should be encouraged today in Germany" ("Commitment," trans. Frances McDonagh, *Aesthetics and Politics: The Key Texts of the Classic Debate within German Marxism*, ed. Rodney Livingstone, Perry Anderson, and Francis Mulhern, trans. Ronald Taylor [New York: Verso, 1977], 178–79, 193). It is important to note that Adorno's response came years before the introduction of conceptual art, the movement that would, among other things, challenge neat separations between discourse and artistic practice. Of course, this is not to suggest an incompatibility between conceptual art and Adorno; see Osborne, *Anywhere or Not At All*, 10, 11, 48–51, 93.

10 The reference is to Edgard Varèse. During the 1920s, speaking to prevailing conservative responses to his radical musical aesthetic—"but is it music?" for example—the composer suggested to refer to his music as "organized sound" (Edgard Varèse, "The Electronic Medium (1962)," from "The Liberation of Sound," ed. and ann. Chou Wen-chung, *Perspectives of New Music* 5 no. 1 [Autumn–Winter, 1966]: 18).

11 According to Seth Cluett, there were approximately ten sound-themed exhibitions between 1966 and 1972 (Seth Allen Cluett, "Loud Speaker: Towards a Component Theory of Media Sound" [PhD diss., Princeton University, 2013], 49). The term's earliest titular appearance was likely MoMA's 1979 *Sound Art* exhibition.

12 Born discusses sound studies authors as "portray[ing] sound as awaiting discovery, as a radical new paradigm, as incipient in existing work (etc): as

a year zero!" in Georgina Born, "Sound Studies / Music / Affect: Year Zero, Encompassment, Difference?" lecture, *Current Musicology—50th Anniversary Conference* (New York, March 28, 2015).

13 Kim-Cohen, *In the Blink of an Ear*, 39–40. In *Against Ambience*, Kim-Cohen introduces the possibility of an "expanded palette of musical terms"; he suggests that music should borrow Krauss's notion of an "expanded field" which had been originally applied to sculpture (*Against Ambience* [New York: Bloomsbury, 2013], Kindle location 276). See Rosalind Krauss, "Sculpture in the Expanded Field," *October* 8 (Spring, 1979): 30–44.

14 Brian Kane, "Musicophobia, or Sound Art and the Demands of Art Theory," *Nonsite.org*, no. 8 (2013), January 20, 2013, accessed June 20, 2013, http://nonsite. org/article/musicophobia-or-sound-art-and-the-demands-of-art-theory.

15 Branden W. Joseph, "Soundings: A Contemporary Score," *Artforum* (November 2013): 282–83.

16 There are two documented versions of Neuhaus's essay: an online manuscript and a document available from the MoMA archives. The latter was likely the version included in MoMA PS1's 2000 exhibition *Volume: Bed of Sound*, although this second version has remained unacknowledged in related literature. The online version appears in Caleb Kelly, *Sound* (London: Whitechapel Gallery, 2011), 72–73, and it is quoted in Kim-Cohen, *Against Ambience* (Kindle location 1202), Kane, "Musicophobia," and G Douglas Barrett, "Speaking Volumes," Recess, May, 2013, http://www.recessart.org/critical-writing-g-douglas-barrett/.

There are a number of differences between the two versions. The online version includes material only from the second page of the archival version and is roughly half the length of that text. The first page of the archival version sets up a sense of technological continuity between orchestral music and sound art through the advent of the personal computer. The last sentence on page one of the archival version introduces the term sound art, although it appears in a more positive light than on page two.

There are other, less significant differences: the first sentence of page two in the archival version, "Over the past twenty years . . .," becomes "From the early 1980s on . . ." in the online text (presumably to appeal to a later readership). Paragraph breaks are different. There is a date discrepancy: the archival version reads "Max Neuhaus, June, 2000," whereas the online version contains a July, 2000 date. Max Neuhaus, "Sound Art?" accessed June 20, 2015, http://www.max-neuhaus.info/ soundworks/soundart/SoundArt.htm. Max Neuhaus, "Sound Art?" 11.A.1172. MoMA PS Collection, The Museum of Modern Art Archives, NY.

17 Neuhaus, "Sound Art?" (both versions).

18 Kim-Cohen, *Against Ambience*, Kindle location 1242.

19 Neuhaus, "Sound Art?" (both versions).

20   I am drawing from Bruno Latour, "An Attempt at a 'Compositionist Manifesto,'" *New Literary History* 41 (2010): 471–90. Note that while Latour views "composition" as a departure from critique, for me criticality is one of composition's—and critical music's—central concerns.

21   Dahlhaus, *The Idea of Absolute Music*, 8.

22   Drobnick proposes a "sonic turn" as a correlate to W. J. T. Mitchell's "pictoral turn" and the broader "visual studies" paradigm in "Listening Awry," in *Aural Cultures*, ed. Jim Drobnick (Toronto and Banff: YYZ Books/WPG Editions), 10.

23   Another no less problematic perspective is that music is actually a *subset* of sound art. Such a view, however, would fail to take into account music's status before the advent of absolute music, that is, before music had been conceived as a purely "sonic art." Music as a subset of sound art would also introduce the taxonomical issue of a species that historically predates its own genus.

24   Osborne, *Anywhere or Not at All*, 102, emphasis in original.

25   Craig Douglas Dworkin, *No Medium* (Cambridge, MA: MIT Press, 2013); David Joselit, *After Art* (Princeton, NJ: Princeton University Press, 2013), 3.

26   Beyond a casual dismissal of "new music," this statement should be understood in the context of a larger project to reformulate music and its relation to a broader artistic and political field of practice. I make these comments, furthermore, not as a passive critic of "new music," but as someone intimately familiar with its institutions and who, through years of working in "new music" contexts, has participated in various efforts to challenge its premises both from within and without.

27   Of course, this is not to suggest that musicology (or sound art theory, for that matter) has been committed as a discipline to a defense of absolute music. On the contrary, many of absolute music's most penetrating and important critiques have arisen from within musicology.

28   "It is conceivable that music in the future will dispense with sound altogether and become an art of induced psychological, physiological states" (Eaton quoted in Branden W. Joseph, "Biomusic," in "On Brainwashing: Mind Control, Media, and Warfare," ed. Andreas Killen and Stefan Andriopoulos, special issue, *Grey Room* 45 [Fall 2011]: 134). Along these lines, we could also add Mauricio Kagel's *Con Voce for three mute players* (1972) and Dieter Schnebel's *Nostalgie for solo conductor* (1962).

29   Note that Straebel has contributed significantly to the German *Klangkunst* literature. Importantly, however, that movement is situated *within* musicology (or *Musikwissenschaft*). See also Andreas Engström and Åsa Stjerna, "Sound Art or *Klangkunst*? A reading of the German and English literature on sound art," *Organised Sound* 14 (2009): 11–18, doi:10.1017/S135577180900003X.

30   Kim-Cohen, *Against Ambience*, Kindle location 1228.

31 Personal communication with Antoine Beuger, June 15/17, 2011.

32 Beuger quoted in Dan Warburton, "The Sound of Silence: The Music and Aesthetics of the Wandelweiser Group," 2001, accessed June 23, 2011, http://www.wandelweiser.de.

33 Slavoj Žižek, "The True Blasphemy," in *Comradely Greetings: The Prison Letters of Nadya and Slavoj* (London: Verso, 2014), 12.

34 Anya Bernstein, "An Inadvertent Sacrifice: Body Politics and Sovereign Power in the Pussy Riot Affair," *Critical Inquiry* 40, no. 1 (Autumn 2013): 220–41, accessed November 14, 2014, http://criticalinquiry.uchicago.edu/an_inadvertent_sacrifice_body_politics_and_sovereign_power_in_the_pussy_rio.

35 Quoted in *Pussy Riot: A Punk Prayer "Pokazatelnyy Protsess: Istoriya Pussy Riot" (original title)*, director Mike Lerner, Maxim Pozdorovkin, performers Nadezhda Tolokonnikova, Mariya Alyokhina, Yekaterina Samutsevich, 2014, film.

36 Cassie Thornton, "We Make Debt," We Make Debt, accessed November 4, 2013, http://debt-material.tumblr.com/ask.

37 This is Žižek's formulation found in each of the foreword sections of his edited Short Circuits volumes, for example, Lorenzo Chiesa, *Subjectivity and Otherness: A Philosophical Reading of Lacan*, ed. Slavoj Žižek (Cambridge, MA: MIT Press, 2007).

38 Oliveros in Martha Mockus, *Sounding Out: Pauline Oliveros and Lesbian Musicality* (New York: Routledge, 2008), 155.

Chapter 1

1 Ultra-red, "Ultra-red: Organizing the Silence," in *On Horizons: A Critical Reader in Contemporary Art*, ed. Maria Hlavajova, Simon Sheikh, and Jill Winder (Rotterdam: Post Editions, 2011), 199.

2 Quoted in Caroline A. Jones, "Finishing School: John Cage and the Abstract Expressionist Ego," *Critical Inquiry* 19, no. 4 (Summer 1993): 665.

3 While I refer to Ultra-red as an "art/activist" collective, the group situate their own work in relation to sound art ("missionstatement," Ultra-red, 2000, accessed July 28, 2013, http://www.ultrared.org/mission.html), and often classify it explicitly as such ("PS/o6.b. encuentrolosangeles," Ultra-red, 2000, accessed July 28, 2013, http://www.ultrared.org/pso6b.html; "Organized Listening: Sound Art, Collectivity and Politics (Vogue-ology)," Vera List Center for Art and Politics, 2010, accessed July 28, 2013, http://www.veralistcenter.org/engage/event/216/organized-listening-sound-art-collectivity-and-politics). Others such as Roger Hallas refer to Ultra-red as a "sound collective" (*Reframing Bodies: AIDS, Bearing Witness, and the*

Queer Moving Image [Durham: Duke University Press, 2009], 242). Yet despite classifications of their work as "sound art," it is appropriate, for reasons that I hope will become clear throughout this chapter, to frame this work as critical music. See also G Douglas Barrett, "Ultra-red, *URXX Nos. 1–9*," *Tacet: Sound in the Arts*, no. 4 Sounds of Utopia/Sonorités de l'utopie (January, 2016): 540–555.

4   Ultra-red, "Ultra-red: PS/o8.i Silent Listen The Record," Ultra-red, 2006, accessed January 28, 2013, http://www.ultrared.org/pso8i.html.

5   Douglas Crimp, "Pictures," in *Appropriation*, ed. David Evans (London: Whitechapel, 2009), 78.

6   Guy Debord and Gil J. Wolman, "Directions for the Use of Détournement," in *Appropriation*, ed. David Evans (London: Whitechapel, 2009), 35.

7   Ibid.

8   Paul Mann, *Masocriticism* (Albany: State University of New York Press, 1998), 187.

9   Douglas Crimp, *Melancholia and Moralism: Essays on AIDS and Queer Politics* (Cambridge, MA: MIT Press, 2002), 161–62.

10 David Evans, "Introduction: Seven Types of Appropriation," in *Appropriation*, ed. David Evans (London: Whitechapel, 2009), 14.

11 Ibid., 16.

12 For an overview of the scholarship and a discussion of the discrepancies between the British-American and European debates, see Dorottya Fabian, "The Meaning of Authenticity and the Early Music Movement: A Historical Review," *International Review of the Aesthetics and Sociology of Music* 32, no. 2 (2001): 153–67.

13 Lydia Goehr, *The Imaginary Museum of Musical Works: An Essay in the Philosophy of Music* (New York: Oxford University Press, 1994), 115.

14 Ibid., 231.

15 See John Cage, *Silence: Lectures and Writings* (Middletown: Wesleyan University Press, 1961), 35–40.

16 Goehr, *The Imaginary Museum of Musical Works*, 260, 262.

17 Ibid., 262.

18 "Ripe for Embarrassment: For a New Musical Masochism" is, in Overton's words, "a manifesto . . . proposing a new paradigm in composer/performer relations, wherein the composer is a masochist who uses score-based Cagean indeterminacy in hopes of being humiliated by a willing performer" (Adam Overton, "Ripe for Embarrassment: For A New Musical Masochism, Matador Oven/Adam Overton," *The Experimental Music Yearbook*, accessed October 16, 2013, http://www. experimentalmusicyearbook.com/Ripe-for-Embarrassment-For-A-New-Musical-Masochism). See also the section discussing John Baldessari's *Baldessari Sings LeWitt*, "Composing Conceptual Art: *Baldessari Sings LeWitt*," in Chapter 3, and my discussion of Peter Ablinger's *Letter from Schoenberg* in Chapter 4.

19 Quoted in Jones, "Finishing School," 665.

20 Ibid.

21 Cage, *Silence*, 8.

22 T. Nikki Cesare-Bartnicki, "The Aestheticization of Reality: Postmodern Music, Art, and Performance" (PhD diss., New York University, 2008), 133. Another passage unites the themes of silence and death in a manner not unlike Cage's response to the "silence equals death" provocation. Found in "Juilliard Lecture" (*A Year from Monday: New Lectures and Writings* [Middletown: Wesleyan University Press, 1967], 95–111), and in "Lecture on Something" (Cage, *Silence*, 128–45), it provides a Zen-like statement following the image of Morton Feldman "submerged" in silence: "The nothing that goes on is what Feldman speaks of when he speaks of being submerged in silence. The acceptance of death is the source of all life" (Cage, *Silence*, 35; *A Year from Monday*, 98). For a sustained engagement with the themes of death and Cagean silence, see Jones, "Finishing School."

23 Jones, "Finishing School," 651–52.

24 Philip M. Gentry, "The Cultural Politics of 4′33″: Identity and Sexuality," *Tacet Experimental Music Review*, no. 1. Who Is John Cage? (2011): 36.

25 Jonathan Katz, "John Cage's Queer Silence; or, How to Avoid Making Matters Worse," *GLQ: A Journal of Lesbian and Gay Studies* 5, no. 2 (1999): 231–52, accessed July 27, 2012, http://www.queerculturalcenter.org/Pages/KatzPages/KatzWorse.html.

26 See *Empty Words: Writings '73–'78* (Middletown: Wesleyan University Press, 1981).

27 Katz, "John Cage's Queer Silence," 231.

28 Thomas S. Hines, "'Then Not Yet "Cage"': The Los Angeles Years, 1912–1938," in *John Cage: Composed in America*, ed. Marjorie Perloff and Charles Junkerman (Chicago: University of Chicago Press, 1994), 99n60.

29 Cage, *Silence*, 35–40.

30 Ultra-red, "Time for the Dead to have a Word with the Living: The AIDS Uncanny," *Journal of Aesthetics and Protest* 4 (2005): 91.

31 Ultra-red, "ps/o8publicmuseum," Ultra-red, 2000, accessed January 28, 2013, http://www.ultrared.org/pso8.html.

32 "Aesthetics of Indifference" is a phrase coined by Moira Roth. The "historically specific [mode of] queer resistance" is from Katz, "John Cage's Queer Silence," 241. See the section below, "Performing Silence."

33 Luke Nicholson, "Being Framed by Irony: AIDS and the Art of General Idea" (MA thesis, Concordia University, 2006), 53.

34 Bordowitz describes the ambivalent reception *Imagevirus* initially received in some cases—including his own—as being at odds with the work of activist groups like ACT UP; later, however, Bordowitz saw "General Idea's work [as] no less

political than the AIDS activists' work of the 1980s" (Gregg Bordowitz, *General Idea: Imagevirus* [London: Afterall, 2010], 77).

35 Bordowitz, *General Idea*, 17.

36 Douglas Crimp and Adam Rolston, *AIDS Demo Graphics* (Seattle: Bay, 1990), 15.

37 Crimp, *Melancholia*, 160–61. Regarding avant-garde theory, Peter Bürger has argued that Duchamp's ready-mades challenged the category of individual creation, signaling a turn toward collectivity (*Theory of the Avant-Garde*, trans. Michael Shaw [Minneapolis: University of Minnesota Press, 1984], 51–53).

38 Crimp and Rolston, *AIDS Demo Graphics*, 18.

39 The "logo" was created by the Silence = Death Project, a group of six gay men who were present at ACT UP's first meeting in 1987. As Avram Finkelstein notes, however, while often referred to as such, the SILENCE = DEATH design was not intended to serve as ACT UP's official insignia (Avram Finkelstein, "AIDS 2.0," Artwrit, December 2012, accessed January 28, 2013, http://www.artwrit.com/article/aids-2-0).

40 Robert Sember and David Gere, "'Let the Record Show . . .': Art Activism and the AIDS Epidemic," *American Journal of Public Health* 96, no. 6 (2006): 967, accessed January 28, 2013, http://www.ncbi.nlm.nih.gov/pmc/articles/PMC1470625.

41 Ibid.

42 Douglas Crimp, "AIDS: Cultural Analysis/Cultural Activism," *October* 43 (Winter 1987): 15.

43 Crimp, *Melancholia*, 31.

44 The full text is available from the New Museum's digital archive. ACT UP, "Let the Record Show . . .," New Museum Digital Archive, accessed January 28, 2013, http://archive.newmuseum.org/index.php/Detail/Occurrence/Show/occurrence_id/158.

45 Crimp and Rolston, *AIDS Demo Graphics*, 16.

46 *Kissing Doesn't Kill* was originally commissioned by "Art against AIDS on the Road," a public art project benefiting the American Foundation for AIDS Research (AmFAR); without giving a reason, AmFAR rejected Gran Fury's project containing the original rejoinder text (Richard Meyer, *Outlaw Representation: Censorship and Homosexuality in Twentieth-Century American Art* [New York: Oxford University Press, 2002], 237).

47 Meyer, *Outlaw Representation*, 236.

48 Ibid.

49 Crimp, *Melancholia*, 38.

50 Chantal Mouffe, *Democratic Politics and Agonistic Public Spaces* (Cambridge, MA: Harvard Graduate School of Design, April 17, 2012), lecture. See also Mouffe, *Agonistics*, 144.

51 Debord, "The Situationists and the New Forms," 164.

52 Ibid.

53 Debord quoted in Claire Bishop, *Artificial Hells: Participatory Art and the Politics of Spectatorship* (London: Verso, 2012), 83.

54 Chantal Mouffe, "Artistic Activism and Agonistic Spaces," *ART & RESEARCH: A Journal of Ideas, Contexts and Methods* 1, no. 2 (2007): 5, accessed January 28, 2013, http://www.artandresearch.org.uk/v1n2/mouffe.html.

55 Ibid., 4.

56 Ibid., 4–5.

57 Chantal Mouffe, "Beyond Cosmopolitanism," World Biennial Forum No. 1. Gwangju, South Korea, lecture, December 31, 2012, https://www.youtube.com/watch?v=VuNzi1rutIc.

58 Hallas, *Reframing Bodies*, 247.

59 Lauren Berlant, *Cruel Optimism* (Durham: Duke University Press, 2011), 248.

60 John Cage, *4'33"* (New York: Henmar Press, 1962).

61 Benjamin Piekut, *Experimentalism Otherwise: The New York Avant-Garde and Its Limits* (Berkeley: University of California Press, 2011), 143.

62 Ibid.

63 Ibid., 172.

64 Eastman's performance was the subject of a collaboration between artist Adam Overton and myself. Working first from the audio recording available at the SUNY at Buffalo Music Library, he and I constructed a "transcription" of the stage actions and speech following a series of interviews with two of the audience members (Arnold Dreyblatt and Ronald Kuivila), and Petr Kotik, who also performed in the original 1975 June in Buffalo concert. We realized the project as a homoerotic reinterpretation of Eastman's performance, involving a series of choreographed sex acts, champagne drinking, and three other performers reading Eastman's speech, all of which took place as part of Overton's *BESHT (Bureau of Experimental Speech and Holy Theses)* series at the Pomona College Museum on December 6, 2012.

65 From State University of New York at Buffalo. Music Dept., *Recordings of June in Buffalo, 1975-1978, 1980*, 1980, Buffalo Music Library, Mus. Arc., 30. Transcribed as "any GOD DAMN THING" in Steven Schlegel, "John Cage at June in Buffalo, 1975" (MA thesis, State University of New York, Buffalo, 2008), 31.

66 Quoted in Schlegel, "John Cage at June in Buffalo, 1975," 31.

67 Ibid.

68 Douglas Kahn, "John Cage: Silence and Silencing," *The Musical Quarterly* 81, no. 4 (1997): 557.

69 Ibid.

70 Ibid., 556.

71 While Kahn's work is regularly associated with "sound art," he is careful not to endorse the term as such, preferring the "more generic [phrase] *sound in the arts*"

(Douglas Kahn, "The Arts of Sound Art and Music," *The Iowa Review* [2006]: 1, accessed July 28, 2014, http://www.douglaskahn.com/writings/douglas_kahn-sound_art.pdf).

72 Kahn, "John Cage: Silence and Silencing," 557.

73 Moira Roth and Jonathan Katz, *Difference/Indifference: Musings on Postmodernism, Marcel Duchamp and John Cage* (Amsterdam: G+B Arts International, 1998), 35.

74 Ibid., 37–38.

75 Ibid., 40.

76 Ibid., 53.

77 Ibid., 54–55.

78 Ibid., 53.

79 Ibid., 62.

80 Ibid., 64.

81 Ibid.

82 Debord, "The Situationists and the New Forms," 164.

83 Ultra-red, "Ultra-red: Organizing the Silence," 201.

84 Ibid., 195.

85 Edgard Varèse, "The Electronic Medium (1962)," 18.

86 Hallas, *Reframing Bodies*, 248. See Paulo Freire, *Pedagogy of the Oppressed*, 30th Anniversary ed. (New York: Continuum, 2000). See also the section "Materialism: Science, Education, (Social) Practice" in Chapter 5 for more on critical pedagogy.

87 Ultra-red, "Ultra-red: Organizing the Silence," 201.

88 A 2012 survey concluded that in 2010 there were approximately three deaths every hour in the United States due to a lack of health insurance (Families USA, "Dying for Coverage: The Deadly Consequences of Being Uninsured," accessed May 29, 2015, http://familiesusa.org/product/dying-coverage-deadly-consequences-being-uninsured). This number has likely dropped since 2010; however, even since the introduction of "Obamacare" in 2010, the percentage of uninsured Americans has only fallen from 16 percent to 14.6 percent. See "Lack of Health Insurance," America's Health Rankings, accessed May 29, 2015, http://www.americashealthrankings.org.

89 See Irene Hall, Ruiguang Song, Philip Rhodes, Joseph Prejean, Qian An, Lisa M. Lee, John Karon, Ron Brookmeyer, Edward H. Kaplan, Matthew T. McKenna, and Robert S. Janssen, "Estimation of HIV Incidence in the United States," *JAMA: The Journal of the American Medical Association* 300, no. 5 (2008): 520–29. I thank AIDS activist James Krellenstein for this reference and for his presentation on current HIV statistics given during an ACT UP meeting at the LGBT Center, New York, on April 29, 2013.

90 "Good people of Woodstock, let's drive these people out of town," was the reaction of one member of the crowd (quoted in David Revill, *The Roaring Silence: John*

Cage: A Life [New York: Arcade, 1993], 165–66). Relevantly, Christopher Butler has argued that the "critical point" of *4'33"* was its ability to startle audiences (quoted in Paul Mann, *The Theory-Death of the Avant-Garde* [Bloomington: Indiana University Press, 1991], 26).

91 I thank ACT UP member Michael Tikili for sharing with me his account of the action. See documentation at https://vimeo.com/54410856.

Chapter 2

1 Stephen Chase and Clemens Gresser, "Ordinary Matters: Christian Wolff on His Recent Music," *Tempo* 58, no. 229 (July 2004): 22.

2 Radu Malfatti quoted in Dan Warburton, "The Sound of Silence: The Music and Aesthetics of the Wandelweiser Group," 2001, accessed June 23, 2011, http://www.wandelweiser.de.

3 Personal communication, June 15/17, 2011.

4 Michael Pisaro, "erstwards: September 2009," September 2009, accessed August 28, 2011, http://erstwords.blogspot.com/2009_09_01_archive.html.

5 Beuger quoted in Warburton, "The Sound of Silence."

6 See Andreas Schlothauer, *Die Diktatur Der Freien Sexualität: AAO, Mühl-Kommune* (Vienna: Verlag für Gesellschaftskritik, 1992), 19–20, http://www.agpf.de/Schlothauer-AAO-Muehl.htm; see also Robert Fleck, *Die Mühl-Kommune: Freie Sexualität und Aktionismus: Geschichte eines Experiments* (Köln: Walther König, 2003), 50–51. My translations of both texts are used throughout. My thanks to Sarah M. Schmidt for her translation help.

7 Schlothauer, *Die Diktatur Der Freien Sexualität*, 11.

8 Ibid., 17.

9 Fleck, *Die Mühl-Kommune*, 156.

10 Ibid., 156–57.

11 Gilles Deleuze and Félix Guattari, *A Thousand Plateaus: Capitalism and Schizophrenia*, trans. Brian Massumi (Minneapolis: University of Minnesota Press, 1987), 21.

12 Fleck, *Die Mühl-Kommune*, 156.

13 Personal communication, June 15/17, 2011.

14 Ibid.

15 Schlothauer, *Die Diktatur*, 172–73; Fleck, *Die Mühl-Kommune*, 213.

16 Personal communication, June 15/17, 2011.

17 Schlothauer, *Die Diktatur Der Freien Sexualität*, 13.

18 Fleck, *Die Mühl-Kommune*, 142.

19   Personal communication, June 15/17, 2011.

20   Samuel Vriezen, "Componistengroep Wandelweiser. Samuel Vriezen," 2007, accessed June 27, 2011, http://sqv.home.xs4all.nl/wandelweiser.html. My thanks to Taylan Susam for his translation from the Dutch original.

21   Personal communication, June 15/17, 2011.

22   Fleck, *Die Mühl-Kommune*, 255.

23   Or was it a quiet music seminar? The multiple translations of *Stille* add a subtle ambiguity to the character of the event.

24   Fondation Foyer Des Artistes Boswil, "10. Internationales Kompositionsseminar Boswil, 10-14.11.91 Juryentscheidung [letter]," September 14, 1991, 4. My thanks to Nicholas Melia for sharing his research on the *Stille Musik* seminar. See Nicholas Melia, "*Stille Musik*—Wandelweiser and the Voices of Ontological Silence," in "Wandelweiser," ed. James Saunders, special issue, *Contemporary Music Review* 30, no. 5 (December 2011): 471–95.

25   In Germany at least, Schnebel has been associated with Cage to the extent that *Stille Musik* jury member Marianne Schroeder was compelled to wonder if he could be called "*Ein deutscher Cage*"? (in *Schnebel 60*, ed. Werner Grünzweig, Gesine Schröder, and Martin Supper [Hofheim: Wolke, 1990], 65–67). It is not clear, however, to what extent Schnebel saw the work of Cage as related to the seminar theme, *Stille Musik*.

26   Regarding the reception of Cage at this time, Werder notes a general aura in Europe in which American experimental music (Morton Feldman, Wolff, Cage) was particularly influential (personal communication, November 21, 2010). Wolff recalls that the jurists were "all serious in their appreciation of John Cage," but notes that this was not to be assumed of all European new music circles at the time (personal communication, June 26, 2011).

27   Jürg Frey, "And On it Went," 2004, accessed July 3, 2011, http://www.wandelweiser. de/frey/JFand.pdf.

28   Christian Wolff, "Quiet Music: On a Composition Seminar in Boswil," in *Cues: Writings & Conversations/Hinweise: Schriften und Gespräche*, ed. Christian Wolff (Köln: MusikTexte, 1998), 232.

29   Ibid.

30   Following their participation in the Boswil seminar, Jürg Frey and Chico Mello were both invited to join Wandelweiser during its first year of operation. Werder, a native of Boswil, attended some of the concerts presented as part of the seminar and was impressed by Frey's work. The two did not meet, however, until 1995 during Werder's residence in Paris. Werder was invited to join Wandelweiser and, as mentioned in this chapter's introduction, became a member in 1997.

31   Chase and Gresser, "Ordinary Matters," 22.

32 Bruno Latour, *Reassembling the Social: An Introduction to Actor-Network-Theory* (Oxford: Oxford University Press, 2005), 31.

33 Ibid.

34 Members have cited George Brecht, James Tenney, and La Monte Young among many others. Closely associated with Wandelweiser, the work of Hungarian-born Swiss artist and composer István Zelenka contains many ostensible similarities to Fluxus. See, for example, his *Versuchen wir die Sachen so zu ordnen, dass das Resultat nie endgültig wird* (2005), a score containing a broad range of instructions for producing various actions and instrumental and vocal sounds.

35 Hannah Higgins, *Fluxus Experience* (Berkeley, CA: University of California Press, 2002), 81.

36 Renato Poggioli, *The Theory of the Avant-Garde* (Cambridge, MA: Belknap of Harvard University Press, 1968), 17.

37 Ibid., 25, emphasis in original.

38 One can appropriately cite Adorno in this regard. In his *Introduction to the Sociology of Music,* trans. E. B. Ashton (New York: Continuum, 1988), music's claim to autonomy since the Enlightenment is seen as false consciousness in light of its commodity status. There are, however, enough differences between Wandelweiser and the music championed by Adorno, the "classical avant-garde," to warrant a theoretical departure as well.

39 Bürger, *Theory of the Avant-Garde*, 35–36.

40 Mann, *The Theory-Death of the Avant-Garde*, 8.

41 Pisaro, "erstwards."

42 Higgins, *Fluxus Experience*, 81.

43 Malfatti quoted in *Audio Culture: Readings in Modern Music*, ed. Christoph Cox and Daniel Warner (London: Continuum, 2004), 64.

44 While it is not a primary focus, certain Wandelweiser works have addressed popular music in some instances. Michael Pisaro's *Tombstones* (2006/10), for example, consists of a series of pieces composed from fragments of existing blues, rock, and rap songs. Pisaro has elsewhere emphasized his ongoing appreciation of rock 'n' roll and Motown ("Hit or miss [*Treffer oder daneben*]," in *MusikDenken: Texte der Wandelweiser-Komponisten,* ed. Eva-Maria Houben and Burkhard Schlothauer [Zürich: Edition Howeg, 2008], 55–59, published online 2004, accessed October 28, 2011, http://www.wandelweiser.de/pisaro/MPTexte_e.html#hit).

45 Quoted in Warburton, "The Sound of Silence," emphasis added.

46 Ibid.

47 Vriezen, "Componistengroep Wandelweiser."

48 Quoted in Warburton, "The Sound of Silence."

49 James Pritchett, "What silence taught John Cage," *L'anarquia del silenci: John Cage i l'art experimental, Museu d'Art Contemporani de Barcelona*, Barcelona, October 23, 2009 to January 10, 2010, accessed July 3, 2011, http://www.rosewhitemusic.com/ cage/texts/What SilenceTaughtCage.html.

50 See Kahn, "John Cage: Silence and Silencing."

51 John Cage, "Defense of Satie (1948)," in *John Cage: An Anthology*, ed. Richard Kostelanetz (New York: Da Capo, 1991), 77–84.

52 See Kahn, "John Cage: Silence and Silencing," 581.

53 Liz Kotz, *Words to Be Looked At: Language in 1960s Art* (Cambridge, MA: MIT Press, 2007), 18. Containing a 1960 copyright, the score's 1961 publication date has been contested (ibid., 268–269n10).

54 Ibid.

55 Quoted in Warburton, "The Sound of Silence."

56 Ian Pepper, "From the 'Aesthetics of Indifference' to 'Negative Aesthetics': John Cage and Germany. 1957–1972," *October* 82 (1997): 34.

57 In James Saunders, "Antoine Beuger," in *The Ashgate Research Companion to Experimental Music,* ed. James Saunders (Farnham, UK: Ashgate, 2004), 231.

58 Osborne quoted in Kim-Cohen, *In the Blink of an Ear*, 158. See the next chapter for an extended discussion of conceptual art and music.

59 Kim-Cohen, *In the Blink of an Ear*, 167.

60 Quoted in Mann, *The Theory-Death of the Avant-Garde*, 26.

61 Ibid., 27.

62 Jacques Derrida, *The Truth in Painting*, trans. Geoffrey Bennington and Ian McLeod (Chicago: University of Chicago Press, 1987), 212, 331.

63 Martina Viljoen, "Questions of Musical Meaning: An Ideology-Critical Approach / Problemi Glazbenog Značenja: Ideološko-Kritički Pristup," *International Review of the Aesthetics and Sociology of Music* 35, no. 1 (June 2004): 21.

64 Pritchett, "What silence taught John Cage."

65 Derrida, *The Truth in Painting*, 7.

66 Mann, *Theory-Death*, 30.

67 Recently, in the US press, Wandelweiser were called "a small coterie of mostly European post-John Cage composers" (Peter Margasak, "Best Place to Hear Work by Wandelweiser Group Composers | Best of Chicago 2011 | Music & Nightlife | Chicago Reader. Chicago Reader | Chicago's Guide to Music, Movies, Arts, Theater, Restaurants, and Politics 2011," accessed June 27, 2011, http://www. chicagoreader.com/chicago/best-place-to-hear-work-by-wandelweiser-group-composers/BestOf?oid1/44102977).

68 Manfred Werder, "2006[1] [CD liner notes]," in *2006[1]*, perfs. Tetuzi Akiyama, Masahiko Okura, and Toshiya Tsunoda (Tokyo: Skiti, 2006).

69   Michael Pisaro, "Writing, Music," in *The Ashgate Research Companion to Experimental Music*, ed. James Saunders (Farnham, UK: Ashgate, 2009), 63.

70   Quoted in Warburton, "The Sound of Silence."

71   Personal communication, June 15/17, 2011.

72   Antoine Beuger, "Grundsätzliche Entscheidungen," in *MusikDenken: Texte der Wandelweiser-Komponisten*, ed. Eva-Maria Houben and Burkhard Schlothauer (Zürich: Edition Howeg, 2008), 120, published online 1997, accessed July 3, 2011, http://www.wandelweiser.de/beuger/ABTexte.html#grund. My translation.

73   Volker Straebel, "Aspects of Conceptual Composing," *The Open Space Magazine* 10 (Fall 2008): 70–71.

74   Ibid., 76.

75   Ibid., 71, emphasis added.

76   Beuger quoted in Warburton, "The Sound of Silence," emphasis added.

77   Bürger, *Theory of the Avant-Garde*, 91.

78   My thanks to Lindsey Lodhie for her suggestions pertaining to this interpretation.

79   John Cage, / 4'33" andrestorresREVOC, accessed July 3, 2007, https://www.youtube.com/watch?v=WYQhXN1UFbU.

80   Ultra-red, "missionstatement," 2000, accessed July 28, 2013, http://www.ultrared.org/mission.html.

81   Terre Thaemlitz, "Please Tell My Landlord Not to Expect Future Payments Because Attali's Theory of Surplus-Value-Generating Information Economics Only Works if My Home Studio's Rent and Other Use-Values are Zero," in *Immediacy and Non-Simultaneity: Utopia of Sound*, ed. Diedrich Diederichsen and Constanze Ruhm (Vienna: Schlebrügge, 2010), 78.

82   Ibid.

83   Ibid.

84   Ibid., 84.

85   Ibid.

86   Although Ultra-red's work is often contextualized as sound art, the term remains inadequate for an understanding of their work, as I argued in the previous chapter.

87   Manfred Werder, "Statement on Indeterminacy," in *Word Events: Perspectives on Verbal Notation*, ed. John Lely and James Saunders (New York: Continuum, 2012), 381.

88   In Patrick Müller, *Manfred Werder. Contemporary Swiss Composers* (Zürich: Pro Helvetia, 2002), 4.

89   Michel Foucault, *Archaeology of Knowledge*, trans. A. M. Sheridan Smith (London: Routledge, 2002), 119, 122.

90   Ibid., 122.

91   Gilles Deleuze, *Foucault*, trans. Sean Hand (London: Continuum, 2006), 4.

92 Foucault, *Archaeology of Knowledge*, 126.

93 Derrida, *The Truth in Painting*, 121.

94 In this case, however, the score was in fact displayed to the audience following Werder's *2010¹* performance at the Incidental Music event in Zürich.

95 In James Saunders, "Manfred Werder," in *The Ashgate Research Companion to Experimental Music*, ed. James Saunders (Farnham, UK: Ashgate, 2004), 353.

96 Personal communication, June 28, 2011.

97 Michel Foucault, "What is An Author? (1969)," in *The Essential Foucault: Selections from Essential Works of Foucault, 1954–1984,* ed. Paul Rabinow and Nikolas S. Rose (New York: The New Press, 2003), 382.

98 Ibid., 391.

99 Bürger, *Theory of the Avant-Garde*, 51–53.

100 Werder in Müller, *Manfred Werder*, 4.

101 Latour, *Reassembling the Social*, 41.

102 Leo Bersani uses the phrase "new relational modes" to describe the urgent social and ethical project Foucault had conceived wherein homosexuality was to be given a privileged role. See Leo Bersani, *Is the Rectum a Grave?: And Other Essays* (Chicago: University of Chicago Press, 2010) and Michel Foucault, "Friendship as a Way of Life," in *Ethics: Subjectivity and Truth*, ed. Paul Rabinow, trans. Robert Hurley (New York: New Press, 1997), 135–62.

103 Werder, "*2006¹* [CD liner notes]."

Chapter 3

1 Gleb Bryanski, "Russian patriarch calls Putin era 'miracle of God,'" *Reuters* (February 8, 2012), http://uk.reuters.com/article/2012/02/08/uk-russia-putin-religion-idUKTRE81722Y20120208.

2 Quoted in Marc Bennetts, *Kicking the Kremlin: Russia's New Dissidents and the Battle to Topple Putin* (London: Oneworld, 2014), 138.

3 Ibid.

4 Anya Bernstein, "An Inadvertent Sacrifice. Body Politics and Sovereign Power in the Pussy Riot Affair," *Critical Inquiry* 40, no. 1 (Autumn 2013): 220–41, accessed November 14, 2014, http://criticalinquiry.uchicago.edu/an_inadvertent_sacrifice_body_politics_and_sovereign_power_in_the_pussy_rio.

5 RT, "Putin: Assange case exposes UK double standards (Exclusive Interview)," September 6, 2012, https://www.youtube.com/watch?v=UB45clPRNoc&feature=youtu.be&t=20m52s.

6 BBC News, "Russian MPs back harsher anti-blasphemy law," April 10, 2013, http://www.bbc.com/news/world-europe-22090308.

7   Masha Gessen and Joseph Huff-Hannon, introduction to *Gay Propaganda: Russian Love Stories*, ed. Masha Gessen and Joseph Huff-Hannon (New York and London: OR Books, 2014).

8   A significant influence on Pussy Riot, Moscow conceptualist poet Dmitri Prigov, prior to his death, collaborated on an action with Voina, the art collective that contained members who went on to form Pussy Riot. See Masha Gessen, *Words Will Break Cement: The Passion of Pussy Riot* (New York: Penguin, 2014), e-book ed., 29–37. Relevantly, Groys has contended that "contemporary Russian art perceives itself as remaining in the tradition of Moscow conceptualism and still relates to this tradition—be it in a positive or polemical way" (*History Becomes Form: Moscow Conceptualism* [Cambridge, MA: MIT Press, 2010], 33).

9   Nadieszda Kizenko, "Feminized Patriarchy? Orthodoxy and Gender in Post-Soviet Russia," *Signs* 38, no. 3 (2013): 596.

10 Jeffers Engelhardt, "Right Singing in Estonian Orthodox Christianity: A Study of Music, Theology, and Religious Ideology," *Ethnomusicology* 53, no. 1 (2009): 36.

11 Ibid., 42.

12 Engelhardt, "Right Singing," 33.

13 Ibid., 32.

14 Ibid., 37.

15 Several Pussy Riot actions have revolved around gay rights in Russia, and Samutsevich has been a vocal supporter of the Russian LGBT community. See Anastasia Kirilenko, "Freed Pussy Riot Member Yekaterina Samutsevich: 'Art Must Be Political,'" October 12, 2012, accessed January 26, 2015, http://www.theatlantic.com/international/archive/2012/10/freed-pussy-riot-member-yekaterina-samutsevich-art-must-be-political/263561.

16 Ruth Wallace, "Catholic Women and the Creation of a New Social Reality," *Gender and Society* 2, no. 1 (1998): 24. Cited in Nadieszda, "Feminized Patriarchy?" 597.

17 Quoted in *Pussy Riot: A Punk Prayer "Pokazatelnyy Protsess: Istoriya Pussy Riot" (original title)*, director Mike Lerner, and Maxim Pozdorovkin, performers Nadezhda Tolokonnikova, Mariya Alyokhina, Yekaterina Samutsevich, 2014, film.

18 Quoted in Gessen, *Words Will Break Cement*, 139.

19 Slavoj Žižek, "The True Blasphemy," in *Comradely Greetings: The Prison Letters of Nadya and Slavoj* (London: Verso, 2014), 12.

20 Consider, for example, Žižek's offhanded remarks on Andreas Serrano's well-known 1987 work *Piss Christ* in *Living in the End Times* (London: Verso, 2011), 325. The philosopher parodies a *New York Times* article on Serrano by describing himself defecating in explicit detail.

21 Lucy R. Lippard, "Escape Attempts," in *Six Years: The Dematerialization of the Art Object from 1966 to 1972; A Cross-Reference Book of Information on Some Esthetic Boundaries* . . . (Berkeley: University of California Press, 1973), vii.

22 In an essay on the Moscow conceptualists, Boris Groys provides a poignant inversion of this early contention of conceptual art wherein the art object's "dematerialization" was viewed as an escape from commodification through the use of language. Rather than leading "the artwork to immateriality or liberat[ing] it from commerce," Groys contends, "conceptual art can rather be seen as a crucial step toward objectifying and hence commercializing language" (Groys, *History Becomes Form*, 82–83).

23 With "proposal form" I refer to the ways conceptual art can outline a work to be constructed, performed, etc., without such a construction ever being executed. This is distinguished from Joseph Kosuth's conceptual "proposition." See the section below "Composing Conceptual Art: *Baldessari Sings LeWitt.*"

24 The actual passage from Kosuth's "Art After Philosophy" (1969) essay reads, "All art (after Duchamp) is conceptual (in nature) because art only exists conceptually" (in *Art After Philosophy and After: Collected Writings, 1966-1990* [Cambridge, MA: MIT Press, 1991], 18).

25 Osborne, *Anywhere or Not at All*, 51.

26 Ibid., 48.

27 Kosuth, "Art After Philosophy," 18.

28 Despite authoring numerous textual works, Kosuth has never, to my knowledge, completely abandoned material forms. For example, his *Art as Idea as Idea* series, which began in 1966, consists of single words and their respective definitions rendered as photostat prints. Nevertheless, for Kosuth the material form remains secondary, as the artist claims, "I never wanted anyone to think that I was presenting a photostat as a work of art" (Kosuth, "Art After Philosophy," 30).

29 Krauss, *A Voyage on the North Sea*, 56.

30 Osborne, *Anywhere or Not at All*, 108–9, italics in original.

31 Ibid., 48, emphasis in original.

32 Ibid., 102, emphasis in original.

33 Ibid., 46.

34 My discussion of this topic continues below in "The *Matter(ing)* of Absolute Music."

35 Žižek, "The True Blasphemy," 12.

36 Interestingly, Berkeley's philosophy is described as a form of "immaterialism" in Marc A. Hight, "Idea Ontology and the Early Modern Tale," in *Idea and Ontology: An Essay in Early Modern Metaphysics of Ideas* (University Park, PA: Pennsylvania State University Press, 2008), 1–10.

37 Philosopher and theoretical physicist Karen Barad provides a similar play on the words "matter" and "mattering" in her quantum physics-influenced Derridian materialism. See Karen M. Barad, *Meeting the Universe Halfway: Quantum*

Physics and the Entanglement of Matter and Meaning (Durham: Duke University Press, 2007).

38   Slavoj Žižek, *Absolute Recoil: Towards a New Foundation of Dialectical Materialism* (London: Verso, 2014), 5.

39   Ibid.

40   Slavoj Žižek, *The Parallax View* (Cambridge, MA: MIT Press, 2006), 168.

41   Ibid.

42   Adrian Johnston, *Adventures in Transcendental Materialism: Dialogues with Contemporary Thinkers* (Edinburgh: Edinburgh University Press, 2014), 128.

43   Ibid.

44   Slavoj Žižek, *Less Than Nothing: Hegel and the Shadow of Dialectical Materialism* (London: Verso, 2012), 920.

45   Žižek, *The Parallax View*, 245.

46   Žižek, "The True Blasphemy," 12.

47   Kosuth, "Art After Philosophy," 30. Compare to Lippard's "dematerialization."

48   Maria Chehonadskih, "Commentary: What Is Pussy Riot's 'Idea'?" *Radical Philosophy* 176 (November/December, 2012): 1–7, published online, http://www.radicalphilosophy.com/commentary/what-is-pussy-riots-idea.

49   Quoted in *Pussy Riot: A Punk Prayer*, film.

50   Alexander Alberro, "Reconsidering Conceptual Art, 1966–1977," in *Conceptual Art: A Critical Anthology*, ed. Alexander Alberro and Blake Stimson (Cambridge, MA: MIT Press, 1999), xx.

51   Sol LeWitt, "Paragraphs on Conceptual Art," in *Conceptual Art: A Critical Anthology*, ed. Alexander Alberro and Blake Stimson (Cambridge, MA: MIT Press, 1999), 12. Regarding the link between LeWitt's 1969 work *Sentences on Conceptual Art* (see next section) and mechanization, Osborne concludes that LeWitt is "a *romantic in the age of mechanization*—not romantically *against* mechanization, but romantically appropriating, or coming to terms with mechanization itself, as the means for romanticization" (Osborne, *Anywhere or Not At All*, 66).

52   Žižek, *Absolute Recoil*, 55, emphasis removed.

53   Ibid., 56.

54   If we take the second part of Kosuth's famous line *literally*, "All art (after Duchamp) is conceptual (in nature) because art only exists conceptually" (Kosuth, "Art After Philosophy," 18), then he is an idealist: art *only* exists conceptually, as an idea. Regarding sound and music, Kane has characterized Kim-Cohen as a Derridian "sonic idealist" ("Musicophobia").

55   There are other important historical links between music and conceptual art that deserve mention. Artist and musician Henry Flynt, for example, coined the musically derived notion of "concept art" as early as 1961, years before "conceptual art" had been proposed. Interestingly, Flynt's point of departure for

"concept art"—and "concept music"—was not texted music but the mathematical "structures" of musical high modernism (e.g., integral serialism). See Branden W. Joseph, "Concept Art," in *Beyond the Dream Syndicate: Tony Conrad and the Arts after Cage* (New York: Zone Books, 2008), 153–212.

I have chosen not to concentrate on Flynt's work here for various reasons. As opposed to Kosuth's goal of transcending individual mediums, for example, "concept art" can be seen as proceeding through a "medium-based conception of conceptual art" (Osborne, *Anywhere or Not at All*, 103). Extending such an understanding to music, Flynt explains, "*Concept art* is first of all an art of which the material is *concepts*, as the material of e.g. music is sound" ("Essay: Concept Art [Provisional Version]," in *An Anthology*, ed. La Monte Young [New York: La Monte Young and Jackson Mac Low, 1963], n.p.). It is important to acknowledge Flynt's preeminent contribution to the intersections between conceptual art and music, especially since his work is often underrepresented in art-historical accounts. Yet his expressedly "medium-based" conception of music as sound ("the material of . . . music is sound") is one the present volume seeks to challenge. I thank Seth Kim-Cohen for his questions related to this subject in preparation for *Singing LeWitt: Sound and Conceptualism*, a panel discussion organized by Kim-Cohen for the 104th Annual College Art Association Conference, February 5, 2016, Washington, DC.

56 Dahlhaus, *The Idea of Absolute Music*, 11.

57 Written toward the end of 1968, the *Sentences* were published in 1969 in the journals *0–9* and *Art-Language* (Osborne, *Anywhere or Not at All*, 53–54).

58 Osborne, *Anywhere or Not at All*, 53–69. Incidentally, fragment number 444 of Schlegel's *Anathenaeum Fragments* contains an early reference to "pure music" (or absolute music).

59 Mel Bochner also notes a connection between the serial*ity* of conceptual art and serial*ism* in the dodecaphonic, or twelve-tone music of composers such as Arnold Schoenberg or Milton Babbitt in "The Serial Attitude," in *Conceptual Art: A Critical Anthology*, ed. Alexander Alberro and Blake Stimson (Cambridge, MA: MIT Press, 1999), 24. Organizationally, serial music and seriality are both concerned with ordering, iteration, and repeatability. For a recent perspective on (contemporary experimental) music and seriality in conceptual art, see James Saunders, "Testing the Consequences: Seriality in the work of the Wandelweiser composers" in "Wandelweiser," ed. James Saunders, special issue, *Contemporary Music Review* 30, no. 5 (December 2011): 497–524.

60 Osborne, *Anywhere or Not at All*, 66.

61 David Platzker, "Art by Telephone" (Chicago: Museum of Contemporary Art, 1969), Specific Object, accessed January 22, 2015, http://www.specificobject.com/projects/art_by_telephone/#.VaV2axaNuRk. I thank Lindsey Lodhie for suggesting this reference.

62   LeWitt, "Paragraphs," 12.

63   Baldessari's 1970 text score *Fifteen Musical Projects. An Exchange with Pauline Oliveros* also provides an explicit connection between conceptual art's "proposal form" and music composition. The work consists of a list of fifteen descriptions of inventive, somewhat tongue-in-cheek proposals for musical performances. In many instances the difficulty or absurdity of the "project" in question only seems to heighten the work's character as "proposal." Number 6, for example, reads, "Musicians dress like various birds, use assorted bird whistles, sit in trees. An outdoor composition." In that excerpt, Baldessari and Oliveros make reference to composition; elsewhere in the work they refer to scores, conductors, music critics, audience members, performers, and participants. *Fifteen Musical Projects* is also constructed in a series, which can be compared to the serial form of LeWitt's *Sentences on Conceptual Art*.

64   Straebel, "Aspects of Conceptual Composing," 72.

65   Krauss, *Voyage*, 10.

66   One is tempted here to elaborate these features as part of a more generalized aesthetic of masculine abjection also characteristic of several other artists of the era (e.g., Vito Acconci).

67   Alenka Zupančič, *The Odd One in: On Comedy* (Cambridge, MA: MIT Press, 2008), 52.

68   Ibid., 32.

69   Lawrence Weiner, *Statement of Intent*, 1968, first published in *January 5–31, 1969*, exhibition catalogue (New York: Seth Siegelaub, 1969), unpaginated. Weiner dates the *Statement* 1968 despite its 1969 publication.

70   In Alberro, *Conceptual Art: A Critical Anthology*, xxii. Note, however, that Weiner also stated, "There's no way to build a piece incorrectly" (quoted in Alberro, xxxiii, note 20).

71   The numerous parodies of *Baldessari Sings LeWitt* found through even a cursory web search might be indicative of the powerful crossover appeal between appropriation art and music "covers"—or, by a similar token, contemporary art and the (pop) song. See, for example, "Justin Bieber Sings John Baldessari Sings Sol Lewitt," http://vimeo.com/43132365.

72   Stefan Gronert, "Trying to See the World Differently," in *John Baldessari: Music*, ed. Stefan Gronert and Christina Végh (Köln: König, 2007), 114.

73   The phrase "male homosocial desire" was first elaborated by Eve Kosofsky Sedgwick in her classic 1985 text *Between Men: English Literature and Male Homosocial Desire* (New York: Columbia University Press). In coining the term, she intended to hypothesize the "unbrokenness of a continuum between homosocial and homosexual—a continuum whose visibility, for man, in our society, is radically disrupted" (1–2). Nadine Hubbs is one of a small group of

writers who focus on gender and sexuality in twentieth-century American music. ✓
See *The Queer Composition of America's Sound: Gay Modernists, American Music, and National Identity* (Berkeley: University of California, 2004), particularly "Being Musical: Gender, Sexuality, and Musical Identity in Twentieth-Century America" (64–102).

74 Rosalind Krauss, "Video: The Aesthetics of Narcissism," *October* 1 (Spring 1976): 50–64.

75 A viewer may expect the first-person pronoun if only given other titles of Baldessari's art works, for example, the above-cited 1971 video *Some Words I Mispronounce.*

76 Groys, *Art Power*, 2.

77 This paradox-contradiction structure shared between jokes and conceptual art is evident in the reaction, "Ah, I get it . . ."

78 Bonds, "Idealism and the Aesthetics of Instrumental Music at the Turn of the Nineteenth Century," 387.

79 Fragment number 444: "Many people find it strange and ridiculous when musicians talk about the ideas in their compositions. . . . Doesn't pure instrumental music have to create its own text? And aren't the themes in it developed, reaffirmed, varied, and contrasted in the same way as the subject of meditation in a philosophical succession of ideas?" *Philosophical Fragments*, trans. P. Firchow (Minneapolis: University of Minneapolis Press, 1991), 92.

80 Quoted in Bonds, "Idealism," 391.

81 Dahlhaus, *The Idea of Absolute Music*, 9.

82 Ibid., 7.

83 Ibid., 8.

84 Ibid., 18.

85 Eduard Hanslick, *The Beautiful in Music (Musikalisch-Schönen)*, trans. Gustav Cohen (New York: H. W. Gray, 1891), 12.

86 In his reading of Otakar Hostinský's *The Beautiful in Music and the Complete Art Work from the Viewpoint of Formal Esthetics* (1877), Dahlhaus makes a similar point regarding Hostinský's attempts to mediate between Wagner and Eduard Hanslick: "Strikingly, even the [a]estheticians of content accepted Hanslick's risky distinction between 'musical' and 'extra-musical' forces instead of reverting to the older [a]esthetic paradigm that had preceded the romantic metaphysics of instrumental music, i.e., that 'music' incorporated *logos* as well as *harmonia* and *rhythmos*. Without their perceiving it, the position they in fact held had already been yielded terminologically" (Dahlhaus, *The Idea of Absolute Music*, 37).

87 This, the considerably bolder version of the passage, is found in the January 1987 issue of the *Minnesota Composers Forum*, 8, before it appeared in *Feminine*

Endings: Music, Gender, and Sexuality (Minneapolis: University of Minnesota Press, 1991), 127–28.

88 In her 2004 essay, "Questions of Musical Meaning: An Ideology-Critical Approach," Martina Viljoen lists some of these critiques (9n10) including Tia DeNora, *Beethoven and the Construction of Musical Genius: Musical Politics in Vienna, 1792-1803* (Berkeley: University of California Press, 1995); Stephen Miles, "Critics of Disenchantment," *Notes* 52, no. 1 (September 1995): 11–38; and Nicholas Cook, "Theorising Musical Meaning," *Music Theory Spectrum* 23, no. 2 (2001): 170–95. Viljoen's own engagement with McClary stems from a unique encounter between formalism and musical meaning.

89 Lawrence Kramer, *Musical Meaning: Toward a Critical History* (Berkeley: University of California Press, 2002), 146.

90 As an illustration of having "terminologically lost" the argument of absolute music, in the new preface to *Feminine Endings*, McClary explains that "the essays performed cultural interpretations not only of lyrics and dramatic plots but also *of the music itself*" (x). Surely, by "*the music itself*" we wouldn't expect anything more (or less) than absolute music.

91 Kim-Cohen, *In the Blink of an Ear*, 39.

92 Ibid., 40.

93 It is important to note that Kim-Cohen has more recently offered a conception of music somewhat at odds with *In the Blink of an Ear*. In *Against Ambiance* he introduces the possibility of an "expanded palette of musical terms" and implies that music should borrow Krauss's notion of an "expanded field" as formerly applied to sculpture (Kindle location 276).

94 Žižek, *Comradely Greetings*, 34.

95 Ibid., 58. Žižek first criticizes Tolokonnikova's invocation of the Nietzschean couple of Dionysus and Apollo and cites Brian Massumi's Deleuze-inspired characterization of the way capitalism supposedly overcomes these kinds of binaries and hierarchies (ibid., 48–49). Tolokonnikova responds by asserting that contemporary capitalism thrives on "anti-hierarchic" and "rhizomatic" structures, which, taken together, amount to "good advertising" (54). "Don't waste your time worrying about giving in to theoretical fabrications," she writes, "while I supposedly suffer from 'empirical deprivations'" (55). Following her reply, Žižek responds with an apology for his "deeply entrenched chauvinism" (58). Others have pointed to a latent "heterosexism" in Žižek: see Chris Coffman, "Queering Žižek," *Postmodern Culture* 23, no. 1 (2012).

96 Quoted from *Manufacturing Reality: Slavoj Žižek and the Reality of the Virtual*, dir. Ben Wright, perf. Slavoj Žižek, 2004, DVD.

97 Slavoj Žižek, *Violence: Six Sideways Reflections* (New York: Picador, 2008), 1. Incidentally, Žižek's 2008 book *Violence* was the sole bit of reading material Tolokonnikova managed to smuggle past prison censors in the corrective labor colony formerly home to a Soviet Gulag (Žižek, *Comradely Greetings*, 28; it was a Russian translation, according to Gessen, *Words Will Break Cement*, 14).

98 "Huuuh! Das Pressegespräch am 16. September 2001 im Senatszimmer des Hotel Atlantic in Hamburg," *MusikTexte* 91 (2002): 69–77.

99 Žižek, *Absolute Recoil*, 31.

100 Quoted in translator's introduction to *Philosophy of the Encounter: Later Writings, 1978-87*, ed. François Matheron and Oliver Corpet, trans. G. M. Goshgarian (London: Verso, 2006), xxii.

101 Žižek, *Absolute Recoil*, 52.

102 Žižek was accused of plagiarizing passages from a white separatist magazine in an essay that appeared in a recent issue of *Critical Inquiry*. See Annalisa Quinn, "Book News: Famed Philosopher Accused of Plagiarizing White Separatist Journal," July 14, 2014, accessed November 12, 2014, http://www.npr.org/blogs/thetwo-way/2014/07/14/331320060/book-news-famed-philosopher-accused-of-plagiarizing-white-separatist-journal. See Žižek's response: Euguen Wolters, "'I Nonetheless Deeply Regret the Incident,' Zizek Responds to Plagiarism Allegations," July 12, 2014, accessed November 12, 2014, http://www.critical-theory.com/i-nonetheless-deeply-regret-the-incident-zizek-responds-to-plagiarism-allegations.

On the subject of potentially inadvertent citations of right-wing materials, it is rather ironic to note that Žižek's "ideas matter" was a phrase earlier penned by Ayn Rand. See "The 'Inexplicable Personal Alchemy,'" in Ayn Rand and Peter Schwartz, *Return of the Primitive: The Anti-industrial Revolution*, New Expanded ed. (New York: Meridian, 1999), 119.

103 Quoted from the lecture version of "Towards a Materialist Theory of Subjectivity," Birkbeck Institute, London, May 22, 2014.

104 If one contends then that we are thus living in "as Althusserian times as ever," perhaps that assertion should account for the kinds of latent patriarchal violence that accompany such a situation. Only two years after writing "Marx in his Limits," as it is widely known, Althusser strangled and killed his wife. Notably, Geraldine Finn contended in her essay "Why Althusser Killed His Wife" (1981) that the event cannot be fully extricated from Althusser's philosophy (Geraldine Finn, *Why Althusser Killed His Wife: Essays on Discourse and Violence* [Atlantic Highland, NJ: Humanities, 1996]).

105 In *Pussy Riot: A Punk Prayer* (film).

106 Žižek, *Absolute Recoil*, 56.

107 This is the case, I think, despite growing support for the so-called New Conceptualism movement found largely in German-speaking new music contexts. See the recent survey of writings on "Neuen Konzeptualismus" in *MusikTexte* 145 (May, 2015).

108 Latour, "An Attempt at a 'Compositionist Manifesto,'" 473–74.

Chapter 4

1 For a complete list of Ablinger's *Weiss/Weisslich* works, see http://ablinger.mur.at/ werke.html/#a27.

2 Kosuth, "Art After Philosophy," 30.

3 Peter Ablinger, "Keine Überschreitung/No Transgression," in *Hören hören/Hearing Listening*, ed. Katja Blomberg (Berlin: Haus am Waldsee, 2008), 87.

4 Ablinger, "Die Klänge interessieren mich nicht/The Sounds Do Not Interest Me," in *Hören hören*, 93, translation slightly modified.

5 See, for example, Ablinger's *Sehen und hören* ("Seeing and Hearing") series (1994– 2013), http://ablinger.mur.at/docu03.html. A subseries of his *Musik ohne Klänge* cycle, *Sehen und hören* includes "Photographs, Photo-series, Photos and Chairs, Photo Projections." The work *Two Part Invention, 32 Fotos* (2003), for example, is described as a score. "The required instrument is a camera with variable exposure time," and the text describes movements and exposure times for photographing a pair of single-colored postcards.

6 Note that Ablinger refers to the computer-controlled device that sits atop the ordinary piano as an "auto-piano player" (Peter Ablinger, "Quadraturen," accessed October 26, 2015, http://ablinger.mur.at/docu11.html), while he describes the instrument as a whole (the piano along with the fitted device) as a "player piano" ("A Letter From Schoenberg reading piece with player piano," accessed January 9, 2010, http://ablinger.mur.at/txt_qu3schoenberg.html).

7 Derrida defines the *parergon* as that which "separates the internal from the external," a double border which "joins together what it splits" (*The Truth in Painting*, 331). I refer here to scores, recordings, and musical automata in this sense as "neither [the] work nor outside the work" (ibid., 121).

8 Documentation of Ablinger's *A Letter from Schoenberg*, which includes Ablinger's transcription of Schoenberg's letter, can be found at "A Letter From Schoenberg reading piece with player piano." For the original recording of Schoenberg's dictation of the letter, see "VR48: BRIEF, LOS ANGELES, AN ROSS RUSSELL, NEW YORK," *Arnold Schönberg Center*, published January 13, 2010, accessed

October 19, 2015, http://www.schoenberg.at/index.php?option=com_content&view =article&id=983&lang=en. The transcriptions of Schoenberg's letter respectively provided by Ablinger and the Arnold Schönberg Center contain potentially important discrepancies (see note 56 below).

9   Deleuze and Guattari, *A Thousand Plateaus*, 21.

10   Ablinger, "Keine Überschreitung," 87.

11   Ablinger, "Die Klänge interessieren mich nicht," 97.

12   This topic continues in Chapter 6.

13   See "Sacrificing" in Jacques Attali, *Noise: The Political Economy of Music* (Minneapolis: University of Minnesota Press, 1985), 21–45; also cited in Paul Hegarty, *Noise/Music: A History* (New York: Bloomsbury, 2007), 7.

14   Paul Hegarty has written extensively about Merzbow; see, for example, the eponymous chapter in *Noise/Music* (153–166). For an "ethnographic" study of Japanese noise, see David Novak, *Japanoise: Music at the Edge of Circulation* (Durham: Duke University Press, 2013). For a discussion of historical connections between noise and various music genres emerging from punk, see Mary Russo and Daniel Warner, "Rough Music, Futurism, and Postpunk Industrial Noise Bands," *Discourse* 10, no. 1 (Fall–Winter 1987–88): 55–76.

15   Hegarty, *Noise/Music*, 5.

16   Mann, *The Theory-Death of the Avant-Garde*, 98.

17   Luigi Russolo, *The Art of Noises: A Futurist Manifesto*, trans. Barclay Brown (New York: Pendragon, 1987), 23.

18   Ibid., 24, emphasis removed.

19   Ibid., 27.

20   Ibid., 24.

21   Poggioli, *The Theory of the Avant-Garde*, 31.

22   *The Art of Noises*, 25.

23   Ibid., 25, 30.

24   Luciano Chessa, *Luigi Russolo, Futurist: Noise, Visual Arts, and the Occult* (Berkeley: University of California Press, 2012). In his discussion of the *intonarumori*, Chessa contends that "the futurists consistently opposed the positive notion of continuity against the negative one of fragmentation" (144), citing the writings of Boccioni and Russolo.

25   Pierre Schaeffer, "Acousmatics," in *Audio Culture: Readings in Modern Music*, 76–81.

26   Nattiez, *Music and Discourse*, 94. For an extensive study of *acousmatic* sound and Schaeffer, see Brian Kane, *Sound Unseen: Acousmatic Sound in Theory and Practice* (New York: Oxford University Press, 2014).

27   Quoted in Nattiez, *Music and Discourse*, 52.

28 Nattiez, *Music and Discourse*, 52.

29 See http://ablinger.mur.at/werk89anfangen.html. For further commentary, see Christian Scheib, "Static's Music - Noise Inquiries," ed. Bill Dietz, 1997/98. Last updated 2002. Accessed January 12, 2010, http://ablinger.mur.at/noise.html.

30 Deleuze and Guattari, *A Thousand Plateaus*, 23.

31 Ibid.

32 Ablinger, "Die Klänge interessieren mich nicht," 94.

33 Dahlhaus, *The Idea of Absolute Music*, 8.

34 Hanns Eisler and Theodor W. Adorno, "The Politics of Hearing," in *Audio Culture: Readings in Modern Music*, 73–75.

35 Theodor W. Adorno, "Music, Language, Composition" (1956), *Essays on Music*, trans. Susan H. Gillespie (Berkeley: University of California Press, 2002), 113–226.

36 Deleuze and Guattari, *A Thousand Plateaus*, 343, 348.

37 Ibid., 349.

38 Ibid.

39 Ibid., 267.

40 Ibid., 23.

41 Deleuze and Guattari suggest that "the objection will be raised that music is not a language, that the components of sound are not pertinent features of language," yet they add: "We keep asking that the issue be left open, that any presupposed distinction be rejected" (*A Thousand Plateaus*, 96).

42 Eric Prieto, "Deleuze, Music, and Modernist Mimesis," *Word and Music Studies: Essays on Music and the Spoken Word and on Surveying the Field*, ed. Suzanne M. Lodato and David F. Urrows (Amsterdam: Radopi, 2005), 10.

43 Deleuze and Guattari, *A Thousand Plateaus*, 11–12.

44 Ibid., 11.

45 Chico Mello, "Zwischen Abbild und Selbst-Referenzialität: Mimesis und Rauschen bei Peter Ablinger/Between Representation and Self-Reference: Mimesis and Noise in Peter Ablinger," in *Hören hören/Hearing Listening*, ed. Katja Blomberg (Berlin: Haus am Waldsee, 2008), 103.

46 Michel Chion, *Audio-Vision: Sound on Screen*, ed. and trans. Claudia Gorbman (New York: Columbia University Press, 1994), 129.

47 Ibid.

48 There is an extensive bibliography around this narrative. See, for example, Friedrich Kittler, *Gramophone, Film, Typewriter* (Stanford, CA: Stanford University Press, 1999), or Jonathan Sterne, *The Audible Past: Cultural Origins of Sound Reproduction* (Durham: Duke University Press, 2003).

49 See Carolyn Abbate, *In Search of Opera* (Princeton, NJ: Princeton University Press, 2001), 203.

50   Ablinger's process works according to principles elaborated by eighteenth-century mathematician Joseph Fourier. See "Quadraturen," http://ablinger.mur.at/docu11.html. Also compare Ablinger's process to the French spectralists (Tristan Murail, Gérard Grisey, Hugues Dufourt). For a technical explanation of spectral analysis, see "Spectrum Analysis" in Curtis Roads, *The Computer Music Tutorial* (Cambridge, MA: MIT Press, 1996), 533–610.

51   Mello, "Zwischen Abbild," 103.

52   Abbate, *In Search of Opera*, 202.

53   Douglas Kahn, *Noise, Water, Meat: A History of Voice, Sound, and Aurality in the Arts* (Cambridge, MA: MIT Press, 1999), 91, 214.

54   Ibid., 91.

55   "The female voice was chosen here for its greater flexibility and adaptability to the instrumental background," the liner notes argue further, "the male voice having a tendency to overpower the music and turn it into a mere accompaniment."

56   Ablinger transcribes the phrase as "You are not only a bugger . . ." But the *Arnold Schönberg Center* ("VR48: BRIEF") cites the passage as "You are not only a . . . (paragraph)," as though Schoenberg had indicated a paragraph break to the transcriber.

57   Writing of the decision to compose *Ode to Napoleon*, Schoenberg states, "I knew it was the moral duty of intelligentsia to take a stand against tyranny," quoted in "Ode to Napoleon op. 41," *Arnold Schönberg Center*. Last updated July 30, 2009. Accessed March 4, 2015, http://www.schoenberg.at/index.php/en/joomla-license-sp-1943310036/ode-to-napoleon-op-41-1942.

58   In a letter addressed to Welles, Schoenberg writes:

> I have heard you over the radio, and I was deeply impressed by your reading; by the great number of characters and shades your voice is capable to produce; by the very artistic and unconventional manner of structural composition; by the sincerity and by the purity of your expression. When the problem came about, who could take the part of the recitation I suggested—primo loco—your name. (Quoted in Sabine Feisst, "Ode to Napoleon Buonaparte, op. 41," in *Schoenberg's New World: The American Years* [New York: Oxford University Press, 2011], 144–49)

I thank Ben Piekut for that reference and his related comments on *Ode to Napoleon*. Although he refers to radio, Schoenberg's preference for Welles's cinematic male voice (and the composer's subsequent scorn of Adler) can be seen in light of what Amy Lawrence calls a widespread "'cultural distaste' for women" developed through Hollywood film of that era (*Echo and Narcissus: Women's Voices in Classical Hollywood Cinema* [Berkeley: University of California Press, 1991]).

59   See, for example, Barbara Engh, "Adorno and the Sirens: tele-phono-graphic bodies," in *Embodied Voices: Representing Female Vocality in Western Culture*, ed. Leslie C. Dunn and Nancy A. Jones (Cambridge, UK: Cambridge University Press, 1997), 120–35. Engh provides an excellent critique of Adorno's 1928 article "*Nadelcurven*," *Musikblätter des Anbruch* 10 (February 1928): 47–50; "The Curves of the Needle," trans. Thomas Y. Levin, *October* 55 (Winter 1990): 48–55. Specifically, Engh responds to Adorno's claim that "male voices can be reproduced better than female voices" ("Curves," 54) and that female voices require the "body as complement" (ibid., 52). I thank Bill Dietz for suggesting this reference.

60   Judith Halberstam, *In a Queer Time and Place: Transgender Bodies, Subcultural Lives* (New York: New York University Press, 2005), 55–56. Note that Judith has more recently identified as Jack Halberstam.

61   For a survey of the development of the term transgender that considers both activist and scholarly perspectives, see David Valentine, *Imagining Transgender: An Ethnography of a Category* (Durham: Duke University Press, 2007). Valentine analyzes the history of transgender as a category, noting its emergence and acceptance in collective and institutional terms in the early 1990s.

62   This is the question my own project *Two Transcriptions/Ode to Schoenberg* attempts to pose. In 2013, I recorded two alternative versions of Schoenberg's *Ode to Napoleon* featuring the voices of transgender artist Zackary Drucker and musician Theodore Baer. See http://gdouglasbarrett.com/two_transcriptions.html. I thank Che Gossett, Theodore Baer, and Ben Piekut for their participation in the roundtable discussion event *Two Transcriptions*, May 25, 2013, Incubator Arts Project, New York.

63   We can also include written language since Schoenberg likely had access to the record's liner notes.

64   Mladen Dolar, *A Voice and Nothing More* (Cambridge, MA: MIT Press, 2006). For a more recent take on the voice, see Brandon LaBelle, *Lexicon of the Mouth: Poetics and Politics of Voice and the Oral Imaginary* (New York: Bloomsbury, 2014).

65   Schaeffer, "Acousmatics," 77. For more on gender and the disembodied voice, see Engh, "Adorno and the Sirens" and Kaja Silverman, *The Acoustic Mirror: The Female Voice in Psychoanalysis and Cinema* (Bloomington: Indiana University Press, 1988).

66   Hegarty, *Noise/Music*, 5.

67   Michel Foucault, *The History of Sexuality Volume 1: An Introduction*, trans. Robert Hurley (New York: Pantheon Books, 1978), 101.

68   Deleuze and Guattari, *A Thousand Plateaus*, 9.

69   Ibid., 10.

70   Ibid.

Chapter 5

1 Ruth Simon and Rob Barry, "A Degree Drawn in Red Ink: Graduates of Arts-Focused Schools Are Shown to Rack Up the Most Student Debt," *The Wall Street Journal*, updated February 13, 2013, http://www.wsj.com/articles/SB10001424127887324432004578306610055834952.

2 Andrew Ross, *Creditocracy: And The Case For Debt Refusal* (New York and London: OR Books, 2014), 104.

3 Ibid., 108.

4 As in, for instance, the "USC Seven": see Hannah Ghorashi, "Entire Class of First-Year MFA Students Dropping out of USC," May 15, 2015, accessed July 15, 2015, http://www.artnews.com/2015/05/15/entire-class-of-first-year-mfa-students-dropping-out-of-usc.

5 These disparities are perhaps also difficult to generalize. While, for instance, many music programs have adopted interdisciplinary approaches, art schools have felt an increased need to incorporate sound into their curricula. Much less common, at least in the United States, is the combination of both paradigms, as is the case, for example, with CalArts.

6 David Graeber, "The Axial Age (800 BC–600 AD)," in *Debt: The First 5,000 Years* (New York: Melville House, 2011), 223–50.

7 Ibid., 245.

8 Moishe Postone, *Time, Labor, and Social Domination: A Re-interpretation of Marx's Critical Theory* (Cambridge, UK: Cambridge University Press, 1993), 170–71.

9 Cassie Thornton, "We Make Debt," We Make Debt, accessed November 4, 2013, http://debt-material.tumblr.com/ask.

10 Graeber, *Debt*, 391.

11 Randy Martin, *Financialization of Daily Life* (Philadelphia: Temple University Press, 2002), 105.

12 Ross contends that "education debt is an especially immoral kind of labor contract. Since it involves the capture of future wages, we could think of it as precocious wage theft" (*Creditocracy*, 149).

13 I borrow this idea from Postone, who defines the "treadmill effect" as a phenomenon in which "increased productivity results neither in a corresponding increase in social wealth nor in a corresponding decrease in labor time, but in the constitution of a new base level of productivity—which leads to still further increases in productivity" (*Time, Labor, and Social Domination*, 347).

14 Dyson begins her book *The Tone of Our Times: Sound, Sense, Economy, and Ecology* (Cambridge, MA: MIT Press, 2014) with a discussion of the homonyms "eco(nomy)" and "echo" and refers to this "eco-echo" relation throughout the text.

She also makes similar note of the dual economic and philosophical registers of "speculation": "'Speculation,' that eminently philosophical term, has little to do with thought, and everything to do with finance" (ibid., 113).

15 The question as to whether Meillassoux is to be considered a materialist or a realist becomes complicated not only by the philosopher's equivocations regarding the latter term, but also by the relationship between the two terms. According to philosopher Peter Gratton, "Even 'materialists' are really 'matter' realists" (*Speculative Realism: Problems and Prospects* [New York: Bloomsbury, 2014], 22), suggesting that the former are in fact a subset of the latter. However, Gratton later explains, "Meillassoux identifies the 'absolute' as the principle of contingency, yet he also rejects realism in favor of a 'materialism,' though he cannot, for all that, be clear on how a *relation* (however absolute) is itself *material*" (ibid., 222n14). Is not debt marked by a similar problem, namely, how an immaterial relation can be made material?

16 Quentin Meillassoux, *After Finitude: An Essay on the Necessity of Contingency* (New York: Bloomsbury, 2009), 3, 7.

17 Christoph Cox, "Beyond Representation and Signification: Toward a Sonic Materialism," *Journal of Visual Culture* 10, no. 2 (2011): 145–61.

18 Peter Hallward, "Anything Is Possible: A Critique of Meillassoux," in *The Speculative Turn: Continental Materialism and Realism*, ed. Levi R. Bryant, Nick Srnicek, and Graham Harman (Melbourne: Re.press, 2011), 139.

19 Alexander R. Galloway, "The Poverty of Philosophy: Realism and Post-Fordism," *Critical Inquiry* 39, no. 2 (Winter 2013): 347–66.

20 Nathan Brown, "The Speculative and the Specific: On Hallward and Meillassoux," in *The Speculative Turn*, 142.

21 Žižek's formulation is found in each of the foreword sections of his edited Short Circuits volumes, for example, Lorenzo Chiesa, *Subjectivity and Otherness: A Philosophical Reading of Lacan*, ed. Slavoj Žižek (Cambridge, MA: MIT Press, 2007).

22 Meillassoux, *After Finitude*, 7.

23 In *ARTnews* (January 22–39, 1971): 67–71.

24 See "Reading Group: AUTONOMIA, OCCUPY, COMMUNISM: LEGACIES AND FUTURES | e-flux," accessed December 30, 2013, http://www.e-flux.com/program/reading-group-autonomia-occupy-communism-legacies-and-futures.

25 Adolf Grünbaum, "Logical Foundations of Psychoanalytic Theory," *Erkenntnis* 19, No. 1/3, Methodology, Epistemology, and Philosophy of Science (May, 1983): 109.

26 Ono's score appeared in a slightly different format before its inclusion in the 1971 Simon and Schuster reissue of her book *Grapefruit*. This original note card version of *Voice Piece for Soprano* was also included in the recent MoMA exhibition *Yoko Ono: One Woman Show, 1960-1971*. In addition to a dedication to Simone Morris

(Forti), the card contained the letter "M" in the upper-right-hand corner, which, according to another card on display, indicated that it was one of the fifty-two "Instructions for Music."

27 Cassie Thornton, "A wild place with a boring facade," accessed August 14, 2013, http://www.cassiethornton.com/about.html.

28 Maurizio Lazzarato, *The Making of the Indebted Man: An Essay on the Neoliberal Condition* (Cambridge, MA: Semiotext(e), 2011), 29, 122.

29 To the primacy of debt climate change offers a worthy challenge. Ross proposes, however, an inherent relationship between the two phenomena, referring, for instance, to debts incurred by Hurricane Sandy victims (*Creditocracy*, 181–215).

30 Ross, *Creditocracy*, 143.

31 Lazzarato, *The Making of the Indebted Man*, 25.

32 Leigh Claire La Berge and Dehlia Hannah, "Debt Aesthetics: Medium Specificity and Social Practice in the Work of Cassie Thornton," *Postmodern Culture* 5, no. 2 (2015).

33 The measure was referred to in 2005 as "one of the most comprehensive overhauls of the [US] Bankruptcy Code in more than twenty-five years" (Susan Jensen, "Legislative History of the Bankruptcy Abuse Prevention and Consumer Protection Act of 2005, A," *Am. Bankr, LJ* 79 [2005]: 485). See Scott Pashman, "Discharge of Student Loan Debt under 11 USC 523 (A)(8): Reassessing under Hardship after the Elimination of the Seven-Year Exception," *NYL Rev.* 44 (2000): 605.

34 The number was actually 1-707-8-EnDeBt.

35 See Seth Borenstein, "NASA To Privatize Space Travel After Last Shuttle Lands," *Huffington Post*, June 20, 2011, http://www.huffingtonpost.com/2011/07/20/nasa-privatize-space-future-changes_n_905186.html. Private Dutch firm Mars One, for example, intends to send humans to Mars by 2026, according to CEO Bas Lansdorp. See the organization's website at www.mars-one.com.

36 Gregory Sholette, *Dark Matter: Art and Politics in the Age of Enterprise Culture* (London: Pluto, 2011), 39, cited in Joshua Simon, *Neomaterialism* (Berlin: Sternberg, 2013), 111–12n107.

37 Karl Marx, *Capital: A Critique of Political Economy*, trans. Ben Fowkes (London: Penguin in Association with New Left Review, 1976), 643.

38 Claire Bishop, *Artificial Hells*, 269.

39 Meillassoux, *After Finitude*, 10.

40 "How Old Is the Universe?" *WMAP—Age of the Universe*, accessed November 4, 2013, http://map.gsfc.nasa.gov/universe/uni_age.html. It is important to note that out of the four preeminent speculative realists (Meillassoux, Graham Harman, Iain Hamilton Grant, Ray Brassier), Brassier is more often cited for his references to science, while Meillassoux is noted for his engagement with mathematics.

Meillassoux's reliance upon the "arche-fossil" argument, however, provides ample reason to consider Meillassoux's materialism in continuity with the "scientific socialism" advocated by Althusser. Regarding the latter, see Paul Thomas, *Marxism and Scientific Socialism: From Engels to Althusser* (London: Routledge, 2008).

41 Meillassoux, *After Finitude*, 21, emphasis removed.

42 Ibid., 36.

43 Louis Althusser, *Lenin and Philosophy, and Other Essays* (New York: Monthly Review, 1972), 71.

44 Adrian Johnston, *Prolegomena to Any Future Materialism: The Outcome of Contemporary French Philosophy* (Evanston, IL: Northwestern University Press, 2013), 13.

45 Meillassoux, *After Finitude*, 38.

46 Marx, *Capital Vol. I*, 494n4, cited in Jacques Rancière, *Althusser's Lesson*, trans. Emiliano Battista (London: Continuum, 2011), 12.

47 Postone, *Time, Labor, and Social Domination*, 170–71.

48 Wildhagen-Héraucort German-English Dictionary quoted in Thomas, *Marxism and Scientific Socialism*, xi. Thomas notes that for the most part the French translation "la science" is generally closer in meaning to the German than the English, "though not to M. Althusser and his followers" (ibid., 30).

49 Marx and Engels, "Theses on Feuerbach [1845]," cited from https://www.marxists.org/archive/marx/works/1845/theses, accessed July 30, 2014. A different translation is published in *The German Ideology Parts I & II* (Mansfield Centre, CT: Martino Publishing, 2011), 197–99.

50 Rancière, *Althusser's Lesson*, 15.

51 Marx and Engels, *The German Ideology Parts I & II* (Mansfield Centre, CT: Martino Publishing, 2011), 28.

52 Althusser, *Lenin and Philosophy, and Other Essays*, 27.

53 Rancière, *Althusser's Lesson*, 12.

54 Randy Martin, *Under New Management: Universities, Administrative Labor, and the Professional Turn* (Philadelphia: Temple University Press, 2011). The term "academic capitalism" comes from Sheila Slaughter and Larry L. Leslie, *Academic Capitalism: Politics, Policies, and the Entrepreneurial University* (Baltimore, MD: Johns Hopkins University Press, 1999), cited in *Artificial Hells*, 268–74. Additionally, Thomas Frank indicts the corporatization of higher education, including the record profiteering and rising tuition costs, and Frank Donoghue laments the gradual extinction of the tenured (humanities) professor (*The Last Professors: The Corporate University and the Fate of the Humanities* [New York: Fordham University Press, 2008]). These writers link the student debt crisis to the thoroughgoing penetration of higher education by a neoliberal market logic.

55 See the group's letter to the Department of Education (much of the debt came from US federal student loans) and their list of supporters at https://debtcollective.org/ studentstrike. See also Chris Kirkham, "Corinthian closing its last schools; 10,000 California students displaced," *Los Angeles Times*, April 27, 2015, http://www. latimes.com/business/la-fi-corinthian-shutdown-20150427-story.html#page=1.

56 See the group of related articles in a forum hosted by the *Chronicle of Higher Education*, "Has Higher Education Become an Engine of Inequality?" July 2, 2012, http://chronicle.com/article/Has-Higher-Education-Become-an/132619.

57 Ted Purves, introduction to *What We Want Is Free: Generosity And Exchange In Recent Art*, ed. Ted Purves (Albany: SUNY Press, 2005), x.

58 Heavily influenced by Paulo Freire's 1968 *Pedagogy of the Oppressed*, critical pedagogy and social practice literature cite Rancière's *The Ignorant Schoolmaster: Five Lessons in Intellectual Emancipation* [1987] (Stanford, CA: Stanford University Press, 1991) as a key text.

59 Bishop, *Artificial Hells*, 3.

60 Ibid., 63–66. For more on the subject of music as social practice, see Michael Chanan, *Musica Practica: The Social Practice of Western Music from Gregorian Chant to Postmodernism* (New York: Verso, 1994).

61 The "Deep Listening" practice of Oliveros can be seen as another experimental music precedent for social practice art. Of particular relevance to Thornton's *Debt 2 Space Program*, Oliveros's *Echoes from the Moon* (1987), for example, is an interactive performance installation that uses a device for bouncing radio signals off the surface of the moon. For a 1996 performance, four hundred participants lined up to "touch the moon" with their voices (*Echoes from the Moon* technical director Gresham-Lancaster quoted in Douglas Kahn, *Earth Sound Earth Signal: Energies and Earth Magnitude in the Arts* [Berkeley: University of California Press, 2013], 181–82). I thank Bill Dietz for his suggestions related to this reference.

62 Ibid., 219–39.

63 Ibid., 224.

64 Ibid., 2, 39, 284.

65 Theodor W. Adorno, *Aesthetic Theory*, trans. Robert Hullot-Kentor, ed. Gretel Adorno and Rolf Tiedermann (New York: Bloomsbury, 2013), 228.

66 For a general overview of the *Klangkunst* literature and a comparison with sound art theory, see Andreas Engström and Åsa Stjerna, "Sound Art or *Klangkunst*?"

67 Born, "Sound Studies / Music / Affect: Year Zero, Encompassment, Difference?" lecture.

68 Kane, "Musicophobia."

69 Cox describes his aim "to contribute to the general revival of realism in contemporary philosophy and its challenge to the idealism and humanism that

have characterized philosophy and cultural theory since the 'linguistic turn'"
("Beyond Representation," 146), and clarifies the reference to Harman, Grant,
and Meillassoux in a footnote (158n1). In that note Cox also includes De Landa,
a philosopher often associated with speculative realism, but not considered one of
its four primary exponents.

70 Jim Drobnick's phrase, "sonic turn," appears in "Listening Awry," in ed. Jim
    Drobnick, *Aural Cultures*, 10. The "speculative turn" appears in *The Speculative
    Turn: Continental Materialism and Realism*, ed. Levi R. Bryant, Nick Srnicek, and
    Graham Harman (Melbourne: Re.press, 2011).

71 Cox, "Beyond Representation and Signification," 145.

72 Neuhaus, "Sound Art?"

73 Kane refers to Kim-Cohen's project as a form of "sonic idealism"
    ("Musicophobia"), whereas this distinction is, perhaps, only implied in Cox's
    description of Kim-Cohen as adopting a "textualist paradigm" ("Beyond
    Representation and Signification," 147).

74 Kim-Cohen, *In the Blink of an Ear.*

75 Incidentally, these three figures are criticized by Meillassoux as positing "vitalist
    hypostatization[s] of the correlation" (*After Finitude*, 37). De Landa, for one, has
    argued for a materialist interpretation of Deleuze.

76 Cox, "Beyond Representation and Signification," 146.

77 Compare this to the "myopic and narcissistic tendencies" attributed to
    contemporary theory by Nick Srnicek ("Capitalism and the Non-Philosophical
    Subject," in *The Speculative Turn*, 164).

78 Cox, "Beyond Representation and Signification," 147.

79 Ibid., 148–49.

80 Ibid.

81 However, Cox does provide a reference to Lukács in the context of "the musical
    score [as] an exemplary instance of the reification characteristic of capitalism, in
    which processes are transformed into exchangeable, saleable products and objects"
    ("Beyond Representation and Signification," 154).

82 Ibid., 148.

83 Graeber, *Debt: The First 5,000 Years*, 387.

84 Meillassoux, *After Finitude*, 5.

85 Ibid., 10.

86 Ibid., 56.

87 Ibid., 52, emphasis removed.

88 Ibid., 67, emphasis removed.

89 In considering Meillassoux's "Deuil à venir, dieu à venir," *Critique*, no. 704/705
    (January/February, 2006): 105–15, along with the philosopher's unpublished
    dissertation of 1997, *L'inexistence divine*, Johnston suggests that Meillassoux

"smuggles idealist religiosity back into materialist atheism via non-dialectical 'materialism'" (*Prolegomena to Any Future Materialism*, 174). See also Johnston's postface to *Prolegomena to Any Future Materialism*.

90 Meillassoux, *After Finitude*, 64.

91 Johnston, *Prolegomena to Any Future Materialism*, 158.

92 Hallward, "Anything Is Possible," 133.

93 Andreas Huyssen, *Twilight Memories: Marking Time in a Culture of Amnesia* (New York: Routledge, 1995), 204.

94 Johan Siebers, *The Method of Speculative Philosophy: An Essay on the Foundations of Whitehead's Metaphysics* (Kassel: Kassel University Press, 1998), 69.

95 Ibid. Regarding the history of the term, speculation can be traced as back as far as Plato and Aristotle. Speculative philosophy is found later in Hume's *An Enquiry Concerning Human Understanding* (1740) and Kant's *Critique of Pure Reason* (1781). In 1839 Feuerbach used the term in his well-known critique of Hegel.

96 Alfred North Whitehead, *Process and Reality*, ed. David Ray Griffin and Donald Wynne Sherburne (New York: Free, 1978), 3. The speculative component of Whitehead's definition would be more evident if he were to accent the word "every" in the quotation (as in "*every* element of our experience"). Meillassoux might take issue with the implicit limitation of the real to human experience.

97 Ibid., 14.

98 Urs Stäheli, *Spectacular Speculation: Thrills, the Economy, and Popular Discourse* (Stanford, CA: Stanford University Press, 2013), 2.

99 I thank Leigh Claire La Berge for her suggestions pertaining to this argument.

100 uncertain commons, *Speculate This!* (Durham: Duke University Press, 2013), published online, http://speculatethis.pressbooks.com.

101 This, despite the fact that, as Latour observes, in the face of the dual threat of economic and ecological catastrophe, the notions of first and second nature have apparently switched roles:

> First nature has entered the Anthropocene where it is hard to distinguish human action from natural forces and which is now full of tipping points, peaks, storms and catastrophes, while only second nature [referring to the economy], it seems, has kept the older features of an indifferent, timeless and fully automatic nature governed by a few fundamental and [in]disputable laws totally foreign to politics and human action! ("On Some Affects of Capitalism," Lecture, Royal Academy, Copenhagen, February 26, 2014, http://www.bruno-latour.fr/sites/default/files/136-AFFECTS-OF-K-COPENHAGUE.pdf, 6).

Nature is now directly under human influence, according to Latour, whereas the economy is beyond governability.

102 Meillassoux, *After Finitude*, 108, emphasis added.

103 Ibid., 108.

104 Quoted in Johnston, *Prolegomena to Any Future Materialism*, 170.

105 Meillassoux's *After Finitude* and Lenin's *Materialism and Emperio-Criticism*
are compared, for example, in Ray Brassier, *Nihil Unbound: Enlightenment and
Extinction* (Basingstoke: Palgrave Macmillan, 2007), 246–47; Johnston, *Prolegomena
to Any Future Materialism*, 151–53; and Žižek, *Less than Nothing*, 625.

106 Hallward, "Anything Is Possible," 139.

107 "In [an] ambiguous (mis)reading of Hegel," Žižek argues, "Meillassoux claims
that the dialectical principle of contradiction (contradictions are really present
in things) excludes any change: change means a transformation of p into non-p,
of a feature into its opposite, but since, in a contradiction, a thing already *is* its
opposite, it has nowhere to develop into" (*Less than Nothing*, 628). Žižek adds
a distinctly Lacanian twist in asserting, "The problem is not to think the Real
outside of transcendental correlation, independently of the subject; the problem
is to think the Real inside the subject, the hard core of the Real in the very
heart of the subject, its ex-timate center" (ibid., 644). Elsewhere Žižek refers to
Meillassoux's project, characterized as "we are stuck in our representations," as
a "pseudo-problem." "The true [arche-]fossil," he insists succinctly, "is *objet petit
a*" ("Badiou VS Žižek—Is Lacan An Anti-Philosopher? 06," YouTube, November
26, 2012, accessed December 31, 2013. https://www.youtube.com/watch?v=bRD-
tBTRbLc). Meanwhile, Toscano invokes Lucio Colletti, asking, "is there not a
need [in Meillassoux] to pre-emptively reduce the real to a domain of entities
rather than relations?" ("Against Speculation, Or, A Critique of the Critique:
A Remark on Quentin Meillassoux's *After Finitude* [After Colletti]," in The
Speculative Turn, 85n8).

108 Brown, "The Speculative and the Specific," 142, 159. Somewhat unexpectedly,
Brown also attempts to show how Hallward's own work supports his argument
as well.

109 Quoted in Thomas, *Marxism and Scientific Socialism*, 105. Thomas points out that
neither the term "historical materialism" nor "dialectical materialism" was ever
actually used by Marx, even though the "materialist interpretation of history"
appears in Engels's 1859 review of *A Contribution to the Critique of Political
Economy* (ibid., 86–87).

Chapter 6

1 Hong-Kai Wang, "Music While We Work" (documentary of Recording Workshops),
June 7, 2012, accessed November 13, 2013, https://vimeo.com/43627255.

2   Hong-Kai Wang, "Music While We Work," accessed November 14, 2014, http://www.w-h-k.net/mwww.html.

3   Jean-Luc Nancy, *Listening*, trans. Charlotte Mandell (New York: Fordham University Press, 2007), 10; also cited in Georgina Born, introduction to *Music, Sound and Space: Transformations of Public and Private Experience*, ed. Georgina Born (Cambridge, UK: Cambridge University Press, 2013), 3.

4   Paul Hegarty, *Rumour and Radiation: Sound in Video Art* (New York: Bloomsbury, 2015), 2–3.

5   Holly Rogers, *Sounding the Gallery: Video and the Rise of Art-Music* (New York: Oxford University Press, 2013), 2, 8, 41.

6   Hegarty, *Rumour and Radiation*, 3.

7   Ibid., 7.

8   On the subject of offscreen sound, see Michel Chion, *Audio-vision: Sound on Screen*.

9   Another notable comparison is Phill Niblock's *The Movement of People Working* (2003, Microcinema International, DVD), a series of film sequences depicting laborers throughout Peru, Mexico, China and Japan originally shot by Niblock throughout the 1970s and 1980s and set to the artist's characteristic drone music.

10 Wynford Reynolds, *Music While You Work* (London: British Broadcasting Corporation, 1942), 4–5.

11 Karin Bijsterveld, *Mechanical Sound: Technology, Culture, and Public Problems of Noise in the Twentieth Century* (Cambridge, MA: MIT Press), 84.

12 See Alexandra Hui, "Muzak-While-You-Work: Programming Music for Industry, 1919–1948," *Historische Anthropologie* 22, no. 3 (December, 2014): 364–83.

13 Slavoj Žižek, *The Sublime Object of Ideology* (London: Verso, 2008), 30.

14 Žižek, *The Parallax View*, 365–66.

15 *The German Ideology*, 14.

16 "Relevant action is theatrical (music [imaginary separation of hearing from the other senses] does not exist), inclusive and intentionally purposeless" (emphasis removed, *Silence*, 14).

17 Quoted in Annette Michelson, introduction to *Kino-Eye: The Writings of Dziga Vertov* (Berkeley: University of California Press, 1984), xv.

18 Marx and Engels, *The German Ideology*, 14.

19 Ibid., emphasis added.

20 Sarah Kofman, *Camera Obscura: Of Ideology* (Ithaca, NY: Cornell University Press, 1999), 3.

21 Marx and Engels, *The German Ideology*, 15.

22 Roland Barthes, *Camera Lucida: Reflections on Photography* (New York: Hill and Wang, 1981), 106.

23 Rancière, *The Philosopher and His Poor*, trans. Andrew Parker (Durham: Duke University Press, 2004), 76. For an analysis of the relationships between Marx, Marxism, and science, see Thomas, *Marxism and Scientific Socialism*.

24 *The Politics of Aesthetics*, 12.

25 Jacques Rancière, "Revising 'Nights of Labour': Talk by Jacques Ranciere," February 16, 2009, accessed March 22, 2014, https://www.youtube.com/watch?v=pwW_LiwCKlg.

26 "I always try to think in terms of horizontal distributions, combinations between systems of possibilities, not in terms of surface and substratum" (*The Politics of Aesthetics*, 50).

27 See Jonathan Sterne's "audiovisual litany" list outlining biases found in recent sound studies texts in Jonathan Sterne, *The Audible Past*, 15; cited in Kim-Cohen, *Against Ambience* (Kindle locations, 1378–79).

28 Martin Jay, *Downcast Eyes: The Denigration of Vision in Twentieth-century French Thought* (Berkeley: University of California, 1993), 329–80.

29 Ibid., 374.

30 Louis Althusser, *Lenin and Philosophy, and Other Essays* (New York: Monthly Review, 1972), 134–36.

31 The metaphor of the *camera obscura* is also integral to apparatus theory. Unlike Marx–Engels's concept of inversion, in apparatus theory the *camera obscura* is equated with filmic realism and the artificial construction of Western perspective. See Jean-Louis Baudry, "Ideological Effects of the Basic Cinematographic Apparatus," *Film Quarterly* 28, no. 2 (Winter, 1974–75): 40.

32 Baudry's essay on the "ideological effects" of cinema moved film scholarship from the formal aspects of representation to the apparatus behind the scenes. Rather than image, he discussed cinema as labor: "Cinematographic specificity . . . thus refers to a *work*, that is, to a process of transformation" (ibid., 40).

33 Žižek, *The Sublime Object of Ideology*, 30.

34 With little historical evidence, however, film historians have relegated the story to a mythical history of cinema. As Tom Gunning has discussed in his groundbreaking work on the "astonished" viewer, this myth is nonetheless part of how cinema was historically received and conceived as a medium of shock or "cinema of attractions." See Tom Gunning, "An Aesthetic of Astonishment: Early Film and the (In)Credulous Spectator," in *Viewing Positions: Ways of Seeing Film*, ed. Linda Williams (New Brunswick, NJ: Rutgers University Press, 1995), 114–33.

35 The first public cinema screening was held on December 28, 1895 at the Salon Indien du Grand Café in Paris. The program featured ten films, each of approximately fifty seconds, by the Lumière brothers beginning with *La Sortie de l'Usine*.

36 Introduction to *Kino-Eye: The Writings of Dziga Vertov*, xi, xxxviii.

37 Ibid., xxxvii–xxxviii.

38 Ibid., xxxix

39 "I must get a piece of equipment that won't describe but will record, photograph these sounds. Otherwise it's impossible to organize, to edit them. They rush past, like time. But the movie camera perhaps?" Vertov, "The Birth of Kino-Eye," in *Kino-Eye: The Writings of Dziga Vertov*, 40.

40 Vertov, "IV. On Radio-Eye," in *Kino-Eye: The Writings of Dziga Vertov*, 91. On Vertov's involvement with sound, see Lucy Fischer, "*Enthusiasm*: From Kino-Eye to Radio-Eye," *Film Quarterly* 31, no. 2 (1977/78): 25–34; Oksana Bulgakowa, "The Ear against the Eye: Vertov's Symphony"; and "Russian Revolutionary Film" in Kahn, *Noise, Water, Meat: A History of Sound in the Arts*, 139–56.

41 Jay Leyda, *Kino: A History of the Russian and Soviet Film* (New York: Collier Books, 1960), 176–77, cited in Kahn, *Noise, Water Meat*, 144. During the silent film-era, live musical accompaniment was standard practice, and *Man with a Movie Camera* was no exception. For the latter, Vertov wrote detailed composition notes.

42 Susan Buck-Morss, *The Origin of Negative Dialectics: Theodor W. Adorno, Walter Benjamin and the Frankfurt Institute* (New York: Free, 1977), 33.

43 Kahn, *Noise*, 66.

44 "My article . . . speaks of radio-eye as eliminating distance between people, as the opportunity for workers through the world not only to see, but also, simultaneously, to hear one another" (Vertov, "From Kino-eye to Radio-Eye," in *Kino-Eye: The Writings of Dziga Vertov*, 91).

45 Jacques Rancière, *Aisthesis: Scenes from the Aesthetic Regime of Art* (London: Verso, 2013), 230, emphasis added, 240.

46 Jacques Derrida, *Of Grammatology*, trans. Gayatri Chakravorty Spivak (Baltimore, MD: Johns Hopkins University Press, 1997), 15.

47 Ibid., 35.

48 Jacques Lacan, *Ecrits: The First Complete Edition in English*, trans. Bruce Fink, Héloïse Fink, and Russell Grigg (New York: W. W. Norton & Company, 2006), 507.

49 Quoted in Leslie J Ureña, "Hong-Kai Wang," ARTiT, June 7, 2011, accessed June 15, 2015, http://www.art-it.asia/u/admin_ed_itv_e/dOSMEibzRUhnL3PlIyFW/?lang=en.

50 Leslie Doelle, *Environmental Acoustics* (Toronto: McGraw-Hill, 1972), 361. Cited in Jonathan Sterne, *MP3: The Meaning of a Format* (Durham: Duke University Press, 2012), 120.

51 "Masks of de-individualization . . .," Žižek, *Comradely Greetings*, 12.

52 Jean-Luc Nancy, *The Sense of the World* (Minneapolis: University of Minnesota Press, 1997), 85.

53 *Aesthetics of Politics*, 49.

54 Žižek, *The Parallax View*, 365–66; Žižek, *The Sublime Object of Ideology*, 30.

55 Jacques Derrida, "White Mythology: Metaphor in the Text of Philosophy," *New Literary History* 6, no. 1 "On Metaphor" (Autumn, 1974): 28.

56 See also eldritch Priest, "Nonsense," in *Boring Formless Nonsense: Experimental Music and the Aesthetics of Failure* (New York: Bloomsbury, 2013), 195–277.

57 See, for example, Peter Gratton, "Time for a Conclusion," in *Speculative Realism: Problems and Prospects*, 201–16.

58 Joseph, "Soundings," 283.

59 Against the equation of medium with material, Kim-Cohen also insisted upon medium as a "social category" (*Against Ambience*, Kindle location 1191).

Conclusion

1   Neuhaus, "Sound Art?"

2   Gregg Bordowitz characterizes Boudry–Lorenz's inclusion of musicians across a "gender continuum" as the artists' "radical transformation of the original material." Quoted from the roundtable discussion *An Evening with Pauline Boudry/Renate Lorenz with Gregg Bordowitz and Pauline Oliveros*, Museum of Modern Art, May 19, 2014.

3   Boudry in *An Evening with Pauline Boudry/Renate Lorenz*.

4   See *Not Now! Now! Chronopolitics, Art & Research*, ed. Renate Lorenz (Berlin: Sternberg Press, 2014).

5   Oliveros in Martha Mockus, *Sounding Out: Pauline Oliveros and Lesbian Musicality* (New York: Routledge, 2008), 155.

6   See also Breanne Fahs, "The Radical Possibilities of Valerie Solanas," *Feminist Studies* 34, no. 3, The 1970s Issue (Fall, 2008): 595.

7   Ibid., 597.

8   Pauline Oliveros, "To Valerie Solanas and Marilyn Monroe in Recognition of Their Desperation (1970)," accessed June 23, 2015, http://www.deeplistening.org/site/content/valerie-solanas-and-marilyn-monroe-recognition-their-desperation-1970-0.

9   Valerie Solanas, *SCUM Manifesto*, introduction by Avital Ronell (New York: Verso, 2004), 49.

10 See Kim-Cohen, *Against Ambience*.

11 Joselit, *After Art*, 3.

12 Quoted in Edward Helmore and Paul Gallagher, "Doyen of American critics turns his back on the 'nasty, stupid' world of modern art," *The Guardian*, October 28, 2012, accessed June 24, 2015, http://www.theguardian.com/artanddesign/2012/oct/28/art-critic-dave-hickey-quits-art-world.

13   Andrea Fraser, "There's No Place Like Home," in *Whitney Biennial 2012*, ed. Elisabeth Sussman and Jay Sanders (New York: Whitney Museum of American Art, 2012), 28.

14   See abstract: Reza Negarestani, "The Human Centipede, A View From the Art World," *Deracinating Effect: November 2013*, Archives, November 7, 2013, accessed June 27, 2015, http://blog.urbanomic.com/cyclon/archives/2013/11.

15   Suhail Malik, *On the Necessity of Art's Exit from Contemporary Art* (Falmouth, UK: Urbanomic, forthcoming). The book version was unavailable at the time of writing. See a video of Malik's original talk at https://www.youtube.com/watch?v=fimEhntbRZ4.

16   Compare to Peter Osborne's "structural libertarianism of contemporary art" (*Anywhere or Not at All*, 87).

17   The passage appeared in the label text for Graham's 1994 exhibition *Two-way Mirror Punched Steel Hedge Labyrinth* held in the Minneapolis Sculpture Garden, Walker Art Center, Minneapolis, 1998. Also quoted in Bishop, *Artificial Hells*, 1. Compare to Negarestani: "Dreams of acceleration or deceleration, speculative enthusiasm for the outside or critical self-reflection are revealed to be simply changes of frequency in the rate of the said iteration" ("The Human Centipede").

18   Fraser, "There's No Place Like Home," 28.

19   Mockus, *Sounding Out*, 2.

20   Joselit, *After Art*, 96.

Selected Bibliography

Abbate, Carolyn. *In Search of Opera*. Princeton, NJ: Princeton University Press, 2001.

Ablinger, Peter. "A Letter From Schoenberg Reading Piece with Player Piano." Accessed January 9, 2010. http://ablinger.mur.at/txt_qu3schoenberg.html.

Ablinger, Peter. "Peter Ablinger: Weiss/Weisslich 18 (1992/96)." August 25, 2006. Accessed January 2, 2009. http://ablinger.mur.at/ww18.html.

Ablinger, Peter. "Die Klänge interessieren mich nicht/The Sounds Do Not Interest Me." In *Hören hören/Hearing Listening*, edited by Katja Blomberg, 93. Berlin: Haus am Waldsee, 2008.

Ablinger, Peter. "Keine Überschreitung/No Transgression." In *Hören hören/Hearing Listening*, edited by Katja Blomberg, 89–98. Berlin: Haus am Waldsee, 2008.

ACT UP. "Let the Record Show . . ." New Museum Digital Archive. Accessed January 28, 2013. http://archive.newmuseum.org/index.php/Detail/Occurrence/Show/occurrence_id/158.

Adorno, Theodor W. *Aesthetic Theory* (1970). Translated by Robert Hullot-Kentor. Edited by Gretel Adorno and Rolf Tiedermann. New York: Bloomsbury, 2013.

Adorno, Theodor W. "Commitment." In *Aesthetics and Politics: The Key Texts of the Classic Debate within German Marxism*. Translated by Frances McDonagh and Ronald Taylor. Edited by Ronald Taylor, Rodney Livingstone, Perry Anderson, and Francis Mulhern. New York: Verso, 1977.

Adorno, Theodor W. "Music, Language, Composition (1956)." *Essays on Music*. Translated by Susan H. Gillespie, 113–226. Berkeley: University of California Press, 2002.

Adorno, Theodor W. *Introduction to the Sociology of Music*. Translated by E. B. Ashton. New York: Continuum, 1988.

Adorno, Theodor W. "*Nadelcurven*," *Musikblätter des Anbruch* 10 (February 1928): 47–50.

Adorno, Theodor W. "The Curves of the Needle." Translated by Thomas Y. Levin, *October* 55 (Winter 1990): 48–55.

Alexander Alberro. "Reconsidering Conceptual Art, 1966–1977." In *Conceptual Art: A Critical Anthology*. Edited by Alexander Alberro and Blake Stimson, xvi–xxxvii. Cambridge, MA: MIT Press, 1999.

Althusser, Louis. *Lenin and Philosophy, and Other Essays*. New York: Monthly Review, 1972.

Althusser, Louis. *Philosophy of the Encounter: Later Writings, 1978-87.* Edited by François Matheron and Oliver Corpet. Translated by G.M. Goshgarian. London: Verso, 2006.

An Evening with Pauline Boudry/Renate Lorenz with Gregg Bordowitz and Pauline Oliveros. Roundtable discussion. Museum of Modern Art, May 19, 2014.

Attali, Jacques. *Noise: The Political Economy of Music.* Minneapolis: University of Minnesota Press, 1985.

"Badiou VS Žižek - Is Lacan An Anti-Philosopher? 06." YouTube, November 26, 2012. Accessed December 31, 2013. https://www.youtube.com/watch?v=bRD-tBTRbLc.

Barad, Karen M. *Meeting the Universe Halfway: Quantum Physics and the Entanglement of Matter and Meaning.* Durham: Duke University Press, 2007.

Barrett, G Douglas. "Speaking Volumes." Recess, May, 2013. http://www.recessart.org/critical-writing-g-douglas-barrett/.

Barrett, G Douglas. "Ultra-red, *URXX Nos. 1-9.*" *Tacet: Sound in the Arts* No. 4. Sounds of Utopia/Sonorités de l'utopie (January 2016): 540-55.

Barrett, G Douglas. *Two Transcriptions/Ode to Schoenberg,* 2013. http://gdouglasbarrett.com/two_transcriptions.html.

Barthes, Roland. *Camera Lucida: Reflections on Photography.* New York: Hill and Wang, 1981.

Baudry, Jean-Louis. "Ideological Effects of the Basic Cinematographic Apparatus." *Film Quarterly* 28, no. 2 (Winter, 1974-75): 39-47.

BBC News. "Russian MPs back harsher anti-blasphemy law." April 10, 2013. http://www.bbc.com/news/world-europe-22090308.

Bennetts, Marc. *Kicking the Kremlin: Russia's New Dissidents and the Battle to Topple Putin.* London: Oneworld, 2014.

Berlant, Lauren. *Cruel Optimism.* Durham: Duke University Press, 2011.

Bernstein, Anya. "An Inadvertent Sacrifice: Body Politics and Sovereign Power in the Pussy Riot Affair." *Critical Inquiry* 40, no. 1 (Autumn 2013): 220-41. Accessed November 14, 2014. http://criticalinquiry.uchicago.edu/an_inadvertent_sacrifice_body_politics_and_sovereign_power_in_the_pussy_rio.

Bersani, Leo. *Is the Rectum a Grave?: And Other Essays.* Chicago: University of Chicago Press, 2010.

Beuger, Antoine. "Grundsätzliche Entscheidungen." In *MusikDenken: Texte der Wandelweiser-Komponisten,* edited by Eva-Maria Houben and Burkhard Schlothauer, 116-121. Zürich: Edition Howeg, 2008. Published online 1997. Accessed July 3, 2011. http://www.wandelweiser.de/beuger/ABTexte.html#grund.

Bijsterveld, Karin. *Mechanical Sound: Technology, Culture, and Public Problems of Noise in the Twentieth Century.* Cambridge, MA: MIT Press, 2008.

Bishop, Claire. *Artificial Hells: Participatory Art and the Politics of Spectatorship.* London: Verso, 2012.

Bochner, Mel. "The Serial Attitude." In *Conceptual Art: A Critical Anthology,* edited by Alexander Alberro and Blake Stimson, 22–27. Cambridge, MA: MIT Press, 1999.

Bonds, Mark Evan. *Absolute Music: The History of An Idea.* New York: Oxford University Press, 2014.

Bonds, Mark Evan. "Idealism and the Aesthetics of Instrumental Music at the Turn of the Nineteenth Century." *Journal of the American Musicological Society* 50, no. 2/3 (Summer–Autumn, 1997): 387–420.

Bordowitz, Gregg. *General Idea: Imagevirus.* London: Afterall, 2010.

Borenstein, Seth. "NASA To Privatize Space Travel After Last Shuttle Lands." *Huffington Post.* June 20, 2011. http://www.huffingtonpost.com/2011/07/20/nasa-privatize-space-future-changes_n_905186.html.

Born, Georgina. "Sound Studies / Music / Affect: Year Zero, Encompassment, Difference?" Lecture. *Current Musicology—50th Anniversary Conference.* New York, March 28, 2015.

Born, Georgina. Introduction to *Music, Sound and Space: Transformations of Public and Private Experience.* Edited by Georgina Born. Cambridge, UK: Cambridge University Press, 2013.

Bourriaud, Nicolas. *Relational Aesthetics.* Dijon: Les Presses du réel, 1998/2002.

Brassier, Ray. *Nihil Unbound: Enlightenment and Extinction.* Basingstoke: Palgrave Macmillan, 2007.

Brown, Nathan. "The Speculative and the Specific: On Hallward and Meillassoux." In *The Speculative Turn: Continental Materialism and Realism.* Melbourne: Re.press, 2011, 142–64.

Bryanski, Gleb. "Russian Patriarch Calls Putin Era 'Miracle of God.'" *Reuters.* February 8, 2012. http://uk.reuters.com/article/2012/02/08/uk-russia-putin-religion-idUKTRE81722Y20120208.

Bryant, Levi R., Nick Srnicek, and Graham Harman, eds. *The Speculative Turn: Continental Materialism and Realism.* Melbourne: Re.press, 2011.

Buck-Morss, Susan. *The Origin of Negative Dialectics: Theodor W. Adorno, Walter Benjamin and the Frankfurt Institute.* New York: Free, 1977.

Bulgakowa, Oksana. "The Ear against the Eye: Vertov's Symphony." *Kieler Beiträge zur Filmmusikforschung* 2 (2008): 142–58. Published online. http://www.filmmusik.uni-kiel.de/beitraege.htm.

Bürger, Peter. *Theory of the Avant-Garde.* Translated by Michael Shaw. Minneapolis: University of Minnesota Press, 1984.

Cage, John. *4'33".* New York: Henmar Press, 1962.

Cage, John. *A Year from Monday: New Lectures and Writings.* Middletown: Wesleyan University Press, 1967.

Cage, John. "Defense of Satie (1948)." In *John Cage: An Anthology,* edited by Richard Kostelanetz, 77–84. New York: Da Capo, 1991.

Cage, John. *Empty Words: Writings '73-'78.* Middletown: Wesleyan University Press, 1981.

Cage, John. *Silence: Lectures and Writings.* Middletown: Wesleyan University Press, 1961.

Cesare-Bartnicki, T. Nikki. "The Aestheticization of Reality: Postmodern Music, Art, and Performance." PhD diss., New York University, 2008.

Chase, Stephen and Clemens Gresser. "Ordinary Matters: Christian Wolff on His Recent Music." *Tempo* 58, no. 229 (July 2004): 19–27.

Chehonadskih, Maria. "Commentary: What Is Pussy Riot's 'Idea'?" *Radical Philosophy* 176 (November/December, 2012): 1–7. Published online. http://www. radicalphilosophy.com/commentary/what-is-pussy-riots-idea.

Chessa, Luciano. *Luigi Russolo, Futurist: Noise, Visual Arts, and the Occult.* Berkeley: University of California Press, 2012.

Chiesa, Lorenzo. *Subjectivity and Otherness: A Philosophical Reading of Lacan.* Edited by Slavoj Žižek. Cambridge, MA: MIT Press, 2007.

Chion, Michel. *Audio-Vision: Sound on Screen.* Translated and Edited by Claudia Gorbman. New York: Columbia University Press, 1994.

Chronicle of Higher Education. "Has Higher Education Become an Engine of Inequality?" July 2, 2012. http://chronicle.com/article/Has-Higher-Education-Become-an/132619.

Chua, Daniel K. L. *Absolute Music and the Construction of Meaning.* Cambridge: Cambridge University Press, 1999.

Cluett, Seth Allen. "Loud Speaker: Towards a Component Theory of Media Sound." PhD diss., Princeton University, 2013.

Coffman, Chris. "Queering Žižek." *Postmodern Culture* 23, no. 1 (2012).

Cook, Nicholas. "Theorising Musical Meaning." *Music Theory Spectrum* 23, no. 2 (2001): 170–95.

Cox, Christoph. "Beyond Representation and Signification: Toward a Sonic Materialism." *Journal of Visual Culture* 10, no. 2 (2011): 145–61.

Crimp, Douglas and Adam Rolston. *AIDS Demo Graphics.* Seattle: Bay, 1990.

Crimp, Douglas. "Pictures." In *Appropriation,* edited by David Evans, 76–79. London: Whitechapel, 2009.

Crimp, Douglas. "AIDS: Cultural Analysis/Cultural Activism." *October* 43 (Winter 1987): 3–16.

Crimp, Douglas. *Melancholia and Moralism: Essays on AIDS and Queer Politics.* Cambridge: MIT Press, 2002.

Dahlhaus, Carl. *The Idea of Absolute Music.* Translated by Roger Lustig. Chicago: University of Chicago Press, 1989.

Debord, Guy and Gil J. Wolman. "Directions for the Use of Détournement." In *Appropriation,* edited by David Evans, 35–39. London: Whitechapel, 2009.

Debord, Guy. "The Situationists and the New Forms of Action in Politics or Art." In *Guy Debord and the Situationist International: Texts and Documents,* edited by Tom McDonough, 159–66. Cambridge: MIT Press, 2002.

Deleuze, Gilles and Félix Guattari. *A Thousand Plateaus: Capitalism and Schizophrenia.* Translated by Brian Massumi. Minneapolis: University of Minnesota Press, 1987.

Deleuze, Gilles. *Foucault.* Translated by Sean Hand. London: Continuum, 2006.

DeNora, Tia. *Beethoven and the Construction of Musical Genius: Musical Politics in Vienna, 1792-1803.* University of California Press, 1995.

Derrida, Jacques. "White Mythology: Metaphor in the Text of Philosophy." *New Literary History* 6, no. 1 "On Metaphor" (Autumn, 1974): 5–74.

Derrida, Jacques. *Of Grammatology.* Translated by Gayatri Chakravorty Spivak. Baltimore, MD: Johns Hopkins University Press, 1997.

Derrida, Jacques. *The Truth in Painting.* Translated by Geoffrey Bennington and Ian McLeod. Chicago: University of Chicago Press, 1987.

Doelle, Leslie. *Environmental Acoustics.* Toronto: McGraw-Hill, 1972.

Dolar, Mladen. *A Voice and Nothing More.* Cambridge, MA: MIT Press, 2006.

Donoghue, Frank. *The Last Professors: The Corporate University and the Fate of the Humanities.* New York: Fordham University Press, 2008.

Drobnick, Jim. "Listening Awry." In *Aural Cultures,* edited by Jim Drobnick, 9–18. Toronto and Banff: YYZ Books/WPG Editions.

Dworkin, Craig Douglas. *No Medium.* Cambridge, MA: MIT Press, 2013.

"Dying for Coverage: The Deadly Consequences of Being Uninsured." Accessed May 29, 2015. http://familiesusa.org/product/dying-coverage-deadly-consequences-being-uninsured.

Dyson, Frances. *The Tone of Our Times: Sound, Sense, Economy, and Ecology.* Cambridge, MA: MIT Press, 2014.

Eisler, Hanns and Theodor W. Adorno. "The Politics of Hearing." In *Audio Culture: Readings in Modern Music,* edited by Christoph Cox and Daniel Warner, 73–75. New York: Continuum, 2004.

Engelhardt, Jeffers. "Right Singing in Estonian Orthodox Christianity: A Study of Music, Theology, and Religious Ideology." *Ethnomusicology* 53, no. 1 (2009): 32–57.

Engh, Barbara. "Adorno and the Sirens: Tele-phono-graphic Bodies." In *Embodied Voices: Representing Female Vocality in Western Culture,* edited by Leslie C. Dunn and Nancy A. Jones, 120–35. Cambridge, UK: Cambridge University Press, 1997.

Engström, Andreas and Åsa Stjerna. "Sound Art or *Klangkunst*? A Reading of the German and English Literature on Sound Art." *Organised Sound* 14 (2009): 11–18, doi:10.1017/S1355771809000003X.

Evans, David. "Introduction: Seven Types of Appropriation." In *Appropriation,* edited by David Evans, 12–23. London: Whitechapel, 2009.

Fabian, Dorottya. "The Meaning of Authenticity and the Early Music Movement: A Historical Review." *International Review of the Aesthetics and Sociology of Music* 32, no. 2 (2001): 153–67.

Fahs, Breanne. "The Radical Possibilities of Valerie Solanas." *Feminist Studies* 34, no. 3, The 1970s Issue (Fall, 2008): 591–617.

Feisst, Sabine. "Ode to Napoleon Buonaparte, Op. 41." In *Schoenberg's New World: The American Years*, 144–49. New York: Oxford University Press, 2011.

Finkelstein, Avram. "AIDS 2.0." Artwrit, December 2012. Accessed January 28, 2013. http://www.artwrit.com/article/aids-2-0.

Finn, Geraldine. *Why Althusser Killed His Wife: Essays on Discourse and Violence.* Atlantic Highland, NJ: Humanities, 1996.

Fisher, Lucy. "*Enthusiasm*: From Kino-Eye to Radio-Eye." *Film Quarterly* 31, no. 2 (1977/78): 25–34.

Fleck, Robert. *Die Mühl-Kommune: Freie Sexualität und Aktionismus: Geschichte eines Experiments.* Köln: Walther König, 2003.

Flynt, Henry. "Essay: Concept Art [Provisional Version]." In *An Anthology*, edited by La Monte Young. New York: La Monte Young and Jackson Mac Low, 1963, n.p.

Fondation Foyer Des Artistes Boswil. "10. Internationales Kompositionsseminar Boswil, 10-14.11.91 Juryentscheidung [letter]." September 14, 1991.

Foucault, Michel. *Archaeology of Knowledge*. Translated by A. M. Sheridan Smith. London: Routledge, 2002.

Foucault, Michel. "Friendship as a Way of Life." In *Ethics: Subjectivity and Truth.* Translated by Robert Hurley. Edited by Paul Rabinow, 135–62. New York: New Press, 1997.

Foucault, Michel. *The History of Sexuality Volume 1: An Introduction*. Translated by Robert Hurley. New York: Pantheon Books, 1978.

Foucault, Michel. "What is An Author? (1969)." In *The Essential Foucault: Selections from Essential Works of Foucault, 1954–1984*, edited by Paul Rabinow and Nikolas S. Rose, 377–91. New York: The New Press, 2003.

Fraser, Andrea. "There's No Place Like Home." In *Whitney Biennial 2012*. Edited by Elisabeth Sussman and Jay Sanders, 28–33. New York: Whitney Museum of American Art, 2012.

Freire, Paulo. *Pedagogy of the Oppressed*, 30th Anniversary edn. New York: Continuum, 2000.

Frey, Jürg. "And On it Went." 2004. Accessed July 3, 2011. http://www.wandelweiser.de/frey/JFand.pdf.

Galloway, Alexander R. "The Poverty of Philosophy: Realism and Post-Fordism." *Critical Inquiry* 39, no. 2 (Winter 2013): 347–66.

Gentry, Philip M. "The Cultural Politics of 4'33": Identity and Sexuality." *Tacet Experimental Music Review* No. 1. Who Is John Cage? (2011): 19–39.

Gessen, Masha. *Words Will Break Cement: The Passion of Pussy Riot,* E-book edn. New York: Penguin, 2014.

Gessen, Masha and Joseph Huff-Hannon. Introduction *to Gay Propaganda: Russian Love Stories.* Edited by Masha Gessen and Joseph Huff-Hannon. New York and London: OR Books, 2014.

Ghorashi, Hannah. "Entire Class of First-Year MFA Students Dropping out of USC." May 15, 2015. Accessed July 15, 2015. http://www.artnews.com/2015/05/15/entire-class-of-first-year-mfa-students-dropping-out-of-usc.

Goehr, Lydia. *The Imaginary Museum of Musical Works: An Essay in the Philosophy of Music.* New York: Oxford University Press, 1994.

Graeber, David. *Debt: The First 5,000 Years.* New York: Melville House, 2011.

Gratton, Peter. *Speculative Realism: Problems and Prospects.* New York: Bloomsbury, 2014.

Greenberg, Clement. "Towards a Newer Laocoon." In *Pollock and After: The Critical Debate,* edited by Francis Frascina, 60–70. New York: Routledge, 2000.

Gronert, Stefan. "Trying to See the World Differently." In *John Baldessari: Music,* edited by Stefan Gronert and Christina Végh, 111–20. Köln: König, 2007.

Groys, Boris. *Art Power.* Cambridge, MA: MIT Press, 2008.

Groys, Boris. *History Becomes Form: Moscow Conceptualism.* Cambridge, MA: MIT Press, 2010.

Gunning, Tom. "An Aesthetic of Astonishment: Early Film and the (In)Credulous Spectator." In *Viewing Positions: Ways of Seeing Film,* edited by Linda Williams, 114–33. New Brunswick, NJ: Rutgers University Press, 1995.

Halberstam, Judith. *In a Queer Time and Place: Transgender Bodies, Subcultural Lives.* New York: New York University Press, 2005.

Hall, Irene, Ruiguang Song, Philip Rhodes, Joseph Prejean, Qian An, Lisa M. Lee, John Karon, Ron Brookmeyer, Edward H. Kaplan, Matthew T. McKenna, and Robert S. Janssen. "Estimation of HIV Incidence in the United States." *JAMA: The Journal of the American Medical Association* 300, no. 5 (2008): 520–29.

Hallas, Roger. *Reframing Bodies: AIDS, Bearing Witness, and the Queer Moving Image.* Durham: Duke University Press, 2009.

Hallward, Peter. "Anything Is Possible: A Critique of Meillassoux." In *The Speculative Turn: Continental Materialism and Realism,* Melbourne: Re.press, 2011, 130–41.

Hanslick, Eduard. *The Beautiful in Music (Musikalisch-Schönen).* Translated by Gustav Cohen. New York: H. W. Gray, 1891.

Hegarty, Paul. *Noise/Music: A History.* New York: Bloomsbury, 2007.

Hegarty, Paul. *Rumour and Radiation: Sound in Video Art.* New York: Bloomsbury, 2015.

Helmore, Edward and Paul Gallagher. "Doyen of American Critics Turns His Back on the 'Nasty, Stupid' World of Modern Art." *The Guardian.* October 28, 2012. Accessed

June 24, 2015. http://www.theguardian.com/artanddesign/2012/oct/28/art-critic-dave-hickey-quits-art-world.

Higgins, Hannah. *Fluxus Experience.* Berkeley, CA: University of California Press, 2002.

Hight, Marc A. "Idea Ontology and the Early Modern Tale." In *Idea and Ontology: An Essay in Early Modern Metaphysics of Ideas,* 1–10. University Park, PA: Pennsylvania State University Press, 2008.

Hines, Thomas S. "'Then Not Yet "Cage"': The Los Angeles Years, 1912–1938." In *John Cage: Composed in America,* edited by Marjorie Perloff and Charles Junkerman, 65–99. Chicago: University of Chicago Press, 1994.

"How Old Is the Universe?" *WMAP—Age of the Universe.* Accessed November 4, 2013. http://map.gsfc.nasa.gov/universe/uni_age.html.

Hubbs, Nadine. *The Queer Composition of America's Sound: Gay Modernists, American Music, and National Identity.* Berkeley: University of California, 2004.

Huyssen, Andreas. *Twilight Memories: Marking Time in a Culture of Amnesia.* New York: Routledge, 1995.

Jay, Martin. *Downcast Eyes: The Denigration of Vision in Twentieth-century French Thought.* Berkeley: University of California, 1993.

Jensen, Susan. "Legislative History of the Bankruptcy Abuse Prevention and Consumer Protection Act of 2005, A." *Am. Bankr, LJ* 79 (2005): 485.

John Cage / 4'33" andrestorresREVOC. Accessed July 3, 2007. https://www.youtube.com/watch?v=WYQhXN1UFbU.

Johnston, Adrian. *Adventures in Transcendental Materialism: Dialogues with Contemporary Thinkers.* Edinburgh: Edinburgh University Press, 2014.

Johnston, Adrian. *Prolegomena to Any Future Materialism: The Outcome of Contemporary French Philosophy.* Evanston, IL: Northwestern University Press, 2013.

Jones, Caroline A. "Finishing School: John Cage and the Abstract Expressionist Ego." *Critical Inquiry* 19, no. 4 (Summer 1993): 628–65.

Joselit, David. *After Art.* Princeton, NJ: Princeton University Press, 2013.

Joseph, Branden W. "Soundings: A Contemporary Score." *Artforum.* November 2013, 282–83.

Joseph, Branden W. "Concept Art." In *Beyond the Dream Syndicate: Tony Conrad and the Arts after Cage,* 153–212. New York: Zone Books, 2008.

Joseph, Branden W. "Biomusic." In "On Brainwashing: Mind Control, Media, and Warfare," edited by Andreas Killen and Stefan Andriopoulos, special issue, *Grey Room* 45 (Fall 2011): 128–50.

Kahn, Douglas. *Earth Sound Earth Signal: Energies and Earth Magnitude in the Arts.* Berkeley: University of California Press, 2013.

Kahn, Douglas. "The Arts of Sound Art and Music." *The Iowa Review* (2006). Accessed July 28, 2014. http://www.douglaskahn.com/writings/douglas_kahn-sound_art.pdf.

Kahn, Douglas. "John Cage: Silence and Silencing." *The Musical Quarterly* 81, no. 4 (1997): 556–98.

Kahn, Douglas. *Noise, Water, Meat: A History of Voice, Sound, and Aurality in the Arts.* Cambridge, MA: MIT Press, 1999.

Kane, Brian. "Musicophobia, or Sound Art and the Demands of Art Theory." *Nonsite. org*, no. 8 (2013), January 20, 2013. Accessed June 20, 2013. http://nonsite.org/ article/musicophobia-or-sound-art-and-the-demands-of-art-theory.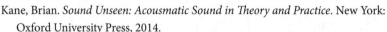

Kane, Brian. *Sound Unseen: Acousmatic Sound in Theory and Practice.* New York: Oxford University Press, 2014.

Katz, Jonathan. "John Cage's Queer Silence; or, How to Avoid Making Matters Worse." *GLQ: A Journal of Lesbian and Gay Studies* 5, no. 2 (1999): 231–52. Accessed July 27, 2012. http://www.queerculturalcenter.org/Pages/KatzPages/KatzWorse.html.

Kelly, Caleb. *Sound.* London: Whitechapel Gallery, 2011.

Kim-Cohen, Seth. *Against Ambience.* New York: Bloomsbury, 2013. Kindle e-Book.

Kim-Cohen, Seth. *In the Blink of an Ear Toward a Non-cochlear Sonic Art.* New York: Continuum, 2009.

Kirilenko, Anastasia. "Freed Pussy Riot Member Yekaterina Samutsevich: 'Art Must Be Political'." October 12, 2012. Accessed January 26, 2015. http://www.theatlantic.com/ international/archive/2012/10/freed-pussy-riot-member-yekaterina-samutsevich-art-must-be-political/263561.

Kirkham, Chris. "Corinthian closing its last schools; 10,000 California students displaced." *Los Angeles Times.* April 27, 2015. http://www.latimes.com/business/la-fi-corinthian-shutdown-20150427-story.html#page=1.

Kittler, Friedrich. *Gramophone, Film, Typewriter.* Stanford, CA: Stanford University Press, 1999.

Kivy, Peter. *Sound and Semblance: Reflections on Musical Representation.* Princeton, NJ: Princeton University Press, 1984.

Kizenko, Nadieszda. "Feminized Patriarchy? Orthodoxy and Gender in Post-Soviet Russia." *Signs* 38, no. 3 (2013): 595–621.

Kofman, Sarah. *Camera Obscura: Of Ideology.* Ithaca, NY: Cornell University Press, 1999.

Kosuth, Joseph. "Art After Philosophy [1969]." In *Art After Philosophy and After: Collected Writings, 1966-1990*, ed. Gabriele Guercio, 13–32. Cambridge, MA: MIT Press, 1991.

Kotz, Liz. "Post-Cagean Aesthetics and the 'Event' Score." *October* 95 (2001): 55–89.

Kotz, Liz. *Words to be looked at: Language in 1960s Art.* Cambridge, MA: MIT Press, 2007.

Kramer, Lawrence. *Musical Meaning: Toward a Critical History.* Berkeley: University of California Press, 2002.

Krauss, Rosalind. *A Voyage on the North Sea: Art in the Age of the Post-Medium Condition.* New York: Thames & Hudson, 2000.

Krauss, Rosalind. "Video: The Aesthetics of Narcissism." *October* 1 (Spring 1976): 50–64.

Krauss, Rosalind. "Sculpture in the Expanded Field." *October* 8 (Spring, 1979): 30–44.

La Berge, Leigh Claire and Dehlia Hannah. "Debt Aesthetics: Medium Specificity and Social Practice in the Work of Cassie Thornton." *Postmodern Culture* 5, no. 2 (2015).

LaBelle, Brandon. *Lexicon of the Mouth: Poetics and Politics of Voice and the Oral Imaginary.* New York: Bloomsbury, 2014.

Lacan, Jacques. *Ecrits: The First Complete Edition in English.* Translated by Bruce Fink, Héloïse Fink, and Russell Grigg. New York: W. W. Norton & Company, 2006.

"Lack of Health Insurance." America's Health Rankings. Accessed May 29, 2015. http://www.americashealthrankings.org.

Latour, Bruno. "On Some Affects of Capitalism." Lecture, Royal Academy, Copenhagen, February 26, 2014. http://www.bruno-latour.fr/sites/default/files/136-AFFECTS-OF-K-COPENHAGUE.pdf.

Latour, Bruno. "An Attempt at a 'Compositionist Manifesto'." *New Literary History* (2010): 471–90.

Latour, Bruno. *Reassembling the Social: An Introduction to Actor-Network-Theory.* Oxford: Oxford University Press, 2005.

Lawrence, Amy. *Echo and Narcissus: Women's Voices in Classical Hollywood Cinema.* Berkeley: University of California Press, 1991.

Lazzarato, Maurizio. *The Making of the Indebted Man: An Essay on the Neoliberal Condition.* Cambridge, MA: Semiotext(e), 2011.

LeWitt, Sol. "Paragraphs on Conceptual Art." In *Conceptual Art: A Critical Anthology,* edited by Alexander Alberro and Blake Stimson, 12–17. Cambridge, MA: MIT, 1999.

Leyda, Jay. *Kino: A History of the Russian and Soviet Film.* New York: Collier Books, 1960.

Lippard, Lucy R. "Escape Attempts." In *Six Years: The Dematerialization of the Art Object from 1966 to 1972; A Cross-Reference Book of Information On Some Esthetic Boundaries . . .,* vii–xxii. Berkeley: University of California Press, 1973.

Lorenz, Renate, editor. *Not Now! Now! Chronopolitics, Art & Research.* Berlin: Sternberg Press, 2014.

Malik, Suhail. *On the Necessity of Art's Exit from Contemporary Art.* Falmouth, UK: Urbanomic (forthcoming).

Mann, Paul. *Masocriticism.* Albany: State University of New York Press, 1998.

Mann, Paul. *The Theory-Death of the Avant-Garde.* Bloomington: Indiana University Press, 1991.

Margasak, Peter. "Best Place to Hear Work by Wandelweiser Group Composers | Best of Chicago 2011 | Music & Nightlife | Chicago Reader. Chicago Reader | Chicago's Guide to Music, Movies, Arts, Theater, Restaurants, and Politics. 2011." Accessed June 27, 2011. http://www.chicagoreader.com/chicago/best-place-to-hear-work-by-wandelweiser-group-composers/BestOf?oid1/44102977.

Martin, Randy. *Financialization of Daily Life.* Philadelphia: Temple University Press, 2002.

Martin, Randy. *Under New Management: Universities, Administrative Labor, and the Professional Turn*. Philadelphia: Temple University Press, 2011.

Marx, Karl and Friedrich Engels. *The German Ideology Parts I & II*. Mansfield Centre, CT: Martino Publishing, 2011.

Marx, Karl. *Capital: A Critique of Political Economy*. Translated by Ben Fowkes. London: Penguin in Association with New Left Review, 1976.

McClary, Susan. *Feminine Endings: Music, Gender, and Sexuality*. Minneapolis: University of Minnesota Press, 1991.

McClary, Susan. "Comment: Getting Down Off the Beanstalk: The Presence of a Woman's Voice in Janika Vandervelde's *Genesis II*." Minnesota Composers Forum, January 1987.

Meillassoux, Quentin. *After Finitude: An Essay on the Necessity of Contingency*. New York: Bloomsbury, 2009.

Melia, Nicholas. "*Stille Musik*—Wandelweiser and the Voices of Ontological Silence." In "Wandelweiser," edited by James Saunders, special issue, *Contemporary Music Review* 30, no. 5 (December 2011): 471–95.

Mello, Chico. "Zwischen Abbild und Selbst-Referenzialität: Mimesis und Rauschen bei Peter Ablinger/Between Representation and Self-Reference: Mimesis and Noise in Peter Ablinger." In *Hören hören/Hearing Listening*, edited by Katja Blomberg, 99–104. Berlin: Haus am Waldsee, 2008.

Meyer, Richard. *Outlaw Representation: Censorship and Homosexuality in Twentieth-Century American Art*. New York: Oxford University Press, 2002.

Michelson, Annette. Introduction to *Kino-Eye: The Writings of Dziga Vertov*. Berkeley: University of California Press, 1984.

Miles, Stephen. "Critics of Disenchantment." *Notes* 52, no. 1 (September 1995): 11–38.

Mockus, Martha. *Sounding Out: Pauline Oliveros and Lesbian Musicality*. New York: Routledge, 2008.

Mouffe, Chantal. *Agonistics: Thinking the World Politically*. London: Verso, 2013.

Mouffe, Chantal. "Artistic Activism and Agonistic Spaces." *ART & RESEARCH: A Journal of Ideas, Contexts and Methods* 1, no. 2 (2007): 1–5.

Mouffe, Chantal. "Beyond Cosmopolitanism." World Biennial Forum No. 1. Gwangju, South Korea, lecture, December 31, 2012. https://www.youtube.com/watch?v=VuNzi1rutIc.

Mouffe, Chantal. "Democratic Politics and Agonistic Public Spaces." Harvard Graduate School of Design, Cambridge, MA, lecture, April 17, 2012.

Müller, Patrick. *Manfred Werder. Contemporary Swiss Composers*. Zürich: Pro Helvetia, 2002.

Murray, Penelope and Peter Wilson. "Introduction: *Mousikē*, not Music." In *Music and the Muses: The Culture of Mousike in the Classical Athenian City*, edited by Murray and Wilson, 1–8. New York: Oxford University Press, 2004.

Nancy, Jean-Luc. *Listening*. Translated by Charlotte Mandell. New York: Fordham University Press, 2007.

Nancy, Jean-Luc. *The Sense of the World*. Minneapolis: University of Minnesota Press, 1997.

Nattiez, Jacques. *Music and Discourse: Toward a Semiology of Music*. Translated by Carolyn Abbate. Princeton, NJ: Princeton University Press, 1990.

Negarestani, Reza. "The Human Centipede, A View From the Art World." *Deracinating Effect: November 2013*. Archives, November 7, 2013. Accessed June 27, 2015. http://blog.urbanomic.com/cyclon/archives/2013/11.

Neuhaus, Max. "Sound Art?" June, 2000. 11.A.1172. MoMA PS Collection, The Museum of Modern Art Archives, NY.

Neuhaus, Max. "Sound Art?" July, 2000. Accessed June 20, 2015. http://www.max-neuhaus.info/soundworks/soundart/SoundArt.htm.

Nicholson, Luke. "Being Framed by Irony: AIDS and the Art of General Idea." MA thesis, Concordia University, 2006.

Nochlin, Linda. "Why Have There Been No Great Women Artists?" *ARTnews* (January 22–39, 1971): 67–71.

Novak, David. *Japanoise: Music at the Edge of Circulation*. Durham: Duke University Press, 2013.

"Ode to Napoleon op. 41." *Arnold Schönberg Center*. July 30, 2009. Last updated March 4, 2015. http://www.schoenberg.at/index.php/en/joomla-license-sp-1943310036/ode-to-napoleon-op-41-1942.

Oliveros, Pauline. "To Valerie Solanas and Marilyn Monroe in Recognition of Their Desperation (1970)." Accessed June 23, 2015. http://www.deeplistening.org/site/content/valerie-solanas-and-marilyn-monroe-recognition-their-desperation-1970-0.

Ono, Yoko. *Grapefruit*. New York: Simon and Schuster, 1971.

Osborne, Peter. *Anywhere or Not at All: Philosophy of Contemporary Art*. London: Verso, 2013.

Overton, Adam. "Ripe for Embarrassment: For A New Musical Masochism, Matador Oven/Adam Overton." *The Experimental Music Yearbook*. Accessed October 16, 2013. http://www.experimentalmusicyearbook.com/Ripe-for-Embarrassment-For-A-New-Musical-Masochism.

Pashman, Scott. "Discharge of Student Loan Debt under 11 USC 523 (A)(8): Reassessing under Hardship after the Elimination of the Seven-Year Exception." *NYL Rev.* 44 (2000): 605.

Pepper, Ian. "From the 'Aesthetics of Indifference' to 'Negative Aesthetics': John Cage and Germany. 1957–1972." *October* 82 (1997): 30–47.

Piekut, Benjamin. *Experimentalism Otherwise: The New York Avant-Garde and Its Limits*. Berkeley: University of California Press, 2011.

Pisaro, Michael. "erstwards: September 2009." September 2009. Accessed August 28, 2011. http://erstwords.blogspot.com/2009_09_01_archive.html.

Pisaro, Michael. "Hit or miss [*Treffer oder daneben*]." In *MusikDenken: Texte der Wandelweiser-Komponisten,* edited by Eva-Maria Houben and Burkhard Schlothauer, 55–59. Zürich: Edition Howeg. Published online 2004. Accessed October 38, 2011. http://www.wandelweiser.de/pisaro/MPTexte_e.html#hit.

Pisaro, Michael. "Writing, Music." In *The Ashgate Research Companion to Experimental Music,* edited by James Saunders, 27–76. Farnham, UK: Ashgate, 2009.

Platzker, David. "Art by Telephone (Chicago: Museum of Contemporary Art, 1969)." *Specific Object.* Accessed January 22, 2015. http://www.specificobject.com/projects/art_by_telephone/#.VaV2axaNuRk.

Poggioli, Renato. *The Theory of the Avant-Garde.* Cambridge, MA: Belknap of Harvard University Press, 1968.

Postone, Moishe. *Time, Labor, and Social Domination: A Re-interpretation of Marx's Critical Theory.* Cambridge, UK: Cambridge University Press, 1993.

Priest, eldritch. "Nonsense." In *Boring Formless Nonsense: Experimental Music and the Aesthetics of Failure,* 195–276. New York: Bloomsbury, 2013.

Prieto, Eric. "Deleuze, Music, and Modernist Mimesis." In *Word and Music Studies: Essays on Music and the Spoken Word and on Surveying the Field,* edited by Suzanne M. Lodato and David F. Urrows, 3–21. Amsterdam: Radopi, 2005.

Pritchett, James. "What silence taught John Cage." *L'anarquia del silenci: John Cage i l'art experimental, Museu d'Art Contemporani de Barcelona.* Barcelona, October 23, 2009 to January 10, 2010. Accessed July 3, 2011. http://www.rosewhitemusic.com/cage/texts/What SilenceTaughtCage.html.

Purves, Ted. Introduction to *What We Want Is Free: Generosity And Exchange In Recent Art.* Edited by Ted Purves. Albany: SUNY Press, 2005, ix–xii.

Pussy Riot: A Punk Prayer "Pokazatelnyy Protsess: Istoriya Pussy Riot" (original title). Director Mike Lerner, Maxim Pozdorovkin, performers Nadezhda Tolokonnikova, Mariya Alyokhina, Yekaterina Samutsevich, 2014, film.

Rancière, Jacques. "Revising 'Nights of Labour': Talk by Jacques Ranciere." February 16, 2009. Accessed March 22, 2014. https://www.youtube.com/watch?v=pwW_LiwCKlg.

Rancière, Jacques. *Aisthesis: Scenes from the Aesthetic Regime of Art.* London: Verso, 2013.

Rancière, Jacques. *Althusser's Lesson.* Translated by Emiliano Battista. London: Continuum, 2011.

Rancière, Jacques. *The Ignorant Schoolmaster: Five Lessons in Intellectual Emancipation* (1987). Stanford, CA: Stanford University Press, 1991.

Rancière, Jacques. *The Philosopher and His Poor.* Translated by Andrew Parker. Durham: Duke University Press, 2004.

"Reading Group: AUTONOMIA, OCCUPY, COMMUNISM: LEGACIES AND FUTURES | e-flux." Accessed December 30, 2013. http://www.e-flux.com/program/reading-group-autonomia-occupy-communism-legacies-and-futures.

Revill, David. *The Roaring Silence: John Cage: A Life.* New York: Arcade, 1993.

Reynolds, Wynford. *Music While You Work*. London: British Broadcasting Corporation, 1942.

Roads, Curtis. *The Computer Music Tutorial*. Cambridge, MA: MIT Press, 1996.

Rogers, Holly. *Sounding the Gallery: Video and the Rise of Art-Music*. New York: Oxford University Press, 2013.

Ross, Andrew. *Creditocracy: And The Case For Debt Refusal*. New York and London: OR Books, 2014.

Roth, Moira and Jonathan Katz. *Difference/Indifference: Musings on Postmodernism, Marcel Duchamp and John Cage*. Amsterdam: G+B Arts International, 1998.

RT. "Putin: Assange case exposes UK double standards (Exclusive Interview)." September 6, 2012. https://www.youtube.com/watch?v=UB45clPRNoc&feature=youtu.be&t=20m52s.

Russo, Mary and Daniel Warner. "Rough Music, Futurism, and Postpunk Industrial Noise Bands." *Discourse* 10, no. 1 (Fall–Winter 1987–88): 55–76.

Sartre, Jean-Paul. *What is Literature?: And Other Essays*. Cambridge, MA: Harvard University Press, 1988.

Saunders, James. "Antoine Beuger." In *The Ashgate Research Companion to Experimental Music*, edited by James Saunders, 231–42. Farnham, UK: Ashgate, 2004.

Saunders, James. "Manfred Werder." In *The Ashgate Research Companion to Experimental Music*, edited by James Saunders, 353–58. Farnham, UK: Ashgate, 2004.

Saunders, James. "Testing the Consequences: Seriality in the work of the Wandelweiser composers" in "Wandelweiser." Edited by James Saunders, special issue. *Contemporary Music Review* 30, no. 5 (December 2011): 497–524.

Schaeffer, Pierre. "Acousmatics." In *Audio Culture: Readings in Modern Music*, edited by Christoph Cox and Daniel Warner, 76–81. New York: Continuum, 2004.

Scheib, Christian. "Static's Music—Noise Inquiries." Edited by Bill Dietz. 1997/98. Last updated 2002. Accessed January 12, 2010. http://ablinger.mur.at/noise.html.

Schlegel, Friedrich von. *Philosophical Fragments*. Translated by P. Firchow. Minneapolis: University of Minneapolis Press, 1991.

Schlegel, Steven. "John Cage at June in Buffalo, 1975." MA thesis, State University of New York, Buffalo, 2008.

Schlothauer, Andreas. *Die Diktatur Der Freien Sexualität: AAO, Mühl-Kommune*. Vienna: Verlag für Gesellschaftskritik, 1992. Available at http://www.agpf.de/Schlothauer-AAO-Muehl.htm.

Schroeder, Marianne. "Ein deutscher Cage?" In *Schnebel 60*, edited by Werner Grünzweig, Gesine Schröder, and Martin Suppe, 65–67. Hofheim: Wolke, 1990.

Sedgewick, Eve Kosofsky. *Between Men: English Literature and Male Homosocial Desire*. New York: Columbia University Press, 1985.

Sember, Robert and David Gere. "'Let the Record Show . . .': Art Activism and the AIDS Epidemic." *American Journal of Public Health* 96.6 (2006): 967–69. Accessed January 28, 2013. http://www.ncbi.nlm.nih.gov/pmc/articles/PMC1470625.

Sholette, Gregory. *Dark Matter: Art and Politics in the Age of Enterprise Culture.*
    London: Pluto, 2011.

Siebers, Johan. *The Method of Speculative Philosophy: An Essay on the Foundations of
    Whitehead's Metaphysics.* Kassel: Kassel University Press, 1998.

Silverman, Kaja. *The Acoustic Mirror: The Female Voice in Psychoanalysis and Cinema.*
    Bloomington: Indiana University Press, 1988.

Simon, Joshua. *Neomaterialism.* Berlin: Sternberg, 2013.

Simon, Ruth and Rob Barry. "A Degree Drawn in Red Ink: Graduates of Arts-Focused
    Schools Are Shown to Rack Up the Most Student Debt." *The Wall Street Journal.*
    Updated February 13, 2013. http://www.wsj.com/articles/SB10001424127887324432
    004578306610055834952.

Slaughter, Sheila and Larry L. Leslie. *Academic Capitalism: Politics, Policies, and the
    Entrepreneurial University.* Baltimore, MD: Johns Hopkins University Press, 1999.

Solanas, Valerie. *SCUM Manifesto.* Introduction by Avital Ronell. London: Verso, 2004.

Stäheli, Urs. *Spectacular Speculation: Thrills, the Economy, and Popular Discourse.*
    Stanford, CA: Stanford University Press, 2013.

State University of New York at Buffalo. Music Department. *Recordings of June in
    Buffalo, 1975–1978, 1980.* 1980. Buffalo Music Library. Music Archives, 30.

Sterne, Jonathan. *The Audible Past: Cultural Origins of Sound Reproduction.* Durham:
    Duke University Press, 2003.

Sterne, Jonathan. *MP3: The Meaning of a Format.* Durham: Duke University Press, 2012.

Stockhausen, Karlheinz. "Huuuh! Das Pressegespräch am 16. September 2001 im
    Senatszimmer des Hotel Atlantic in Hamburg." *MusikTexte* 91 (2002): 69–77.

Straebel, Volker. "Aspects of Conceptual Composing." *The Open Space Magazine* 10 (Fall
    2008): 69–78.

Thaemlitz, Terre. "Please Tell My Landlord Not to Expect Future Payments Because
    Attali's Theory of Surplus-Value-Generating Information Economics Only Works if
    My Home Studio's Rent and Other Use-Values are Zero." In *Immediacy and Non-
    Simultaneity: Utopia of Sound,* edited by Diedrich Diederichsen and Constanze
    Ruhm, 65–87. Vienna: Schlebrügge, 2010.

Thomas, Paul. *Marxism and Scientific Socialism: From Engels to Althusser.* London:
    Routledge, 2008.

Thornton, Cassie. "A wild place with a boring facade." Accessed August 14, 2013. http://
    www.cassiethornton.com/about.html.

Thornton, Cassie. "We Make Debt." We Make Debt. Accessed November 4, 2013. http://
    debt-material.tumblr.com/ask.

Toscano, Alberto. "Against Speculation, Or, A Critique of the Critique: A Remark
    on Quentin Meillassoux's *After Finitude* (After Colletti)." In *The Speculative Turn:
    Continental Materialism and Realism,* 84–91. Melbourne: Re.press, 2011.

Ultra-red. "Organized Listening: Sound Art, Collectivity and Politics (Vogue-ology)."
    Vera List Center for Art and Politics, 2010. Accessed July 28, 2013. http://www.

veralistcenter.org/engage/event/216/organized-listening-sound-art-collectivity-and-politics.

Ultra-red. "missionstatement." Ultra-red, 2000. Accessed July 28, 2013. http://www.ultrared.org/mission.html.

Ultra-red. "PS/o6.b. encuentrolosangeles." Ultra-red, 2000. Accessed July 28, 2013. http://www.ultrared.org/pso6b.html.

Ultra-red. "ps/o8publicmuseum." Ultra-red, 2000. Accessed January 28, 2013. http://www.ultrared.org/pso8.html.

Ultra-red. "Time for the Dead to have a Word with the Living: The AIDS Uncanny." *Journal of Aesthetics and Protest* 4 (2005): 82–94.

Ultra-red. "Ultra-red: Organizing the Silence." In *On Horizons: A Critical Reader in Contemporary Art,* edited by Maria Hlavajova, Simon Sheikh, and Jill Winder, 193–209. Rotterdam: Post Editions, 2011.

Ultra-red. "Ultra-red: PS/o8.i Silent Listen The Record." Ultra-red, 2006. Accessed January 28, 2013. http://www.ultrared.org/pso8i.html.

uncertain commons. *Speculate This!* Durham: Duke University Press, 2013. Published online. http://speculatethis.pressbooks.com.

Ureña, Leslie J. "Hong-Kai Wang." *ARTiT,* June 7, 2011. Accessed June 15, 2015. http://www.art-it.asia/u/admin_ed_itv_e/dOSMEibzRUhnL3PlIyFW/?lang=en.

Valentine, David. *Imagining Transgender: An Ethnography of a Category.* Durham: Duke University Press, 2007.

Varèse, Edgard. "The Electronic Medium (1962)." From "The Liberation of Sound." Ed. and ann. Chou Wen-chung. *Perspectives of New Music* 5, no. 1 (Autumn–Winter, 1966): 11–19.

Viljoen, Martina. "Questions of Musical Meaning: An Ideology-Critical Approach / Problemi Glazbenog Značenja: Ideološko-Kritički Pristup." *International Review of the Aesthetics and Sociology of Music* 35, no. 1 (June 2004): 3–28.

Vriezen, Samuel. "Componistengroep Wandelweiser. Samuel Vriezen." 2007. Accessed June 27, 2011. http://sqv.home.xs4all.nl/wandelweiser.html.

Wallace, Ruth. "Catholic Women and the Creation of a New Social Reality." *Gender and Society* 2, no. 1 (1998): 24–38.

Wang, Hong-Kai. "Music While We Work (documentary of recording workshops)." June 7, 2012. Accessed November 13, 2013. https://vimeo.com/43627255.

Wang, Hong-Kai. "Music While We Work." Accessed November 14, 2014. http://www.w-h-k.net/mwww.html.

Warburton, Dan. "The Sound of Silence: The Music and Aesthetics of the Wandelweiser Group." 2001. Accessed June 23, 2011. http://www.wandelweiser.de.

Weiner, Lawrence. *Statement of Intent,* 1968. First published in *January 5–31, 1969.* Exhibition catalogue. New York: Seth Siegelaub, 1969.

Werder, Manfred. "*2006*[1] [CD liner notes]." In *2006*[1]. Performers Tetuzi Akiyama, Masahiko Okura, and Toshiya Tsunoda. Tokyo: Skiti, 2006.

Werder, Manfred. "Statement on Indeterminacy." In *Word Events: Perspectives on Verbal Notation,* edited by John Lely and James Saunders, 381. New York: Continuum, 2012.

Whitehead, Alfred North. *Process and Reality.* Edited by David Ray Griffin and Donald Wynne Sherburne. New York: Free, 1978.

Wolff, Christian. "Quiet Music: On a Composition Seminar in Boswil." In *Cues: Writings & conversations/Hinweise: Schriften und Gespräche,* edited by Christian Wolff, 232. Köln: MusikTexte, 1998.

Žižek, Slavoj. *Absolute Recoil: Towards a New Foundation of Dialectical Materialism.* London: Verso, 2014.

Žižek, Slavoj. "Towards a Materialist Theory of Subjectivity." Lecture. Birkbeck Institute, London, May 22, 2014.

Žižek, Slavoj. "The True Blasphemy." In *Comradely Greetings: The Prison Letters of Nadya and Slavoj.* London: Verso, 2014, 11–13.

Žižek, Slavoj. *Less Than Nothing: Hegel and the Shadow of Dialectical Materialism.* London: Verso, 2012.

Žižek, Slavoj. *Living in the End Times.* London: Verso, 2011.

Žižek, Slavoj. *The Parallax View.* Cambridge, MA: MIT Press, 2006.

Žižek, Slavoj. *The Sublime Object of Ideology.* London: Verso, 2008.

Žižek, Slavoj. *Violence: Six Sideways Reflections.* New York: Picador, 2008.

Zupančič, Alenka. *The Odd One in: On Comedy.* Cambridge, MA: MIT Press, 2008.

Index